FAIL BETTER

Also by Mark Kingwell:

A Civil Tongue: Justice, Dialogue, and the Politics of Pluralism (1995)
Dreams of Millennium: Report from a Culture on the Brink (1997)
In Pursuit of Happiness: Better Living from Plato to Prozac (2000)
The World We Want: Restoring Citizenship in a Fractured Age (2001)
Practical Judgments: Essays in Culture, Politics, and Interpretation (2002)
Catch and Release: Trout Fishing and the Meaning of Life (2003)
Nothing for Granted: Tales of War, Philosophy, and Why the Right Was
    Mostly Wrong: Selected Writings 2000-2003 (2005)
Nearest Thing to Heaven: The Empire State Building and American Dreams (2006)
Marginalia: A Cultural Reader (1999)
Classic Cocktails: A Modern Shake (2006)
Concrete Reveries: Consciousness and the City (2008)
The Idler's Glossary (2008)
Opening Gambits: Essays on Art and Philosophy (2008)
Glenn Gould (2009)
The Wage Slave's Glossary (2011)
Unruly Voices: Essays on Democracy, Civility and the Human Imagination (2012)
Measure Yourself Against the Earth (2015)

Fail BETTER

Why Baseball Matters

Mark Kingwell

BIBLIOASIS
WINDSOR, ONTARIO

FIRST EDITION

Library and Archives Canada Cataloguing in Publication

Kingwell, Mark, 1963-, author
    Fail better / Mark Kingwell.

Issued also in electronic format.
ISBN 978-1-77196-153-0 (softcover).--ISBN 978-1-77196-154-7 (ebook)

    1. Baseball--Psychological aspects. 2. Failure (Psychology).
I. Title.

GV867.6.K56 2017   796.35701'9   C2016-907944-9
                                               C2016-907945-7

Edited by Daniel Wells
Copy-edited by Emily Donaldson
Typeset by Chris Andrechek
Cover designed by Gordon Robertson

Canada Council   Conseil des Arts   ONTARIO ARTS COUNCIL
for the Arts   du Canada   CONSEIL DES ARTS DE L'ONTARIO
                                       50 YEARS OF ONTARIO GOVERNMENT SUPPORT OF THE ARTS
                                       50 ANS DE SOUTIEN DU GOUVERNEMENT DE L'ONTARIO AUX ARTS

Canadian   Patrimoine
Heritage   canadien

Published with the generous assistance of the Canada Council for the Arts and the Ontario Arts Council. Biblioasis also acknowledges the support of the Government of Canada through the Canada Book Fund and the Government of Ontario through the Ontario Book Publishing Tax Credit.

PRINTED AND BOUND IN CANADA

Contents

For Alison Gordon,
Paul Quarrington, Linda Williams

"All of old. Nothing else ever. Ever tried. Ever failed. No matter. Try again. Fail again. Fail better."

Samuel Beckett, *Worstward Ho* (1983)

Form

THIS IS A BOOK ABOUT baseball, and like all baseball books it faces a series of choices that reflect the game itself.

Does it concern statistical analysis? Personal reflection? Cultural investigation? Does it address biography and autobiography? Is it a book of history, elegy, and nostalgia? Is it a meditation on fatherhood, or community, or ethics?

Well, the game is all of these, and more, and the pages that follow reflect my own different kinds of engagement with it. I am not a stats geek, but like any fan I feel in baseball the weird tidal pull of averages and projections. My baseball biography is, in itself, entirely insignificant; but in common with every baseball lover I have ever met, the details of life and circumstance seem constantly refracted through the game, the parks visited and plays witnessed. Not sentimental by nature, I likewise feel the strange power of a game—especially in its eternally compromised Major League form—to raise the hairs on the back of my neck or bring a lump to my throat.

"We love baseball," poet Donald Hall says, "because it seizes and retains the past, like the snowy village inside a glass paperweight." Hall is the supreme poet of baseball, but is that actually *right*? A glass paperweight is not life; and surely, whatever else it is, baseball is part of life. And yet, the image captures an undeniable appeal: baseball, played in the present, always seems somehow to contain, and illuminate, the past. Turn the globe upside down, and the settled snow will fall, and fall again. These little globes are purchased as souvenirs, to contain memories. They're already projecting themselves into some future moment when, idly, we will pick up and invert the fluid-filled chamber.

No wonder that the literal snow globe which features so prominently in Orson Welles' *Citizen Kane* (1941), dropped and smashed as Kane utters his immortal "Rosebud...," has become cinematic shorthand. It means any object or feature that instantly communicates longing, especially frustrated or wistful: the green dock light in *The Great Gatsby*, the ruby slippers in *The Wizard of Oz*, the mysterious statuette in *The Maltese Falcon*. And, of course, the snagged home-run ball in Don DeLillo's novella *Pafko at the Wall* (1992), prelude to the monumental *Underworld* (1997). The snow globe is thus related to, but distinct from, Alfred Hitchcock's famous "MacGuffin": the mysterious object of desire, often unseen, around which the film's action revolves. The snow globe is more personal, and particular; it contains a world.

I think a different metaphor is more apt. Baseball is a scrapbook, idiosyncratic and at times personal, elsewhere as theoretical and abstract as the most arcane rule on the official books. Players speak of "chopping up" the game after it's over, considering blown plays and bad pitches—also remarkable homers and clever gap singles—with the relative calm of clubhouse hindsight. One American player I know, who played in a minor league in Japan, said the hardest thing about doing so was not having a chance to chew over the games afterward. How else can we *slow the game down*, stretching the blurring realities of lived game-time into reflection? Players, unlike television fans, do not enjoy the luxury of instant replay and simultaneous commentary.

There is slow, and there is slower. Writing about baseball, like writing about life, is an always-failed attempt to slow down the flow of consciousness, to capture it—some of it— in discourse. If Proust and Woolf could not do it completely, if Ian McEwan spent a whole novel relating one man's single Saturday and Nicholson Baker expanded the thoughts of a shopping-mall escalator ride into another volume, who can hope to seize, in words, even one baseball game, let alone baseball as such? And yet, the diamond's play of equal and opposite forces, baseball's feeling of pent energy, forever calls to us for reflection. My friend, the writer Lauren Oliver, put it this way on one opening day not long ago: "Baseball— it's like the art film of sport: no plot, anti-climactic, beauty in slow-motion and repetition, and the sounds of wood cracking and leather hitting leather."

Slow the game down. In what follows, I will relay facts and indulge narrative impulses, analyze the game and the desires it prompts in us. It is axiomatic in baseball writing that the game is both itself and more than itself. Again, true enough. But baseball is not everything: it does not explain the universe, demystify human consciousness, or settle the relation between the two. Nevertheless, the abiding theme of these reflections—the importance of failure and error to human self-understanding—recurs and mutates across these pages precisely because of baseball's ability, however indirect, to aid philosophical heavy lifting. In particular, there is no better tutor of human failure's enduring significance than this strange, crooked game of base.

We learn best by failing, because failure is the site of success illuminated. Far more often, we fail without learning anything, and think we have learned when we have merely succeeded. A game which embraces failure as its beating heart offers a significance beyond its apparent pointlessness. In this as in other ways, baseball acquires a status akin to art, genuine leisure, and those other non-utilitarian pursuits that

Aristotle long ago recognized as the highest and most divine parts of ourselves.

The book is structured as a series of linked interventions, not exactly essays in the traditional sense, but sometimes essayistic. They try to isolate aspects of this larger argument. Some are short, some long; some personal and some quite theoretical. Several might be considered versions of the seventh-inning stretch, leisurely pauses to refresh the main action. You can sing then, or get a beer, or (more likely) check your phone. I don't mind.

A word about my subtitle. Attempting to say why something matters, especially if it is a game that belongs, in its history and reality, to millions, is clearly some kind of fool's errand. So I'm not claiming I have, in what follows, all the answers about the appeal and meaning of baseball. This isn't a work of sociology: I don't pretend to offer an account of how people come to be attached to baseball teams, or why the church of baseball might have replaced more conventional sites of worship. But for me, *mattering* is a matter of what a thing teaches us, its ability to convey insight. The genius of baseball is the way it can be about so many things that it is not, explicitly, about. Its lessons are deep and various, and the form I adopt here—memories and arguments, these interlocked sorties of history, language, opinion, and statistics—are my attempt to illustrate how the game keeps on teaching us, with every single at-bat and out. That is what mattering means.

There is a narrative arc, if not a single grand argument, that unites the book, It is my own story as a lifetime fan, however conflicted and sometimes ambivalent I remain about organized and professional baseball. Because baseball feels like a game that ought to resist excessive organization and the success-driven imperatives of professional sports, that ambivalence is real and never quite laid to rest. More troubling still, baseball is rife with sexism, racism, and every version of those forces of crude economic calculation that rob life of romance, sanity, and hope—and that's just in the Little League World Series.

By the time we scale the tricky rockface of genetics, luck, and social selection that leads to the Major Leagues, pretty much every depravity and blemish of human character is available on daily view, and twice in those cities with franchises in both leagues. We know this, we cannot fail to know it, because baseball is that rarest of things, a game that is contested by its most elite players on almost every single day of their season, 162 games in all, from May to October. And then it gets really interesting. The lives of those players—the troubled relationships, on-the-road misbehaviour, drug abuse and domestic violence—have been described more than once. It is enough to say here that success in professional baseball is often a direct cause of failure in other aspects of life.

But baseball also exhibits extraordinary beauty, sportsmanship, and the most elusive quality of competitive sports, a feeling of ravishing transcendence. How is it possible that something so devilishly hard can, in exalted moments, be made to look so graceful and right? How can a confrontation between two players, both of whom know *exactly* what the other is trying to do, be so bewitching, even as (at least) seven other on-field players crouch motionless and watch, engaged in a peculiar kind of active waiting? This basic stillness of baseball, the constant renewal of tension out of pause, of action exploding from an apparent standstill, is an ever-recurring wonder.

In Japanese aesthetic thought, *ma* means the quality of negative space: a gap, or pause, or separation between two related things. *Ma* is the silence between the notes of a Bach aria played by Glenn Gould; it is the perfectly timed pause before a poem's final line—or a joke's punchline; it is, more subtly, the feeling of presence exuded by an absent friend

15

whose room we enter. In sport, it pervades the scene of sumo wrestling, where the ritual salt-purification of the ring, the elaborate greetings and foot-stomping gradually gather every particle of energy in the arena into the apparently sudden, in fact elaborately orchestrated, clash of two gargantuan bodies moving with astonishing speed and power.[1]

Baseball is a constant lesson in the deep pull of this quality. It is a game that can, and does, reorder the charge of every molecule in one's known universe. The pitcher faces the batter. The fielders stand waiting. Legendary Yankees radio broadcaster John Sterling, going strong since 1989, takes a characteristic pause when the pitcher begins to deal: "And ... thuh ... *pitch.*" Action initiated, play begun. We dwell in those pauses and gaps, biting our nails or rocking our knees but more often just *waiting.* "The game doesn't change the way you sleep or wash your face or chew your food," the narrator notes in DeLillo's story. "It changes nothing but your life."[2]

Another concept from Asian philosophy, this time Chinese, is relevant here: *wu wei,* a central feature of Taoism, is the idea of *non-doing* — a state of being that is so natural and fluid as to seem effortless, without struggle. *Wu wei* — action without doing — is the paradoxical goal of wise existence.

Baseball's aesthetic appeal is deeply entwined with that feeling of smooth, second-nature success. We can see, too, how one might, according to this wisdom, succeed in one sense and still fail in another, more essential way. Visibly effortful achievement lacks the crowning finesse of genuine baseball grace, the *sprezzatura* of carefully careless execution. Winning ugly is still winning, but it is somehow tainted, debased. In an ideal world, there is no striving in baseball.

Meanwhile, the game itself is structured so that any success — bunching hits, converting an easy pop-up into a towering moonshot, turning a 6-4-3 double play — feels like a hard-won gift. Indeed, various degrees of failure are so pervasive on the diamond that they should remind us how remarkable it is that there is any success at all. Baseball is agonizing, not least because even the players spend most of their time watching and hoping rather than actually acting. How much worse for spectators!

And yet, in a sad failure of appreciation, we routinely forget these lessons about difficulty. That is a fan's right: we are allowed to jeer a player for striking out or booting a grounder. But underneath there should lie a profound gratitude, and admiration. To fail at such a high level is something only the exalted few can experience.

My ambition is a simple but difficult one: nudging one fan's particular, maybe peculiar, baseball story somewhere towards the region of generality. Baseball is a game where exceptionally talented people spend time getting things wrong and then, incredibly, manage to make impossible things look easy. I can't do that, but I hope at least that I will be able to show why the difficult is so difficult.

Every book fails, as Beckett reminds us. That's because books are human projects and every human project, including each human life, fails. There is no perfection in the republic of letters any more than there is in the mortal realm. But an imperfect life can still be a beautiful one, and though all of our lives must end, there is much success in that universal failure of mortality. That is the nature of things: a life finished is not, any more than a game suspended, a final decision. And always, always there is the possibility of *better*.

Failure in achieving the perfection we seek is our lot in life. *Nothing else ever.* How we navigate the channels of earthly contingency, including the biggest contingency of all, is what makes human lives worthy of celebration. Baseball is just one of many routes to insight on these central points of existence, but one with a privileged democratic appeal. Which is to say: not all philosophers are fans of baseball, but all fans of baseball are, after their own fashion, philosophers.

Love

WHAT IS LOVE?

Not all love is romantic love, but for better or worse it remains the standard, conflicted point of reference. Let us say, in accordance with one classical definition of such, that it is *a passage from contingent encounter to necessary relation*. That we met and fell in love is a matter governed to a harrowing degree by chance — not arbitrary, exactly, but highly improbable and unlikely. Not all couples *meet cute*, as Hollywood parlance has it, but there's always a possible-worlds moment when no kind of meeting might have replaced the one that comes to matter so much. Soon, or anyway at some future point, we cannot imagine not being in love. The saddest thing about a love that fades is the memory of those times when it seemed impossible it should ever do so.

Maybe worse, all love is itself a failure — even when it succeeds. Should our love outlast the multitude of contingencies that batter against it, as Shakespeare's sonnets suggest it should, well, what then? Either you or I must go before the other. If it is me, I leave you bereft, which I cannot bear; if it is you, then I am the one bereaved, and that is worse because it must be lived. Love is not happiness, it is vulnerability. "We are never so defenceless against

19

suffering," Freud reminds us, "as when we love." Loving a game is not the same as loving a person, but the feelings of defencelessness — of being at the mercy of the contingent — can sometimes seem similar.

In the film adaptation of Bernard Malamud's heartbreaking novel, *The Natural* (book 1952; movie 1984), the character Roy Hobbs, a conflicted tragic hero, utters an immortal line. It has been voted on some fan polls as one of the top ten baseball-movie quotes of all time, up there with "There's no crying in baseball!" (*A League of Their Own*, 1992) and "If you build it, they will come" (*Field of Dreams*, 1989) — not to mention "Today (*day ... day*) I consider myself (*self ... self*) the luckiest man on the face of the earth" (*Pride of the Yankees*, 1942). Hobbs, attempting a comeback after a mysterious tryst and gunshot wound, says to another character: "God, I love baseball."

It is one of the many liberties the screenwriters and director Barry Levin took with Malamud's original story, which is downbeat and sad to the point of depression. In the novel, Hobbs' comeback is marred by game-fixing schemes and a deliberate echo of the 1919 Black Sox "Eight Men Out" scandal (for which see John Sayles' 1988 drama of that name, with appropriate nods to worker exploitation). In the book, a disgraced Hobbs is confronted by a young newsboy who pressed him for an explanation of how the pristine game has come to be sullied by politics and money. "Say it ain't true, Roy," he implored, an obvious reference to the plaintive "Say it ain't so, Joe," directed at real-life baseball natural and game-thrower "Shoeless" Joe Jackson as he left a Chicago courtroom.

The truth is hard to figure, though. The actual quotation, reported in the *Chicago Daily News*, apparently went this way: "It ain't true, is it Joe?" "Yes, kid, I'm afraid it is," Jackson replied. This version is closer to Malamud's, lacking the so-Joe rhyme, but Jackson would later deny that the exchange ever happened in any form; it was a figment of the reporter's imagination. More seriously, Jackson's culpability in the scandal was questioned repeatedly—a fact reflected in Sayles' film treatment—and a Chicago jury acquitted the eight players implicated in the scandal in 1921. Nevertheless, Major League commissioner Kenesaw Mountain Landis saw fit to ban Jackson for life starting in the 1920 season.

"Regardless of the verdict of juries," Landis said, "no player that throws a ballgame; no player that undertakes or promises to throw a ballgame; no player that sits in a conference with a bunch of crooked players and gamblers where the ways and means of throwing games are planned and discussed and does not promptly tell his club about it, will ever play professional baseball."

Of course this is not true—witness Pete Rose. But that is a story for another time, and another commissioner.

Maybe Levinson was right to salvage Roy Hobbs from the slagheap of moral failure, and instead elevate him into the fireworks-strewn heavens of legend. That's how the movie ends, anyway. Robert Redford's constrained, even tight-lipped performance as Hobbs lends an undeniable, slender elegance to this mythology, even though he can't throw a baseball worth a damn. When he delivers the line in question, there is a traditional superaddition of Redfordian charisma to carry it into the realm of sincere conviction.

I have played baseball at most stages of my life, usually very badly, and I have loved it for even longer and with considerably more success. The two things are not unrelated.

I played T-ball in elementary-school gym class, and stood cluelessly through grade-four games where no throw was ever caught. I played sandlot ball on empty blocks in seaside towns when I was ten, on summer-abandoned schoolyard diamonds made of gravel when I was 13, and on beautiful grass swards of university campus land when I was 19, where the best part was the draft-beer sessions afterwards. I have played for college-newspaper softball teams, for pick-up sides composed of Sunday-morning louts with expansive insult lexicons, for corporate fastball teams with no morale or talent whatsoever, including a bunch of newspaper sports-writers who could not play sports, and for scrub teams of every shape and size.

Aged 12, I was an honorary coach for a Little League team managed by my Uncle Bryan and starring my cousin Jeff, a hothead who always ended his slides by coming up swinging. I was good at chatter and scoring, and I learned from my uncle, coaching the hitters at third base, how signals work. My younger brother Sean sat in the dugout with me, a dugout that was in fact a little enclosure of chain-link wire fencing and grey steel poles built into the backstop wings. When our uncle went out to the mound to talk with the pitcher, Sean trotted out too. He was nine.

I'm not sure what wisdom he thought he would impart to the towering athletic 12-year-olds of Port Credit, Ontario, but he had a serious face under his Pepsi-logo bucket hat and a professional-looking trot. I like to imagine that he was like the coach in *Bull Durham* (1988), who solves wedding-gift dilemmas and bad-juju frights in a rapid-fire conference at the mound. "Okay, well, uh ... candlesticks always make a nice gift, and uh, maybe you could find out where she's registered and maybe a place-setting or maybe a silverware pattern. Okay, let's get two! Go get 'em."

Along the way, like everyone else, I was hit by pitches and called out on bad running decisions. I dropped easy-out flies and more than once threw the ball wide. Way more than once I was guilty of arrogance; for example, pitching against a nerdy English graduate student, who proceeded to school all of us in the art of batting by cricket-placing a string of base hits to every empty patch of grass on the field. He had never stood between the foul lines before or heard of Casey Stengel, but he knew how to hit 'em where they ain't, even as the rest of us tried to swat heroic home runs that ended up as easy dribblers to the pitcher.

Like most people, I was never very good at baseball, because baseball is a difficult game to be good at, at any level. Chubby and somewhat indolent as a child, I didn't make a full Little League team at any point, nor did I play for my high school or college. The only "uniforms" I ever possessed were (1) a red t-shirt advertising the Loewen Windows fastball team, some housing outfit based in Steinbach, Manitoba (just checked; they're still a going concern)—which, come to think of it, was probably a hand-me-down from my older brother Steve; (2) an orange *Globe and Mail* t-shirt from an ill-advised advertising campaign of the 1980s (why orange?); and (3) a white t-shirt with blue three-quarter sleeves that bore the script logo "Varsity Thunderbirds."

This last name was based on a deep inside joke among the staff of the college-newspaper at the University of Toronto. On that squad of nerds and student-politics hacks I fielded neurotically but adequately at shortstop, and managed to hit the opposite way against my natural left-field pull by way of some fancy footwork at the plate. With the shift on, I stepped left across the box and punched the ball into right field. The tactical weakness of a shift: go opposite field, and there's nobody there. On the *Globe* slo-pitch team, bizarrely competitive as these "casual" leagues so often are, there were few notable moments. The mustachioed goons from the tabloid *Toronto Sun* routinely kicked our asses, complete with cry-baby sound effects and Bronx cheers aimed at our presumed paper-of-record pretensions. Meanwhile, the natural athletes over at the *Toronto Star*—Hemingway's old paper, as they never tired of pointing out—were just better than everyone else. I don't imagine Papa ever played fastball for them, or anybody else, but that didn't seem to matter.

The *Globe* team had two good players, our catcher and my friend Jim Davidson, who wrote sports and had recruited me into the team. Jim was old school. He liked to call the newly opened Toronto SkyDome (1989), a marvel of futuristic retractable-roof engineering on the scale of the evil-genius lair in *Moonraker*, "the yard." As in, "I'm going down to the yard to catch the game. Wanna come?" Charmless old Exhibition Stadium, which predated the Dome and witnessed snow-dusted home openers and bone-chilling late-season games, was universally known as the "Mistake by the Lake." It didn't even deserve to be called a yard, let alone a field.

Jim once fielded a pop-up along the first-base line by running full tilt into foul territory, Jeter-Donaldson-style. He neatly snagged the ball and then plowed into the cyclone fence so hard that a sting pattern of the chain-links was lacerated into his thigh. Diamonds on the diamond. He was a good player, fearless and tough. The catcher was good too. The rest of us were pathetic. That *Globe* team boasted a pitcher from the press room, an old guy missing a finger on his right hand, possibly as a result of some tiff with the offset-printing monster machines that resided in the basement of the *Globe* building on Front Street. It was rumoured that this debility actually allowed him some sort of occult spin on the ball, but I never witnessed this particular brand of magic. He was like R. A. Dickey or Tim Wakefield marshalling the capricious knuckleball: some days the pitch was there, other days not so much. We had lots of other days.

Again, like most of us, I have a snapshot album of memories and near-memories. I caught a few decent games for a student team that took on the staff and priests of my Catholic high school in the late 1970s. Among other things, I threw out a trunk-dragging Jesuit at second to end a game. *Unhitch the trailer, padre!* I had a decent arm then, at least with a softball. But I confess that I was also a bit of a jerk on the field, and at this late date I ask Fr. Dave Nazar, then a bearded, young priest-in-training, and Mr. Larry Franz, my brilliant physics teacher, to forgive me my trespasses. Fr. Nazar is these days, I see, a big wheel in the Vatican, and I hope he doesn't remember that time, with their side batting skins in a shirts/skins game, when I tried to rattle him at the plate by noting that he was "scrawny and pudgy at the same time."

During the late 1980s, playing for the hapless *Globe* side, I recall making a sprawling tag out of a stealing runner at second base off a hot throw from the catcher—oblivious to the lead runner breaking from third for a go-ahead run. As I lay in the dust, I noted that the ump actually blew the call—don't tell anyone, but I had missed the tag—and also that the right play would have been to fire the ball directly back to home to prevent the go-ahead run. *D'oh*. I remember matching a high-fly catch in left field one day in the summer of 1981, playing a long-evening softball game with a bunch of other students. I had been daydreaming and thinking about Kierkegaard, suddenly coming to awareness as the ball descended my way in that arc of slightly sickening inevitability that all outfielders recognize. *Mine mine mine*. (Jeebus, I hope I have it.)

Late to the moment, I misjudged the ball almost completely, falling backwards on friendly campus grass and flinging out my glove behind me to *just* sno-cone the catch. Holding up the catch in the approved wannabe-pro manner, I got back to my feet and fired the ball somewhere in the general direction of the pitcher. I heard the cheering from a dark-haired woman on the other team, Jane Coffey, who I fancied I was in love with. *She knows my name!*

Nothing ever came of that. Nothing ever came of my baseball career either, except the stone-cold knowledge that "career" is a wildly inappropriate word for it. But I loved playing baseball. And watching it. And thinking about it. Another snapshot, a sort of aimless home-movie clip that lodges in my mind for no good reason except that it was about baseball. My older brother Steve and I, bored on a family camping trip across the Prairies, find ourselves with a little free time in some po-dunk town between Winnipeg and wherever. North Battleford? Estevan? I don't know.

Bored out of our minds, we hung around the main street and then spotted a couple of teenage boys in baseball uniforms. They had gloves and a bat, and they were older than us. They seemed headed somewhere with a sense of purpose, men at work, so we followed them. I know that maybe sounds weird, but we were *soooooo* bored. If they were going to a baseball game, life suddenly might be interesting for an hour or two. We trailed them along the street, down a couple of side roads, toward what looked like a municipal park. There were two diamonds laid out in opposite corners of a big field. Yay! Baseball!

There was no one else to be seen. The diamonds were empty, the outfields deserted. No canvas bags of bats and balls, no chatter of pepper-playing athletes, no smack of ball into glove. Nothing. The two kids crossed the field and disappeared into a residential neighbourhood on the other side, like ghosts of disappointment and *not at all* like the old-timey players who wander into the tall corn in *Field of Dreams* (1989). This film is loosely based on the novel *Shoeless Joe* (1982) by Canadian Prairie writer W. P. Kinsella, who ended his own life with physician assistance in September 2016, while I was writing this. Neither film nor book existed when I walked the dusty streets of Estevan, if that's where we were, but I can say that neither contains much of the flat, unforgiving grimness pervading that landscape. If you build it, will they come? Maybe in the cornfields of Iowa. In Saskatchewan, they had better get ready for disappointment and bring a jug of Kool-Aid.

I find it hard to convey the depth of everyday despair that freighted the look Steve and I exchanged at this

moment of failure. No game, no strikes and misses, no
grounders to short, no home runs. Nothing. We trudged
back to meet our parents and head for the next campsite,
where Steve would begin an epic-protest bout of soli-
taire-playing in the trailer, not emerging except for meals
and bodily relief over many days. I lacked his commitment
to protesting boredom with boredom, and found solace in
swimming whenever I could.

Why do we love baseball? It is not an easy issue to resolve.
Is it the beauty of the field's abstract geometry, its linear
refusal of territory and conquest? Is it the preternatural
grace of the players, whose bodies are, superficially, so akin
to our own sad ones—not the behemoths of football or the
off-world giants of basketball—but yet so far advanced in
skill, speed, and judgment, these stealth X-Men? Or is it the
sheer difficulty of the game, which started as a sort of picnic
diversion and advanced ever farther towards the vanishing
point of coordinated perfection?

They say hitting a Major-League fastball is the hardest
feat in sports. But then, hitting a curve, the graveyard of
talented-but-limited hitters, is harder. How about tracking
down a screaming fly to right? Or fielding a hot shot to second and then softly tossing the ball in pursuit of a 4-6-3 double play? And what about a double play, anyway? The pitcher's best friend, they call it, as if best friends were easy to
come by. And what about, for crying out loud, a *triple* play?
We can only hope to witness a few of these, if any, in a lifetime. What the hell does that say about this game that seems
so casual in design, so devilish, fascinating, and sublime in
execution?

"I believe in the church of baseball," Susan Sarandon's
character says in *Bull Durham*. It's a goofy line in a fairly
goofy if amiable movie, one that does not hold up over the
span of time—the rest of the monologue is unquotable without a measure of embarrassment: "I've tried all the major

religions and most of the minor ones. I've worshipped Buddha, Allah, Brahma, Vishnu, Shiva, trees, mushrooms, and Isadora Duncan. I know things. For instance, there are 108 beads in a Catholic rosary and there are 108 stitches in a baseball. When I learned that, I gave Jesus a chance. *[sigh]* But it just didn't work out between us. The Lord laid too much guilt on me. I prefer metaphysics to theology." Okay, please stop now.

But, but—there is some basic truth in there, even or especially for non-believers. The church of baseball lies in the same quarter as that church described in the opening lines of Norman Maclean's *A River Runs Through It* (novella 1976; film 1992): "In our family, there was no clear line between religion and fly fishing. We lived at the junction of great trout rivers in western Montana and our father was a Presbyterian minister who tied his own flies and taught others. He told us about Christ's disciples being fishermen, and we were left to assume, as my brother and I did, that all first-class fishermen on the Sea of Galilee were fly fishermen, and that John, the favorite, was a dry-fly fisherman."

I prefer metaphysics to theology too, and like these two fictional voices I find I mostly belong to no church except those of baseball and fly fishing. They are, in my experience, the most comprehensively beautiful pursuits that exist outside the world of books. Here the simple truth of love reigns over all. "Why is it incomparably thrilling?" Thomas McGuane once asked, rhetorically, about fishing. "It's the contest joined, but it's also a kind of euphoric admiration and—this is risky—it feels like love. You watch your fish and you are filled with admiration, transported by beauty. Isn't that love? It was in high school!"

I love baseball. It is the Sabbath, the soul-saving time out of time, the space of sacred observance. You can bring your smartphone to the game, but the game's irrefutable leisure will not submit to the routine logic of swiping and posting.

Your tweets do not capture the game!

We all need sabbaticals, even if they happen on days other than Saturday or Sunday. We crave with a lover's hunger the inimitable openness of a batter walking to the plate, getting set in the box, poised to face the waiting hurler, himself a portrait in classic posture. The waiting is everything. A pause in baseball is always pregnant; a stoppage of play in any other game, in football, say, is just that: nullity without expectation or drama; not play bracketed by the game, merely play suspended by the clock. Can you love a pause? Can you love a logic of pauses? Can you love a game whose essence lies in the motionlessness that opens up between motions, and gives them meaning?

But explaining why is like conveying in words the exaltation—the raising high—one feels when Glenn Gould plays music by William Byrd or Orlando Gibbons.[3] No love so intimate and personal, so wrapped in biography and mortality, is ever easily shared. They say that Lucifer, before the celebrated prideful fall, was the anointed guardian of music in heaven. Now there is an image for the poetic among us! Baseball is the heavenly, devilish music of the physical world. Our love here is a complicated, implicated property. Angels in the outfield, sure. Devils too.

We try to parse this love, so bound up with our lives and sense of being here. We fail, of course, because the recurring lesson here—as so often—is failure. And sometimes it is better to try not to try, that deeper and more complicated metaphysical lesson. If there is success, it is a matter of the great conjunction where moderate skill meets luck, contingency, fate, and circumstance.

Oh, and also weather. In Spanish, *el tiempo* means both "time" and "weather." Baseball tells time in idiosyncratic, non-chronological ways. Its time is, in effect, a matter of weather. I can't help thinking that if one understood just this one grammatical conjunction completely, it would unlock the secret of baseball's deep metaphysical pull.

One cannot do that, not completely or perfectly. And yet we try. Of course we do. It's not like we have a choice — since choosing not to try is itself a choice.

Fail (1)

IT IS A COMMONPLACE AMONG baseball people that the game is about failure. Very true. It comes in many forms.

Most obvious: failure at the plate. Everyone knows that if you fail seven times out of ten to get on base with a hit—walks and struck-batsmen don't count, nor do sacrifices (bunt or fly)—you are a potential Hall-of-Fame hitter. Reaching first base on an error or a fielder's choice also doesn't count as a hit, though it does count as an at-bat, because rewarding somebody just for getting there would give credit where credit is not due, or maybe it would be too easy.

Nowadays, on-base percentage, or OBP, matters a lot more to some managers, and many fans, than batting average. It is a much better mark of offensive potential in a player. Or consider WAR, the abstruse stat concerning "wins above replacement"—a measure, ideally, of how valuable a particular player is compared to any available alternative. Of course, wins happen for a lot of reasons, just like losses. Nevertheless, the stats universe is slow to swing towards reason in baseball. It's probably more important to consider a pitcher's earned-run average (ERA)—the number of runs he has allowed through his own failure, rather than someone else's (errors, or inherited baserunners), averaged over a notional nine innings. But there is far more atavistic magic in the idea of wins per season.

A 20-game winner will always command respect, in other words, even if the details show that more than a few of those wins were squeakers he would have lost but for some mid-game offensive explosion or a couple of rally-killing put-outs. J. A. Happ recorded his 20th win of the 2016 season in late September, capping an outstanding season for a team that doesn't always back up its starting pitchers. I was at the ballpark when Happ won his 18th of the year, a pitching gem that was also a 3-2 nail-biter against the Red Sox, who would go on to lead the division into the final week of the season. The night before, Boston's Rick Porcello won *his* 20th in a 13-3 laugher against the September-doomed Blue Jays. Porcello would rack 22 altogether and win a controversial Cy Young Award over Justin Verlander.

Happ was the first Blue Jay to win 20 since Roy Halladay in 2008. He thus joined Halladay, Pat Hentgen, Jack Morris, Roger Clemens, and David Wells in the Jays' 20-game club—a roster that includes a couple of Cy Young winners, one of them a *seven-time* laureate, and one player who some think should be in the Hall of Fame.

Note for those keeping score: these last two are the same player. And one of the *other* members of the Jays' 20-win club is one of the most vocal opponents of said player's Hall of Fame election because of his—the other guy's—use of performance-enhancing drugs. Okay, what the hell: Roger Clemens is the seven-time Cy Young winner who has been denied election to the Hall because of juice rumours; Roy Halladay is among his ardent critics. Suffice to say that they will not be toasting each other at the Jays Old-Timers's Day picnics.

The Jays outbid 11 other teams to get Happ, late of the Mariners. The long-limbed starter was eventually signed for a $36-million, three-year deal. The contract seemed excessive, if not deranged, at the time; now it is revealed as brilliant and visionary. "Nobody in their wildest dreams thought Happ was going to win twenty games, I don't think," manager John Gibbons said when Happ racked his double-decade win. "He might have, but not many guys would have predicted that, because not many guys win twenty games anymore, really."[4]

Well, they do—but it's harder, especially because the modern five-man pitching rotation means fewer starts for elite pitchers, and the whole notion of middle relief makes it a dice-roll whether a good initial outing will result in a win or a bullpen collapse. (The Jays even went to a six-man rotation in late 2016, to keep youngster Aaron Sanchez in the mix.) Is Happ a better pitcher than rotation-mate Marco Estrada? Or the Dodgers' Clayton Kershaw, who won the 2013 Cy Young with just 16 wins but an ERA of 1.83? Or the Mariners' Félix Hernández, who snagged the 2010 honour with a divey 13-12 mark, one of the worst non-reliever records on the books?

Baseball wins belong to everybody, just like losses, but only pitchers have a score in the column marked "W-L." Note for weirdness geeks: it is possible to have a career ERA of infinity, if a pitcher allowed one or more earned runs in a single Major League appearance without retiring a batter— presumably just before getting back on the bus to some sad one-horse minor-league town. Talk about a bitter cup of coffee! The good news is that there is also the chance to record a lifetime batting average of 1.000, racking a base hit or two without an out before leaving the Bigs. There are, in fact, some eighty Major League players who posted lifetime perfect batting averages; of them, only eighteen-year-old John Paciorek, called up by the Houston Colt .45s for one game in 1963, did better: he went three-for-three against the Mets, with two walks, four runs scored, and three batted in. Then he never saw another pitch in the Show. Career batting line?

Batting average 1.000, on-base percentage 1.000, slugging percentage 1.000. Compare Babe Ruth's career numbers: .342 average, .474 OPB, and .690 slugging. Piker.[5]

Despite theoretical weirdness of that sort, batting average still rules in career hitting tallies, not least because nobody recorded on-base percentage (OBP) for many decades of the game's history. For those who *are* keeping score, OBP is in fact an average, not a percentage and = (hits + walks + hit-by-pitch) / (at-bats + walks + hit-by-pitch + sac flies). Again, batters are not credited with reaching base on an error or fielder's choice, and they are not charged with an opportunity if they make a sacrifice bunt. So, basically, it's times-on-base divided by at-bats, but with the usual exceptions and caveats.

If you combine this figure with slugging percentage, or SLG—a hitter's total number of bases reached, divided by his at-bats—you get the magical OPS measure, or on-base-plus-slugging.

This formula nowadays dominates the minds of general managers. Expressed formally, OPS = at-bats *times* (hits + walks + hit-by-pitch) + total bases *times* (at-bats + walks + hit-pitch + sac flies) *divided by* at-bats *times* (at-bats + walks + hit-by-pitch + sac flies). In other, less tortuous words: this is the number of times you reach, combined with how far you get when you *do* reach, expressed as a function of how many times you try. A very good OBP is .360 or so; a good SLB is in the .450 range, and a good, productive OPS is somewhere around .820.

Okay then! But fans are simple folk, mostly, and batting average still dominates the narrative of success at the plate. Under the game's excruciating extenuating circumstances, which are just normal by the game's standards, if you fail to get a base hit just six times in ten tries you will land among the immortals. No one has hit for .400 during a baseball regular season since Ted Williams in 1941. Williams himself, with a glittering .406 average, was the first player to do it since Bill Terry in 1930. A few more recent players have come close, including, in 1994, San Diego's Tony Gwynn, who was hitting .394 on August 11, when a players' strike ended play for the year.

Then there is a failed season. That was also the season when the Montreal Expos, at 74-40, were clearly the best and most dominant team in the game, and Matt Williams of the Giants had 43 home runs in 112 games, well within reach of Roger Maris' longstanding regular-season record of 61 homers, since bested three times by juiced Sammy Sosa (66 in 1998, 64 in 2001, 63 in 1999), juiced Mark McGwire (70 in 1998, 65 in 1999), and juiced Barry Bonds (73 in 2001).

1994: a season of many might-have-beens. In 1980, with no strike yet looming, Kansas City mainstay George Brett, he of the tar-stained bat and general outrage over umpiring, was hitting .399 as late as September 19 — .39950, in fact — but could not shatter the .400 threshold, finishing the season hitting .390. Like every other Blue Jays fan of the same vintage, I watched charisma-free first baseman John Olerud, an outstanding talent out of Washington State University, flirt with the mark during the hot weeks of the Jays' 1993 season, which would conclude with a second consecutive World Series victory.

For 58 of the 158 games Olerud played that year—itself an impressive roster of appearances in the 162-game season—he hit .400 or better. He was above .400 into August, August 24 in fact, the first player to accomplish that feat since Williams in 1941. Even his slow and steady performances at the plate, with a silky smooth table-clearing swing that was the envy of the league, and a demeanour seemingly impervious to pressure, risk, or ambient temperature, could not keep him at the peak for long. Olerud succumbed to history, inevitability, the laws of physics, and everything else that makes Major League hitting the single most challenging feat in sports.

He fell short of the magic line in the waning days of that fall, consigned to the teeming leagues of the almost-great with a league-leading but merely mortal .363 batting average for the year. Subsequent seasons as a Met, Mariner, Yankee, and Red Sock would never provide such drama again. While with the Mets in 1999 he was touted by *Sports Illustrated* as part of the "best infield in league history," along with Robin Ventura, Edgardo Alfonzo, and Rey Ordóñez; but Olerud's career was one of general decline; he would retire in 2005 after an undistinguished foray in Boston, a member of the College Baseball Hall of Fame but not of the big house in Cooperstown.

Next up: failure in the field. In no other major sport is "error" an official scoring category, feared and respected by fielders at every position. There are unforced errors noted in tennis and volleyball matches, but they are not entered as black marks against the player's name for all time. There are penalties in football for excessively violent or devious play, but they too fall to the wayside after the content is concluded. A ballplayer's errors haunt him, a long statistical contrail of gaffes, misjudged grounders, flubbed pop-ups, and air-mailed throws that follows him around forever.

What do errors mean? There may be, according to another famous movie quotation, "no crying in baseball" (though *pace* Tom Hanks there is lots of crying, in fact maybe more now than ever), but there is certainly a lot of arguing. Managers object to calls, and until recently all they could do was argue—an ump's decision was never reversed, except occasionally post-game by the larger powers that be. But how can you argue about an error, anyway? A bad judgment on the part of the ump may be cause for exasperation and objection, but bad judgment in the field is just failure.

Arguing about error poses some interesting questions, however. Such argument might be a matter not of countervailing correctness ("You got it wrong!") but of what lawyers call mitigation ("Yes, I got it wrong, but for good reasons!"). I am trying to convince you, in each case, either that the error is understandable (by plausible association) or else not an error at all (unwitting rightness). Indeed, the two moves nicely capture the Oxford philosopher J. L. Austin's celebrated distinction between *excuses* and *justifications*. These concepts seem close, if not identical, and are often run together; but as Austin argued in his paper "A Plea for Excuses" (1956), keeping them apart allows us to understand our ordinary language, and hence ourselves, better. An excuse admits the error or miscue but offers some reason or reasons for why it happened; a justification attempts to say that in fact there was no real error or miscue.

Consider a characteristic Austinian example: "You dropped the tea tray: Certainly, but an emotional storm was about to break out: or, Yes, but there was a wasp. In each case the defense, very soundly, insists on a fuller description of the event in its context; but the first is a justification, the second an excuse." Austin's imagination runs typically to garden party or high table for its examples, but his nuanced appreciation of what we say in response to error—how we attempt to deal with muffs—applies as much to ethics and law, and baseball. You shot someone: Certainly, but he was threatening my son (justification): or, Yes, but I mistook him for a deer (excuse).

Just for the record, a *post facto* justification—such as discovering that Istanbul is in fact Constantinople—may shade it towards excuse. The lines are not always hard.

All of which highlights the fact that error, like the deliberate flaw in a Persian rug or the Asian aesthetic theory of deliberate imperfection known as *wabi-sabi*, is far more intriguing than correctness. Error, the psychoanalyst Jacques Lacan said, is the site of truth far more than correctness. We are never closer to the real than when we are making mistakes, sometimes especially when we *realize* we are making them.

As with some kinds of social behaviour, often there is no such thing as correctness except insofar as error deviates it. For example, there is an important difference between doing something mistakenly and doing it inadvertently—did you hit Hot when you meant to hit Cold, or did you hit Hot while reaching for the soap? But there is no corresponding debate about things done "takenly" or "advertently." Even when obvious linguistic pairs exist, care must be exerted: we make a mistake if we think my sometimes being careless means that otherwise I am always being careful.

In baseball, errors are calculated as a function of chances; the resulting fielding percentage is one part (though not the most important) in determining the Gold Glove winner at each position. But what counts as a chance? Well, the player must have, in the scorer's judgment, not just a scant chance—the bare possibility—of making the play. He must be in a position where he, or anyone, should make the play—well, anyone who belongs in that league, whatever it is. Error lurks between the routine and the spectacular. As so often in life, you don't get individual credit for extra-good plays, but you do pay individual penalty for ordinarily bad ones. And also for taking bad chances—that's why fielding percentage alone can't determine the Gold Glove decision.

How much worse is that category of unforced errors, especially in individual games such as tennis or golf? The "unforced" seems gratuitous, but it captures its own kind of Austinian distinction: these aren't just bad shots, like a mis-played return of service or missed fairway; they are mistakes the player brings on him- or herself, like fanning on a smash, or driving into a bunker. Actually, given that a golfer's sole opponent is him- or herself and the course, one might even argue that all golf errors are unforced. Ouch.

Errors in fields of play highlight the expansive role played by error everywhere in our mortal experience, the fraught relation between action, speech, and environment. By far the most interesting unforced errors are the ones analyzed by Sigmund Freud in *The Psychopathology of Everyday Life*—the source from which springs the notion of a Freudian slip. As with the tics of neurosis, everyday spoonerisms, misspellings, revealing substitutions and the like—*parapraxis* was Freud's term—show our unconscious minds forcing some repressed thought into tangled utterance. We say what we don't intend but nevertheless mean.

This was a form of ordinary language that Austin did not consider. In his introduction to a recent Penguin Books reissue of the Freud classic, the critic Paul Keegan notes that, in "A Plea for Excuses," Austin said, "I do not know how many of you keep a list of the kinds of fool you make of yourselves." Freud, Keegan argues, is saying this: "I have made a list of the kinds of fool we make of ourselves." Baseball, we might say, is the game in which it is possible to make a list of the kinds of fool we make of ourselves. The statistics don't lie, even if we do.

"Freud," Keegan goes on to say, "is the first observed to be philosophically struck, not by our failure rate, but by how unintrigued we are by the fact—how feckless, how innocent." Yes, that's right: the Penguin text reads "observed," not "observer." Mere typo or unconscious judgment? Is Freud—are you?—the observer or the observed? Are we, perhaps, most observed when we think we are doing the observing? (Take note, ballpark fans: there are cameras everywhere to capture your embarrassing moments of nacho-gobbling, beer-swilling, nose-picking, and bad kisses.)

Observed? Observer? You're an official scorer; you decide. Just remember that it's your own sheet you're recording.

Here's one thing you should enter on every box score. Sometimes love is like the missing step on a staircase that

Heidegger talks about. The missing piece becomes the most important piece. Absence is presence keyed to high volume — we didn't know how much we depended on something so ordinary, until it was gone.

Boom: now I'm falling down the stairs! Did anyone see that?

Fail (2)

To WIN IN BASEBALL IS to embrace the essence of the game, which is its devious, bucolic difficulty, like a pastoral-scene video game that conceals a thousand superhuman challenges. You cannot win if you don't navigate the target-rich environment of striving against immense odds.

Sometimes, the obverse truth rules the day: you can succeed and still not win. And this offers a deep lesson, does it not, something to ponder beyond the diamond. Baseball is a game so cruel that you can do everything right and still lose. A pitcher can throw a gem, racking a team season-record 13 strikeouts over six innings, and be let down by a suddenly lackluster offensive effort by the members of his league-leading batting order, garnering himself an especially painful L. (I saw Marcus Stroman of the Blue Jays so treated the night before writing this.)

A pitcher can even, theoretically, toss a no-hitter and lose—on a combination of errors and walks, say, in a low-score game. This has in fact happened five times in major league baseball since 1900—though three of those were not technically no-hit complete games, since the starting pitchers, on the visiting team, pitched only eight innings. Maybe the most colourful example of this success-as-failure was

Yankees pitcher Andy Hawkins, who delivered a dominating no-hit performance against the White Sox at Comiskey Park on July 1, 1990.

Hawkins sat down the first two batters he faced in the eighth inning and then Yankees fans everywhere, not to mention students of cosmic irony, watched in appalled fascination as a string of error, walk, walk, error, and error contrived to plate *four* no-hit runs for the Pale Hose. The Yankees had nothing to offer in the top of the ninth, and Hawkins entered baseball history as one of its rarest stooges, the pitcher who can't win for winning.

In fact, Hawkins must be considered among the most star-crossed of baseball's fools of fortune. Also in 1990, he pitched a shutout against the Minnesota Twins into 12 innings—the last time a starting pitcher has gone so far in a game—but suffered an eventual 2-0 loss. In his very next appearance, he hurled the Yankees to six innings of no-hit ball against the White Sox, but rain at Yankee Stadium forced the players off the field in the seventh. After a delay, the game was called and Hawkins was denied another chance to record an official no-hit game. His pitching career, already in jeopardy despite these strong starts, was almost over—his best days, in fact, were in the mid-1980s with the San Diego Padres. His last Major League appearance would be in August of 1991.

Even more cruelly, a pitcher can achieve actual perfection and still be robbed of victory, or at least of glory. On June 2, 2011, the Detroit Tigers' powerful right-hander Armando Galaragga was cruising in an outing against Cleveland. The Tigers were up 3-0 going into the ninth inning, a margin built of one home run (Miguel Cabrera in the second) and some good situational hitting, plus luck, in the eighth (Austin Jackson and Johnny Damon plating after two hits and an error by Cleveland's Shin Soo "Big League" Choo). More importantly, Galaragga had retired side after side of Cleveland hitters. No hits, no errors, no men on base, no-no-nothing — he was in line to become just the twenty-first Major League pitcher to record a perfect game.

Twenty-six batters up, 26 batters down. Including, just for extra drama, a circus catch by Austin Jackson in centre field in the top of the ninth. Then — *qué desastre!* An easy grounder from Cleveland's Jason Donald was fielded by Miguel Cabrera and relayed over to Galaragga, who had correctly and smartly moved over to cover first base. Galaragga clearly had his foot on the base when he received the soft toss from Cabrera, and Donald's swift charge down the first-base line was for naught. Except, except — except that first-base umpire Jim Joyce, who had a good look at the play, somehow decided that Donald had beaten the throw and was safe.

Safe! That is, a base hit — gone the perfect game, gone the no-hitter, gone the glory. Fans who watched the game, or viewed the morning-after highlights with appalled wonder, probably had the same expression on their faces as Galaragga. He looks around, first with satisfaction — 27 men retired, game over, history books here I come! Then his smile goes stiff and unbelieving, his face a mask of bemusement. What? What happened? Did the ump just call that guy *safe?!* Yes, Armando, he did. And in the era before instant replay, as in all the years of ball so far, the umpire's ruling is divinely ordained. You can argue, but you cannot alter.

Joyce apologized after the game, tearfully admitting he had blown the call. "I just cost the kid a perfect game," he said. Yes, you did. Even those of us sympathetic to the plight of the umpire, the lone guardian of order in an otherwise imperfect and chaotic world, wished it otherwise. Human error is not just for the players.

Galaragga, to his enormous credit, never berated Joyce, indeed showed a depth of understanding unlikely to be matched by most of us under similar circumstances—allowing, of course, that there are no similar circumstances. He finished the game with a one-hit shutout, an unofficially imperfect perfect game that is sometimes known as "the 28-out perfect game." Sometimes you have to make one more erasure to finish the day; but you cannot erase the ruling that made it necessary to do so.

But maybe the most memorable example of the perfect failure is an even more notorious imperfect perfect game. On May 26, 1959, St. Louis Cardinals lefty Harvey Haddix was enjoying one of those transcendental afternoons when player meets zone, all pitches feel like strikes, and somehow one rises above oneself in a holy concatenation of awesomeness. Haddix was a good-not-great pitcher who would enjoy a 14-year career with a number of teams, finishing with a 136-113 record, including 99 complete games and 21 shutouts (the latter stats totally remarkable for today's game but not unusual in the postwar period). He recorded 1,575 strikeouts and tallied a very respectable lifetime ERA of 3.63. In 1953 he'd won 20 games, and appeared in one of his three All-Star Games. He also won three Gold Gloves. But most of all, Haddix is remembered as a charter member of the Perfect Fail Club.

That day in May, facing the Milwaukee Braves, Haddix was hurling on point. His opponent, Lew Burdette, was pitching his heart out at the same time, and the two teams took a nothing-nothing tie into 13 innings. Haddix was perfect through 12 of them, retiring 36 consecutive hitters with a combination of fastball and slider. He had retired two batters in the bottom of the thirteenth when an error by third baseman Don Hoak allowed Atlanta's Félix Mantilla to reach. He advanced to second on a sac bunt by Eddie Matthews—a little late-innings small ball, there.

Then, with first base open, Haddix intentionally walked Hank Aaron and stood in to face Joe Adcock. A career .277

hitter, Adcock nevertheless had occasional power, and on this day he found the sweet spot, taking Haddix's fastball all the way to the fences. Maybe even over them—the hit appeared to be a home run, and Aaron, running the bases in what he thought was a walk-off, left the path and was passed by the running Adcock. The second out was charged to Adcock for the pass, and the score tallied as 2-0 in favour of Atlanta. Eventually, the National League head office would rule that Adcock's hit was a double, not a dinger, and Mantilla's run alone would count. But it was enough: just short of 13 perfect innings, and there it goes, a game lost at an official score of 1-0.

Some people say it was the best pitching performance in Major League history. Haddix had pitched, in effect, one-and-a-third perfect games. He was showered with congratulations, though also with at least one Bronx cheer. A letter on university stationery arrived from a Texas A&M fraternity, which read, in its entirety, "Dear Harvey, Tough shit." No love lost there for the failures of near perfection, no respect for the perfect being enemy of the good, or maybe just no feeling at all for human frailty and the cruel twists of baseball fate. "It made me mad," Haddix said, employing what might be judged comic understatement, "until I realized they were right. That's exactly what it was." Yes, because tough shit is still shit.

Did Haddix pitch a perfect game despite the loss? Well, he certainly pitched more perfect innings in a single game than any other pitcher in Major League history. Did he pitch a no-hitter, by the same token? Nope—more tough shit there, alas. In 1991, the league powers changed the definition of a no-hitter to "a game in which a pitcher or pitchers complete a game of nine innings or more without allowing a hit." That "or more" was a death-blow to Haddix's near-perfect outing. His game was taken off the list of official perfect games, and relegated to the stuff of quirky legend: the Perfect Game

Loss. Haddix's response showed once again a Stoicism few others could muster in the same place. "It's okay," he said, of the ruling. "I know what I did."

Rules

THE RULES ARE NOT THE game, just as the map is not the territory. But the rules are no game, as communications theorist Anthony Wilden has said: the rules are there to constrain and punish, with the force of law.[6]

If you ever begin to feel anger or contempt for an umpire who has blown a call or allowed a strike zone to get elastic, recall that the umpire is there as the game's necessary judge, the policeman who guarantees the existence, not just the integrity, of the game. A game with no umpires is tennis without a net. Robert Frost said free verse was such a non-game, and my colleague Ronald de Sousa is associated with a similar charge against arguments in favour of the existence of god (i.e., they are not arguments because they do not respect reason).

Let's be clear on the force of this phrase about force. The problem with netless tennis is not that it is too easy; the problem is that it is not tennis. If you insist that you are still playing tennis, this is a violation of the implicit contract of all games, that they will be contested within a frame. The frame, and the contract about it, are not themselves part of the rules. They cannot be, because they are, instead, the necessary conditions of the rules themselves. A rulebook whose first rule was "The rules of this book must be followed" has, to paraphrase Wittgenstein, misunderstood the grammar of the word "rule." This does not imply, by any means, that it is ever easy to follow the rules.[7] But it *does* imply, insofar as we understand the nature of rules and the games we (have reason to) play, that following the rules makes sense. We accept rules as binding when we acknowledge them as framing the game. This is what is known in the trade as *deontic constraint* governed by practical reason.

Wittgenstein is relevant in another way, because he was the philosopher who urged us to see language not as a repository of static meanings, still less a basket of sticky labels we might attach to things in the world, but as a nested series of games where, famously, "meaning is use." I make what is in effect a *good move* in a given language-game if I utter something that is accepted and taken up by the other participants. Good moves do not need to be agreeable or even polite; they *do* need to be comprehensible to the other players as both standing within the rules and making some novel contribution to the form of life established or enabled by the rules. The game itself gives us the implicit parameters of *how to go on*, to conduct the game in an interesting manner, regardless of whether the game is finite (competitive and results-driven) or infinite (cooperative and dedicated to continuance as the main goal).

What holds for language surely holds for baseball, since the game analogy is not just a metaphor but a conceptual linkage. *Rules* govern *actions* within the game, including moves that are unique and unprecedented but which, for all that, are instantly recognizable as good. (How often have we heard it said of a baseball play, "I have never seen *that* before.") The rules themselves, and within them the game, are in turn governed—though only implicitly—by *conventions*. These spectral features of the game concern things like when and whether to hit a batter: something an objective observer might consider entirely outside the game, but which insiders, players and fans alike, recognize as legitimate.

Have you ever been hit by a pitch while standing at the plate? I have. It was a revelation, because at first I thought it was just a mistake, especially given the common wildness of pitching in the fastball league I was playing in. It was one of those leagues made up of beer-belly guys who thought they transformed into Derek Jeter when they put on cleats and a pair of batting gloves. You know. I went along to play on Sundays not out of any burning desire to win, but to escape from another bout of logic homework and all the reading I was supposed to be doing. In light of what happened, maybe my attitude was obvious. New Haven is a blue-collar sports town, and it tolerates the denizens of Yale as long as they don't get too cocky.

The pitch took me full in the meaty part of my lower back as I turned to try and avoid it, tumbling to the dirt in the process. This was fastball, not hardball, so it didn't hurt *that* much. But it hurt. When I got up and started my wounded trot to first base, I caught the pitcher's eye. He was glaring, entirely unapologetic. *Oh*, I thought. *He did it on purpose. That's weird.* Then I realized the truth: this was retaliation, entirely within the conventions of the game, for the whooping I'd done when I lofted a routine blooper into shallow right field the previous inning. I had celebrated because hits were rare enough for me that any single, however pathetic, was an event. The pitcher entertained a different view: by crowing over a lucky hit I was showing him up.

Were we both right? Both wrong? Yes, and yes.

A recent Big-League exchange, caught on camera, captures the same clash of interpretations and why there will always be a place for plonking in baseball. The Tampa Bay Rays' pitcher Chris Archer, hurling in what would be a futile match during a sad season, struck out his Detroit opponent, ending the inning. Archer bounded off the mound like a

Jack-in-the-Box, fists pumping, until he noticed the batter sending him the death beam. "Act like you've struck somebody out before," the Tiger said. "Come on, man," Archer said." It's a game. I'm just having fun." (This was all caught on video replay, the absence of audio no barrier to understanding what was shouted, er, said.)

Complicating the case is the fact that Archer is known for showboating after strikeouts, including a notorious incident in 2015 when he got Boston's David Ortiz swinging in the fifth inning of a loss, then bounded off the field like he'd clinched the World Series. Big Papi, himself no slouch in the self-presentation department, had slow-trotted a three-run bomb off of Archer in another game. This prompted the young Rays pitcher to complain that the Boston slugger considered himself "bigger than the game"—a common charge, almost a mantra when it comes to finding fault with other players' comportment on the field. The background axiom is obvious: no one is bigger than the game, and thinking otherwise (or even just *seeming* to) therefore qualifies as the cardinal baseball sin of arrogance.

One blogger, writing after the 2015 incident, condemned Archer this way: "Chris Archer is that dude back in middle school who got up and shut off the N64 when you were whipping his ass in Golden Eye, but calls you a pussy when you wanna switch to Mario Kart because you're having an off-day with the KF7 Soviet. When he's whipping your ass, it's, 'Come on, man! It's just a game! I'm havin' fun!' But when you dance on his grave, homeboy unplugs the system so the game doesn't even save your baller ass stats, and then tells his mom that you were being mean to him."[8]

This is unfair to Archer, obviously, because he is not technically a *spoilsport*, the guy who ends the game when the game is not working in his favour. Archer is arguably guilty of a more common crime, so-called emotional conjugation. This is the irrational tendency, first codified by Bertrand Russell, by which we invariably grant more moral flexibility to ourselves than to others. Here are some examples: (1) "I'm firm, you're obstinate, he's a pig-headed fool." (2) "I'm righteously indignant, you're annoyed, he's making a fuss over nothing." (3) "I've reconsidered the matter, you've changed your mind, he's gone back on his word." And of course: (4) "I have an independent mind, you're eccentric, he's round the twist."

And so in baseball we might get versions of the following: "I'm enjoying myself, you're being cocky, and he's a showboating jackass." Then flip it over: "I'm a serious pro, you're being humourless, and he's a sanctimonious prig." This being baseball, you would maybe want to change the final letters of that last word.

The rules will not tell you how to adjudicate exchanges like the one between Archer and Ortiz, in short, because they feature a common tangle of mixed *norms* in baseball: the norm of professionalism ("Act like you belong here") versus the norm of amateurism ("Relax, it's a game, let's have fun"); the norm of traditional civility (*"Respect* the game, be a pro") versus the norm of individual exuberance ("Make the most of your moment!"). Because professional sports are leisure activities contested for money, a great deal of money, there is no resolution possible here. Two sets of norms clash in a mash of conventions that are forever subject to variable interpretation and application.

Complicating things even more, there are common *generational* and *racial* aspects of norm-clash. Older players, especially retired cranky types, tend to see youthful confidence, or self-regard, as heinous. They hear the steps of time coming up behind them. Jonathan Papelbon and Bryce Harper came to blows in the Washington Nationals' dugout during the 2015 season because the older player found fault with Harper's disdain for running out obvious pop flies. Papelbon was offended on behalf of baseball, Harper dismissive on behalf of his version of common sense. (The fact is, even a routine fly can be dropped; it's not just for show that we run hard to first on every struck ball, however hopeless.)

José Bautista's dramatic bat flip after a big home run against the Texas Rangers in 2015 called down a firestorm — well, a Twitter-storm — of abusive ire, much of it subtly, and not so subtly, directed at his Latin heritage and skin colour. Hall of Fame pitcher Rich "Goose" Gossage offered a lengthy and profane tirade. "Bautista is a fucking disgrace to the game," Gossage told ESPN. "He's embarrassing to all the Latin players, whoever played before him. Throwing his bat and acting like a fool, like all those guys in Toronto. (Yoenis) Cespedes, same thing."[9] The implication is clear: *Real ballplayers — that is, white or "proper" Latino ones — don't act that way!* Don't they? I'm pretty sure they do, when they feel like it: witness Harper, whose casual assholery is matched only by his talent. And tossing a bat high in the air is not so different from pointing out where you're going to hit that dinger in the first place — something that Babe Ruth did long before Reggie Jackson took it up. (In 1932, that is, though the truth of the issue is still disputed; perhaps Ruth just talked a little gentle trash.)

Of course both acts, and others like them, risk generating a reaction. The Rangers, sly punks as always, waited until *early the next season* to retaliate. Bautista was plonked at the plate with a stinging inside pitch, and then pasted with a sneaky punch by Rougned Odor after he slid hard into second to break up a potential double play.

Speaking of which, the rules now say you can't slide hard into second any more. As of 2016, a central feature of the game has been outlawed because of the so-called Chase Utley rule. The previous fall, Utley, playing for the Dodgers, badly injured Rubén Tejada of the Mets when he deviated from the basepath in the traditional manner and slid hard into second on a ground ball. The slide was high and late, certainly ill-judged, and Utley's helmet made brutal contact with Tejada's thigh. The slide broke up the double play and allowed a crucial Los Angeles run to score. Tejada writhed on the ground, his leg broken (he would be out for the rest of the postseason). This was in Game Two of the series, which the Mets would go on to win three games to two. They also went on to win the National League pennant but lost the World Series to the Kansas City Royals, four games to one.

As so often, there was some backstory here. Utley had taken out Tejada in another game, five years earlier, when he was a Philly. Tejada was still burned about the 2015 play well into the 2016 season, mostly because Utley had never offered any sort of apology, though Tejada acknowledged that the Dodgers infielder had sent him "a couple of things."[10] (If you're like me, you would really like to know what these things were. What gifts do you get for the guy whose season you ended with a nasty play? There is, after all, no section in a Hallmark display for "Sorry I Shattered Your Leg.")

A majority of players responding to one poll considered the slide legal but dirty; a majority likewise thought the Mets should retaliate, but stopped short of wanting any rule change.[11] Major League Baseball disagreed. Mindful of the value of its prize livestock, the game's higher powers decided to institute a new rule. No longer could a player show any sign of aiming to disrupt the tag-and-turn by the opposing shortstop or second baseman. The era of breaking up double plays was over, sent to historical dust along with the dead ball, the low pitcher's mound, and the Charlie Brown mitt.

How you view this development is a reliable barometer of your baseball-norm attitude. Opinion doesn't quite divide along strict generational lines, but certainly many older fans and players ("traditionalists") view the new rule as an assault on the integrity of the game. Others ("pragmatists") find it eminently sensible to remove a common injury locus from the game. Does this make sense when pitchers are still expected, now and then, to throw at a player with deliberate intent to hurt? But not at his head! And not behind him, either, such that his natural human back-flinch means nasty contact anyway. Okay. I guess.

And so it goes. Norms and conventions are tricky, precisely because they must remain unwritten and therefore open. At a higher level still are those equally invisible, unarticulated but nevertheless rock-solid *presuppositions* that make the game possible. Key among these is that the rules are the rules, that failing to follow them is not just a piece of eccentricity or bad luck, but a *failure*. There can be no room for interpretation or racial prejudice here. If you do not accept the presuppositions of the game, you are not playing the game at all. You are doing something else.

To appreciate what I mean, consider the philosopher R. G. Collingwood's account of *presuppositions*. There are, Collingwood argues, three conceptual levels observable in any practice. Most obvious are (1) *propositions*, those statements and acts within the practice that make for success. In the practice of carpentry, for example, a typical proposition might be "This two-by-four is 30 inches long." Such propositions are the daily currency of the practice, allowing it to go forward. Beneath this level, and making it possible, are (2) *relative presuppositions*, those assumptions of the practice that sustain suitable conditions for generating propositions.

So, in the example, a relative presupposition of the proposition "This two-by-four is 30 inches long" is that I have a tape measure, purchased from a reputable maker, which I have used to do the measuring. It doesn't matter what unit of measurement is employed, only that we are all using the same system. We assume that the tape measure does not alter between uses, and that the carpenter's imperative to "measure twice and cut once" is a matter of thoroughness, not a check to see if the tape has changed any during the interval between measurements.

That combination of proposition and presupposition might seem sufficient to any practice, but Collingwood reminds us that there are also, at a deeper level again, more fundamental presuppositions that make the other two levels possible. These are (3) *absolute presuppositions*, about which there can be no argument. These are not claims subject to examination of truth or falsity, like propositions, nor are they enabling conditions of such truth or falsity, like relative presuppositions. In the case of carpentry, an absolute presupposition might be something like "Measurement is possible" or "There is a unit of measurement" (much the same thing). These are not really claims, though we can phrase them as statements. To do so is to highlight why such statements are odd, however. They mostly reside in the realm of non-stating, underwriting success and failure at higher levels.

When it comes to baseball, *actions* are the propositions, and *rules* are the relative presuppositions. Confusingly, because baseball is a complex practice that includes social, cultural, and economic context, norms and conventions might also be considered relative presuppositions of the game—with the caveat that they are essentially contestable features of it. The absolute presuppositions are not conventional, or relatively normative. They concern, rather, the very nature of the game as game: that there shall be rules, and players, and adjudication of the one against the other. In no other manner is the game possible.

Realism

THE GAME IS ORDERED BY the rules, but it is not contained by them. More mysteriously still, it is not constituted by them: baseball is so much more than the rules laid out to govern its play.

The philosopher David Lewis, chasing down some thoughts about the relation of rules to action, gives an account of the rules of baseball that raises a deep question. Baseball rules, he says, seem to fall into two categories: (a) *constitutive* rules that govern such things as *what counts* as scoring and what counts as, in general, correct play; and (b) *regulative* rules that enjoin the players to behave in such a way *that* they observe the first kind of rules. Neither seems more fundamental to the other; indeed, there is an intertwining here that is itself somewhat mysterious because it is enacted by the gameplay itself.

One way to put this is to say, with Lewis, the following: "Thanks to the definitions constructed from the constitutive rules, the regulative rules become simply directives to strive to see to it that one's present behavior bears a certain rather complicated relation to the history of the players' behavior in previous stages of the game." Or, translated into something a little less bizarre, "What play is correct depends on the score." Well, yes. But that simple proposition speaks volumes.

We needn't follow Lewis' further intricate excursions into the nature of rules—baseball is for him merely one example of various games where presuppositions are exposed by play. We can just stand back and appreciate the following point he makes about the game's larger relation to its rules.

"The rules of baseball could in principle be formulated as straightforward directives concerning behavior, without the aid of definable terms for score and its components," he notes. "Or they could be formulated as explicit definitions of the score function, the components of score, and correct play, followed by directives in which the newly defined terms appear. It is easy to see why neither of these methods of formulation has found favor. The first would pack the entire rulebook into each directive; the second would pack the entire rulebook into a single preliminary explicit definition."[12] The game could not, so heavily burdened, fairly begin.

But then how exactly do we compose the rule book? Where do we begin? We know that there is play, and that there are rules according to which some of it is correct play. Yet, how did we manage that? In this game, once again, we have additional levels of mystery. Because nobody really knows for sure where the rules of baseball came from.

The history of baseball might even be written as a series of myth-busting investigations of the game's origin. Abner Doubleday, Civil War general and man of parts, supposedly invented the game in 1839 in the cow pasture of Cooperstown resident Elihu Phinney, hence the ongoing link between the sport and that quaint town in upstate New York. But this claim is bogus, hotly disputed ever since. In fact, the Cooperstown variant of the game—known as town ball—is still played annually by the attendees at the Cooperstown Symposium on Baseball and Culture. It is immediately clear to anyone who has spent time in England that this game is really a hybrid of cricket and rounders, designed to be contested by young and old alike. Some rudiments of the modern game are there, but runners can scamper around indefinitely, backwards and forwards, like players in a college-town game of Quidditch; and they can be thrown out by the simple expedient of being struck by the thrown ball (which is soft).

A stronger claim had actually come earlier, from William R. Wheaton and William H. Tucker of the Knickerbocker Base Ball Club of New York. In 1845, club members drew up their version of "the game of base" and circulated the rules. Terminology was heavily influenced by card games: outs were known as *aces*, at-bats designated *hands*. But rudiments of the modern game are discernible. Runs and innings were terms later borrowed from cricket. The notion of the baseball *pitch* is enshrined here, with the now-outmoded idea that the ball should be tossed like a horseshoe, not projected overhand.

Other important elements of the Knickerbocker game were the concepts of three strikes, three outs, and foul territory; also that no runner should advance on a foul, and that the batting order was fixed. Hard to recall now, but most American games derived from cricket and rounders had no concept of foul territory at all; a modern cricket pitch has a boundary, but only for convenience (and either four or six runs); in principle it encompasses the whole world. Despite the Knickerbockers' acumen, it would be some time before the field had a "home run" fence, and a batter's first two foul balls were recorded as strikes—essential features of the modern game.

This might seem convincing, but scholars have also disputed the originary status of these rules. The so-called Massachusetts variant of the game, which was first codified in 1858, has four bases, no foul territory, and a wide-open field akin to the Cooperstown game. As in town ball, runners could be retired by *plugging* or *soaking*—that is, being physically struck by the thrown ball. The New York style gradually edged out this variant, in something of the way four-down Ivy League football triumphed over its McGill three-down rival in gridiron contests. But other New York City teams also set down the game's constraints, including a set of rules devised by William R. Wheaton for the Gotham Club in 1837, casting doubt on the canonical status of the Knickerbocker game.

Does it matter? Probably not. In fact, when we consider what philosophers call the *force of law* and the *mystical foundation of authority*, it is as well that the rules of the game should be shrouded in misty disputes.[13] The game, after all, must be larger than the humans who contest and adjudicate its actions. Then, and only then, can we accept the transcendental nature of the game's own status—nobody is bigger than the game—and of routine judgments made within the game.

Consider, in conclusion, the hoary tale of the three umpires.

Three umpires are sitting in a bar, sharing a beer together. They begin talking about their job and the difficulties they face in calling balls and strikes. The first umpire states quite confidently, "There's balls and there's strikes, and I call them as they are!" The second umpire, with a slight look of disapproval, says, "No, no, no. There's balls and there's strikes, and I call them as I see 'em." The third umpire says, "You know, you're both wrong. There's balls and there's strikes, and they ain't nothin' till I call 'em." Call Umpire One a pragmatist, Umpire Two an empiricist, and Umpire Three an authoritarian—or a realist in the legal sense.

David Lewis' account of Umpire Three is a version of baseball where "the score is, by definition, whatever some scoreboard says it is." This could be a real scoreboard, with lit bulbs or metal numbers, or it could be the scoreboard in the Crew Chief umpire's head, or it could be (most plausibly) the collective scoreboard in the heads of a not-yet-acrimonious softball game. "Under this analysis," Lewis says, "it is impossible that this scoreboard fails to give the score. What is possible is that the score is in an abnormal or undesired relation to its causes, for which someone may perhaps be blamed." Normativity, and error, are where we choose to find them.[14]

Or, if that's too arcane, spare a thought for Hall of Fame umpire Bill "Catfish" Klem (1874-1951), "the Old Arbitrator." Klem pioneered chest protectors and the over-shoulder umpire's stance at home, and did much in his 26 Major League seasons (including 18 World Series) to solidify the umpire's position as the game's loyal arbiter. It's probably apocryphal, but it is said that in response to a query about whether a pitch was a ball or a strike, Klem has been the model for every aspiring Umpire Three since: "It ain't nothing until I call it."

He hated the nickname "Catfish," which started as an insult about his sour puss, and was reputed to eject players without further warning if they used it on him. That's not in the rules, but it's not against the rules either. Don't poke the law!

A revealing coda: later in life, Klem suffered from a skin condition he believed was related to nervous tension brought on by confrontations with players and managers. "Most baseball fans ... feel that these verbal and physical public humiliations go in one ear and out the other. Well, they don't. They go in one ear and go straight to the nervous system, eating away coordination, self-confidence and self-respect."

The law may be mystical, but its servants are flesh and blood. And the good news in all of this, what must be acknowledged as the most absolute of absolute presuppositions, is that *there can be no failure without the possibility of success*. The reverse also holds, of course; that's what makes the game a game.

Safe

WE MIGHT STILL FEEL JUSTIFIABLY unsatisfied with the status of rules and umpires, those armoured dragoons who go by the general name of "Blue." One feels anger but also, sometimes, pity for someone who must take the field as, at once, less than the game (an obstacle, mere furniture, not a player) and more than the game (the embodiment of judgment and the rules). The rules say that the umpire, when struck by the ball, is considered part of the field of play. This sounds simple but isn't.

"The plate umpire stands mask in hand, nearly blimpish in his outfitting," the narrator says in DeLillo's *Pafko at the Wall*. "He is keeping the numbers, counting the pitcher's warm-up tosses. This is the small dogged conscience of the game. Even in repose he shows a history thick with embranglement, dust-stomping men turning figures in the steep sun."[15]

The umpire's call continues to have an uncertain status even in the age of the instant replay. Consider the traditional sandlot wisdom that "the tie goes to the runner" at first base. The first duty of the umpire would seem to be that there should never arise a tie, because in fact there is no such rule. The actual official rulebook says this: "Rule 6.05(j): After he hits a fair ball, he or first base is tagged before or if he touches first base at the time of the ball getting there (batter is out)." Which seems pretty straightforward until you begin to reflect on the phrase "at the time of the ball getting there." That would seem to suggest that a tie goes to the fielder, not the runner. But worse, what is this time of arrival? How long does it last? As instant replay has shown us, slow-motion cameras record the fact that catching the ball is *a process with duration*, not an instantaneous moment.

A 2014 renumbering of the rules, which incorporated some of the changes already discussed, also altered the language of this rule (now known as 5.09 (a) (10)). The new wording may be no clearer: "[A batter is out when] After a third strike or after he hits a fair ball, he or first base is tagged before he touches first base."

As philosopher Ted Cohen has written, ongoing invocation of the "tie rule" shows both the depth of ignorance most fans harbour about the game *and* the murky reaches of ambiguity into which we venture even when we do know the rules. "We usually don't know what the rules are, and the fact that when we do know a rule we discover that it makes little sense" is cause of justified consternation.[16] Cohen felt so strongly about this, and the apparent contradiction evident in the written rule for the first-base tie, that he petitioned Major League Baseball to change the rule. The gods above decreed that any change to the language of the rule would be "confusing"—even though the rule is evidently confused now, even in its correctly stated form.

That might incline some of the nihilistic among us to revert, once more, to a realist or authoritarian position on the umpire's calls. But what about a different view than any of the Three Umpires manages to espouse? Suppose we view the umpire's decisions as more like contextual performances than as statements of fact. This would once more follow the pioneering "ordinary language" philosophy of J. L. Austin, especially in his influential notion of *performative utterances*.

Suppose I am the harbourmaster or ocean-line president and, in the act of breaking a bottle of champagne over the prow of a ship, I say, "I christen this ship the *Joltin' Joe Carter*." Well, by *saying* that, you have *done* that; the speech-act itself executes the sentence and, via its appropriate utterance, makes itself true.

Performatives are an important class of speech-act because, on Austin's analysis, they are not statements with discernible truth value. They don't describe states of affairs; instead, they create them. In place of truth there is, he argued, *felicity*: whether or not they get the job done. (Later philosophers would argue that a performative sentence is *true* any time it is uttered felicitously; the sentence is verifiable by its happy use.[17]) A large measure of getting the job done, and of this felicity, is a matter of context. There must be a custom of naming ships; I must possess the relevant authority; the occasion must be the actual ceremony and not a dress rehearsal; and so on.

Now consider the umpire. Making a call appears, under certain contextual circumstances, to be a performative utterance and not a descriptive one. When he shouts, "The batter is out!" those words themselves make the batter out. Such an utterance is more like a custodian saying "The library is closed" than someone in the library saying "The library is cold." The former makes its contents the case; the latter reports on something that is not brought about by the contents of the speech.

But wait a second! Isn't this just more realism, umpires making decisions like gods, or tyrants?

Maybe not, because consider all the things that have to hold in order for the umpire's call to be a felicitous utterance. This has to be a suitable occasion, suitably ordered by the teams' joint contesting of the game. The umpire has to be the properly constituted authority, exercising judgment in the service of fairness and the rules. I call batters out all the time, just like most fans, and even though I think I am right, they are not out by virtue of my saying so.

Most of all, umpires cannot perform at whim, nor are they blind to events around them—except in the jaundiced view of fed-up fans. The occasions that call forth their judgments are actions independent of their thoughts and intentions, though not their judgment. Only thus could the execution of the call, making the batter out, continue to hold sway. The context is everything. And the nice thing about the context of baseball, as opposed to the context of some other practices, is that we pretty much know where it begins and ends.

You don't call the umpire blue for nothing. He's only the umpire if and when he occupies the uniform. And as they say in the military, "You salute the uniform, not the man." You can still cheat, bend the rules, or try to find loopholes, but the authority of the game is not open to question. The replay officials are thus like more distant deities, communicating with their earthbound minions by way of headphones. Even they must answer, in the fullness of time, to the collective Olympian power known as Major League Baseball.

And always, always remember that the umpire is the only one on the field who can call time in or time out. You raise your hand after sliding into second, asking for favour. He grants it, allowing you to dust off your jersey and re-tuck your pants. You are about to go into your windup and you see his hand raised in a policeman's stop gesture, the batter not yet poised in the box. And then he points at you: *now* you are free to begin the pitch. *The Umpire is the Lord of Time!* Think about that on the next occasion when you feel like arguing balls and strikes.

When there are games without umpires, of course, all bets are off. New England poet Donald Hall recalled playing some sandlot ball with Robert Frost, the dean of American verse. "We played softball," Hall told Peter Stitt of the *Paris Review*. "This was in 1945, and Frost was born in 1874, so he was 71 years old. He played a vigorous game of softball but he was also something of a spoiled brat. His team had to win and it was well known that the pitcher should serve Frost a fat pitch. I remember him hitting a double. He fought hard for his team to win and he was willing to change the rules. He had to win at everything. Including poetry."[18]

He was willing to change the rules. A virtue in poetry, maybe, though not in baseball. And note the irony of Frost's own attitude toward poetry—no free verse!—differing from his attitude about baseball, where the rules were up for grabs. Winning isn't always everything. That piece of wisdom is not in the rules, because it can't be; but it is in the game.

Night

THE FIRST NIGHT-TIME WORLD SERIES game in baseball history was played on October 13, 1971, at Three Rivers Stadium in Pittsburgh. The hometown Pirates were up against the Baltimore Orioles, champions of the American League.

Starting pitcher Luke Walker gave up a first-inning 3-0 lead to the Os, including two bases-loaded sac flies by Brooks Robinson and Boog Powell. Bucs manager Danny Murtagh pulled Walker for Bruce Kison, who settled down to six shutout innings, with just one hit allowed. Kison hit three Baltimore batters, still a single-game Series record. Resolute Pittsburgh hitting from Willie Stargell and Al Oliver in the bottom of the first frame staked Kison to a 3-2 score for this string of excellence, and Oliver racked again when his RBI single tied the game at 3-all.

In the seventh inning the Pirates mounted a small offensive and, capitalizing on a dropped fly to centre and a scrappy single, backup catcher Milt May, batting for pitcher Kison, stroked the RBI single that gave the Pirates a 4-3 lead. They would hang on for the win, and eventually take the series in seven games. It was a classic matchup, featuring a bushel-full of All-Stars and Hall of Famers, including Jim Palmer and Roberto Clemente, the first Spanish-speaking player to be honoured as Series MVP. But for many fans, the night-time game was the real breakthrough, the game that changed the game.

Night-time baseball has a history longer than most of us would imagine. The first night game was played in 1880, as an exhibition of the power of electric light showcased by two department-store teams keen on the potential of Thomas Edison's commercial lightbulb. A half century would pass before organized baseball would take the lights seriously. Non-standing games were played in 1909 and 1927, and the legendary House of David touring teams used lights mounted on trucks for their barnstorming baseball crusade, but only in 1930 would there be a sanctioned minor-league game under the lights. On April 28 of that year, the Independence, Kansas, Producers of Class C were defeated 9-1 by the visiting Muskogee Chiefs.

After that, night ball was a burgeoning force, and though the Majors resisted in the atavistic manner of all baseball trends, the outcome was inevitable. Wrigley Field, home of the Chicago Cubs, was the last Major League venue to surrender. On August 9, 1988, the Cubs played under the lights for the first time, losing—of course—6-4 to the travelling New York Mets. The Mets would win the NL East that year, losing the NLCS to the Dodgers in seven. The Dodgers would beat Oakland in five games to take the World Series in an all-California affair.

It would be a while longer before the Series surrendered to the night, however. Game six of the 1987 Series was the last game played during the day—but even that was a kind of night game, begun at 4 pm and played under the lights of the sad old Minneapolis Metrodome. The Twins won big that day, 11-5 over the visiting St. Louis Cardinals. In fact, this was the first Series where every game was won by the home team, and the Twins, enjoying home field advantage in this, the first Series to feature indoor games, took their

first franchise title in seven. Outdoor sunshine did not figure prominently, though weekday day games would remain,
for many fans, the gold standard of baseball leisure, the
grown-up version of playing hooky. What better escape from
life's demands than an afternoon at the yard, beer in hand,
when everyone else is toiling away?

Lights and domes are no longer novelties in baseball,
and the idea that there might be weekday day games—in
the World Series—betokens an age so decisively past that
it sometimes seems hard to realize its span lies within my
own. That, surely, is how age takes us: we may feel the same
inside, or mostly, but the facts of history keep battering
away at our minds. I can't claim a direct memory of the 1971
Series, because I was only eight at the time. But I certainly
remember the 1973 Series, which was the first to feature all
weekday games starting at night—three midweek matches
at Shea Stadium. (Weekend games at the Oakland-Alameda
Coliseum still hewed to the afternoon norm.)

The reigning-champ Oakland A's won in seven over the
not-quite-amazing Mets, who were managed by Yogi Berra
and boasted the lowest winning percentage (.509) of any
team ever to win a pennant. The Series MVP was Reggie
Jackson, youthful and dashing and master of feuds with
Oakland owner Charlie Findlay; but my hero was Hall of
Fame pitcher Rollie Fingers, with his exquisitely waxed
moustache and dandy's fastidiousness on the mound. I
made pencil sketches of his face in the margins of my school
notebooks, those pale-green ruled Hilroy staplebacks they
handed out on the first day of class. He shared space with
Mark Spitz, my main hero, who had won an unprecedented
seven gold medals swimming for the U.S. in the 1972 Munich
Olympics.

A few other legends were present during those night games
in October 1973: besides Berra, Jackson, and Fingers, Tom
Seaver, Willie Mays (!), Catfish Hunter, and A's manager

71

Dick Williams would all enter the Hall. I remember some of these faces even now, including the controversial moustache of Jackson, whom legend credits with starting the A's' penchant for facial decoration and upstart styling. Most of all, though, those weekday night games made it possible for me to watch baseball with my father, and for him to teach me to score.

I recall a cartoon from the time, which makes sense only against this historical background. One schoolkid passes another at the door to the principal's office. "You should be happy," he tells the scared-looking boy. "He's got the World Series on in there." That would have been on the radio, of course, and during the day, because it's at school. A trip to the principal's office, the dreaded endgame of all classroom japes and dust-ups, is here flipped into a gift. Yes, you will be chewed out and maybe — every kid's fear, in those days — threatened with the strap. But you'll get to hear who's leading, who's pitching, and what inning it is.

There was a rumour in my grade school that the principal, or in fact the vice-principal who was charged with corporal discipline, was in the habit of placing a long hair along your palm before administering the strap. That way, a single blow would inflict a long painful wound in the tender limb, pushing the hair beneath the skin and maybe drawing a thin line of blood. How do we even imagine such things? And yet, I remember vividly the day on the playground when my rambunctious friend Tommy Decker explained this tiny torture to me, inciting appropriate fear. Just another reason to avoid being sent to the office.

But what if the principal had the Series on in there? If you could distract yourself with a few minutes of play-by-play from Bob Murphy, well … almost worth the dressing down and even the strap, right? I mean, you were there anyway, might as well make the best of it. Thus, we imagined, might those in Luftwaffe prisoner-of-war camps distract themselves from their objectively dire predicament by flirting with the Kommandant Klink's buxom secretary or stealing a glass of schnapps, the way Colonel Hogan slyly did in *Hogan's Heroes* (1965-1971), available to us circa 1973 as after-school reruns?

I got sent to the office a few times, once for the heinous crime of shooting bent sucker sticks with a rubber-band slingshot improvised between my thumb and forefinger—a standard guerilla weapon of the time. But I never got the strap, let alone the strap plus hairline laceration. Nor did I ever hear the World Series playing when I visited the office. I do remember them wheeling big televisions on steel-tube frames into class so we could watch parts of the Apollo missions broadcast live. That was cool.

Pebble

WHAT WAS EVEN COOLER TO me, that fall of 1973, was watching the Series games with my dad. We lived on an air force base a few miles outside of the small Prince Edward Island town of Summerside.

It was a sad place, viewed from the sober perspective of memory. The only store was the base B/X, which was a sort of combination Safeway and Canadian Tire; and there was a single greasy-smelling café, with a couple of pinball machines, that sat under the athletic building, which featured basketball courts and a bowling alley. The base cinema screened horror movies and goofy features every Friday, and we all went. For some reason, George Hamilton's performance as daredevil Evel Knievel sticks in my mind, as does a downmarket sub-Hitchcockian effort called *The Frogs* (1972), nothing to do with the play by Aristophanes by the way, in which—yes—evil frogs encompassed the demise of arrogant humans on some distant jungle island. Vincent Price as Dr. Phibes and Christopher Lee as Dracula made frequent appearances in our entertainment universe, too, as did second-rate Disney films that had no reason to exist. I am maybe the only person who recalls watching *The Three Caballeros* (1944), an animated, proto-*Ishtar* musical that strained to create buddy-movie chemistry between Donald Duck and a couple of Hispanic parrots.

Meanwhile, it remained a big deal to order a pizza by phone and have it delivered to the base—a practice my mother soon scotched in favour of a then-dominant Kraft pizza-making kit. And there were long lines when the first Mr. Submarine shop opened in "downtown" Summerside. My father gamely attempted to get subs for the family on opening weekend and returned empty-handed: the teenage sub-makers were favouring their pals in the long line, he said. *No sub for you!* The actual first-run cinema in town showed the original *Willy Wonka* movie (1971), that piece of Gene Wilder brilliance, and I somehow sat through the whole of *The Way We Were* (1973) with my mother, because my father couldn't stand Barbra Streisand. I was so jazzed about going to an actual adult movie that I overlooked her studied kookiness in favour of glamour-boy Robert Redford—long before he was the cinematic incarnation of Roy "The Natural" Hobbs.

You might say, in sum, that we had to *make our own fun.* Baseball was a big part of it, because pretty much everyone had a mitt, soaked with a ball inside and tied with a shoelace overnight to mould the pocket. And one thing we were never short of was open space. Pick-up games happened every day of the summer. There was one organized team, an elite squad of heroes who were given gold-coloured caps but no other uniform, and whom the rest of us worshipped. The standout player on this Olympian side was a kid whose real name I don't think I ever knew. We all called him Crackerjack. He danced through the infield like Nijinsky, a handsome, lanky presence with a natural athlete's love of display. I also remember him being exceptionally funny and kind, but now I wonder if that was just the usual dispensation about character that we grant to the physically gifted.

I loved playing baseball then, as I still do now when I get the chance, but as already indicated I have never been very good. (Yes, I will keep saying that, because it's true.) Baseball is, in its way, as humbling and revelatory of character as golf. And unlike golf, your failures are ones that hurt the team even more than yourself. Errors mean men on base or runs scored; strikeouts generate offensive stalls and easy low-pitch-count innings for the other side. As anyone knows who has tried, playing even the crudest form of baseball is exceptionally tricky. Soccer and touch football are strolls in the park by comparison. Catching fly balls is something that seems easy, hitting a pitch maybe even easier. But none of the elements of the game actually come without struggle. I knew even then, watching Crackerjack and the other gold-crowned players, that I lacked the easy grace and instinctive body-intelligence of the natural athlete. I was instead, I was made to realize, a *pebble-picker*.

Baseball has lots of inventive and colourful slang, maybe even more than other sports because it is the most leisurely and talky of team games. Chatter and trash are natural properties of minutes and hours spent on the field and in the dugout, the lovely *longeurs* between bursts of action. I will explore more slang terms later on, but this one comes burnished with shame. What is a pebble-picker? Well, he's that guy who, having missed an easy grounder, goes back to the scene of the crime and looks critically at the dirt, maybe even actually picking up a bit of it, to signal that the error just committed was really the groundskeeper's fault. Pebbles! Uneven ground! Crazy hops! I didn't have a chance!

Absolutely true, in one sense. The ground might have been as flat and soft as a billiard table and I still would have muffed that play. Worse, having let the ball go by me, I might stand there in an attitude meant to project a mixture of bafflement and well-judged resentment at the gods of chance. *Come on, fate! Give me a break!* One day, though, striking this posture, a new coach yelled at me from the dugout. "Go *after* that ball!" he shouted. "You missed it, you get it!" This was a new thought for me. I had been very much of the school that suggested, once a grounder was missed by the infielder (me), it was the outfield's job to retrieve it. My work was done; however badly, the ship of failure had sailed, and I was its sole passenger.

This new coach taught me something that I still cherish, even though I am probably no better at shortstop now than I was then. When the ball goes by you, turn around and go get it! You have failed, but no failure is total. There might still be something to retrieve, if only your own sense of commitment to the game. You might even catch the runner trying to stretch his gift of one base into a greedy haul of two. Go after that ball!

Stillness becomes movement, readiness translates into action, because that is the heart of the game.

"The difference is when the ball is hit. Then nothing is the same," the narrator of DeLillo's *Pafko* muses. "[E]verything submits to the pebble-skip of the ball, to rotations and backspins and air-streams. There are drag coefficients. There are trailing vortices. There are things that apply unrepeatably, muscle memory and pumping blood and jots of dust, the narrative that lives in the spaces of the official play-by-play."[19]

The pebble-skip, yes—I know it well, real or imagined. The *pebble* is where physics meets metaphysics.

Score

SCORING A BASEBALL GAME MINIATURIZES play into a graphic art form. Just as the rules are not the game, no graphic representation can capture the feel of a game, or convey the grace of a slick scoop at third that then generates a laser-throw to first. The resulting x at the right-hand corner of the scoring sheet's little diamond, and the note of put out or fielder's choice will never substitute for witnessing the play.

But baseball is the most abstract and angular of all major sports, a contest assayed within a set of mathematical constraints: 90 feet between bases, 60 feet and six inches from the pitching rubber to home plate, walls set eccentrically somewhere (usually) between 350 and 425 feet from home. The foul lines and fences define the universe of the game, but they too are merely abstract. A batter is frequently retired by a play on the ball that had gone outside of fair territory — depending on how generous the home field is with its margins between the line and the first row of seats.

A ball sent beyond the fence is out of play, but therefore considered one of the most successful coups in the game's repertoire of odd, explosive gestures. Runners advance not along a straight path, but crookedly and by sometimes bizarre stages. Consider, on the last point, not only the intentional

walk, the steal, and the error, but also the weird and wonderful sacrifice bunt and fly, or the even weirder balk—especially the so-called Balk Off, a game-ending pitcher's gaffe
that can send a home-team runner on third into the plate,
and glory, in a mixture of celebration and anti-climax that
has no equivalent in any other game.

The scoring sheet captures these physically enacted
abstractions with abstractions of its own. Each frame is a
tiny baseball diamond, a field within the field, where the batter's progress, or lack of it, is marked down with a firm pencil. All the players are numbered, like counters on a board.
First hard thing to remember when you're a kid: shortshop
is six, not five, reflecting the original infield-outfield status of
this mobile position.

A scored run fills in the diamond, so you can see at a glance
just who is on top, and by how much, and who got the ribeyes.
If you're a perfectionist you can keep track of foul balls as
well as outcomes. Most of the scoring codes are obvious—
FO (fly out), PO (put out), FC (fielder's choice). Some are
rare: defensive indifference (DI), left base early (LBE), left
basepath (LBP), infield fly rule (IFR). The common strikeout, by tradition noted with K—and a *backwards* K for a called
strikeout, rather than one executed by the batter's window
shopping—seems anomalous in its symbol. The origin of the K
proves to be an all too typical baseball story, combining happenstance and ingenuity in about equal measure.

Henry Chadwick was born in Exeter, in the English
county of Devon, in 1824. His grandfather had been a close
friend of John Wesley, the religious pioneer whose new
Christian sect of Methodism would flourish on both sides of
the Atlantic. At age 12, Henry's parents took him and their
somewhat unreliable prospects to Brooklyn, where they
lived a life of exceptional moral grace and uncertain financial stability. Henry was brought up to love ethics, God, and
cricket, in about that order—but also, as the game emerged

in mid-century American culture, baseball. In 1856, acting as cricket reporter for the *New York Times* — yes, in the day there was such a position — he observed an organized contest of baseball and was immediately smitten.

He became the game's most important booster and statistician in the early years, alongside such celebrity fans as Mark Twain and, later, Stephen Crane. By focussing on statistics and their relation to game narrative, Chadwick paved the way for every sabermetrician and analytics geek still to come.[20] He invented the ERA stat for pitchers, for example, just when relief pitchers became a normal feature of the game and complete games plus win-loss records were no longer a reliable measure of mound prowess. He also, as an influential journalist, gave us the box score and, among other innovations, the K.

Chadwick's rationale for the scoring mark was that it avoided ambiguity with other notes. The box score itself, derived from traditional newspaper reports of cricket matches, was an exercise in concision and graphic presentation of information. All the essentials of a game could be recorded there, and set down in agate type for the newspaper rounds. Courtesy of Chadwick, the very first box score appeared in 1859 in the *New York Clipper*, although it would not take flight as a newspaper feature until 1925, when *Baseball Magazine* popularized Chadwick's 1859 formula and made it the gold standard for sports pages across the continent.

I can still remember, as I headed off to graduate school in the fall of 1985, following the Blue Jays' pursuit of the AL East pennant via the agate in the print edition of the *International Herald-Tribune*, available at a newsstand in Edinburgh's Waverley Station. In those days before satellite television and (!) the Internet, there was no other way to keep track of the game — 1985 being, in this sense as well as a few others, closer to 1925 than to 2015. The Jays would win the division title that year, their first ever, with 99 wins—still a franchise record. Then they would, as the small type inevitably told me, blow a 3-1 series lead in the championship series against the Kansas City Royals, and be seen off in seven games. The Royals would then go on to beat the Cards in seven for the World Series, but by then, who cared? Well, not me, anyway.

Chadwick knew that scoring the game was more detailed and required more imagination than the basic box score. He was the Edison—or maybe the Einstein—of the scorecard, coming up with inventive solutions to the many salient details of any contest. The hard sound of the K resonated with the hard syllable of "struck" in Struck Out. It also offered a nice incidental resonance with the sharp "K.O." of the boxing knockout, something still preserved in the habitual lingo of saying that the batter—especially if caught looking—has been "punched out." This last association is made even more emphatic by most umpires' third-strike-looking call coming in the form of some sort of punching or, occasionally, bow-and-arrow arm spasm.

Like box scores, scoring is personal when the game is distant. In our house near Summerside, there was a semi-finished basement that we used as the TV room. You went down there by turning left from the main door, which was technically the side door, next to the driveway. The actual front door, at what felt like the back of the house, faced onto a field and another row of houses across the way. This was standard design for Canadian Forces Base PMQs—permanent married quarters—which housed my parents, me, and my two brothers for most of our childhoods. The base design, including the house layout, had been executed by some gang of Ottawa bureaucrats and then dropped unceremoniously and without variation on sites across the country.

I sustained a shock of uncanny recognition when reading the first chapters of Ann-Marie MacDonald's 2003 novel *The*

Way the Crow Flies, which was set on an air force base near London, Ontario. This was the scene of a real-life murder mystery involving the teenaged Stephen Truscott, accused of raping and killing his classmate Lynne Harper. Truscott was convicted and sentenced to death; his conviction was later overturned on appeal.

We had lived on that same base before coming to Prince Edward Island — my younger brother Sean was born there — but I don't remember the house much. It was a time when kids were sent outside to play for large stretches of the day, even in winter, when I would venture out with my mittens on a string, a note pinned to my parka so someone could call my mother if I ran too far afield and got lost. (This tended to happen.) How odd, though, to read in MacDonald's book the narrator's account of the house in which she lived, exactly replicating the floor plan. Left — down the basement. Straight ahead — three steps up to the kitchen. Left from there — the living room where my parents entertained their sideburned and up-do-sporting friends, officers and wives. I don't recall a single female officer.

The basement was not nice. We had parties down there, my brothers and I, where there was music, and dancing, and furtive games of Spin the Bottle and Post Office. Creedence Clearwater Revival and Deep Purple, Alice Cooper and Grand Funk Railroad. Mostly it was just a place to have a couch and a television. In the summer, the dark and coolness attracted infestations of beetles, harmless but repellent. I had a deflated football that I used as a Hammer of Death to deal with them whenever they ventured into the half circle of blueish light thrown by the TV screen. Their squashed corpses formed a perimeter of insect destruction around our pocket of more-or-less civilized human habitation. In this insalubrious quarter, my father patiently taught me the elements of scoring.

Scoring baseball is a way of watching baseball. It combines immediate joy in the spectacle with a scholar's fastidiousness about detail, responsibility, and outcome. It also responds to a dozen hard choices that many fans don't spend time worrying about. Was that an error or a base hit? This is the line between success and failure: a single base hit can push a batter into the .300s or, even more significantly, over the so-called Mendoza Line (about which more later; see "Slang"). Was that a wild pitch or a passed ball? No huge statistical significance to this, one might suppose, at least not anything that will stain a player's record, but the ethical import is considerable. Whose fault was that last goofed play, when the ball went to the backstop and allowed a runner to advance or, even worse, score?

Many times these calls are obvious. A shortstop who boots the ball or fumbles the relay is clearly the culprit, incidentally taking achievement away from the batter. A pitcher who sails the ball over the catcher is not giving his battery-mate a chance. But often enough, the choice of who gets what is not at all clear. The game's official scorer makes this momentous decision, and though some of these judgment calls can later be reversed, once the call is made it is usually made for good: the gods of baseball, and their high priest the scorer, have spoken.

Scoring preserves a sense of proportion in the game. Its combination of abstraction over abstraction makes it an almost ideal metaphysical practice: a graphic account of a non-territorial context whose main feature is inaction punctuated by outbursts of frenetic activity, ruled by a non-temporal measure of time. When one scores, one is doing a peculiar kind of graphematic philosophy, scattering pencil marks across a page to record and notarize the elegant, attenuated running, hitting, and throwing of the diamond. This is not appearance versus reality, that ancient philosophical distinction; the scorecard never pretends to be the play it records. Instead, a distinct and equally ancient mystery is invoked: how can a record stand as a representation of something real?

The scorecard does not depend, except minimally in the convention of the box's miniature diamond, on the relation of mimesis, or imitation. The card does not picture the action. On the contrary, this is a kind of writing, where the meaning-bearing marks carry their import because of a less direct and more conceptual pairing. There are no miniature figures on the card, just names. There are no replays, only the game's progress registered in shorthand. The scored game can be replayed in imagination, but the mental pictures thus conjured are closer to the theatre of the mind we associate with reading fiction than to the image-based media of the post-radio world.

We speak of "keeping" score, as if it were an act of capture; instead, we might recall that "record," whether on stats sheets or in the book of achievement, is a word rooted in the *heart* (*cor*) — to repeat so as to commit to memory, to learn by heart. Writing, and graphic marks more generally, came later. Scoring creates a record. But better still, scoring shall set our hearts free.

Medium

AND THIS, IN TURN, RAISES a question: what is the proper medium for baseball? Like most sports fans, I have a fairly large flat-screen television, though mine is dwarfed by some of the wall-covering entertainment systems installed by my friends, especially one NFL-crazed artist who spends Sundays transfixed by a screen that is so large and vivid it can make you feel sick with vertigo if you use it to play first-person-shooter videogames.

The flat-screen number is not the first TV I've owned, of course. I had a tiny colour set before that, purchased in the delusional belief that a smaller screen would make me watch less television. The set I had before that was a 1950s-vintage black-and-white antique that my friend Charlie gave me when I was in graduate school. It was trapezoidal in shape, heavy, and festooned with decidedly lo-tech buttons and dials. It looked like something from the set of *Lost in Space*. Charlie used it to watch basketball games in the kitchen while he was cooking Sunday dinner, but he got tired of that, and he gave it to me one January day, which happened to be Super Sunday: the day of the National Football League championship game, the Super Bowl.

So the first show I watched on the old b/w was a football game. And not just any football game, but the apotheosis of football games, the all-out celebration of hyped Americana and commercial rapacity that is the Super Bowl. It is the great exploding gourd of American culture, the Super Bowl, and the only way to experience it is via the tube. For, in a sense unimagined by the makers of those frightful disability-of-the-week movies, the Super Bowl is truly *made for TV*.

That was just luck. Where I used to live, in New Haven, Connecticut, the set picked up only one channel, the local ABC affiliate whose transmission tower was just down Orange Street from my house. ABC somehow managed to snag the Super Bowl contract in 1988—something that doesn't often happen—and so I watched the Washington Redskins romp 42-10 over the Denver Broncos in 12-inch black and white. This was, for the record, Super Bowl XXII. I don't usually have much facility for remembering past championship games, even in sports I like a lot more than professional football, but I do recall, as many of us do who were alive then, that Redskins quarterback Doug Williams, a black man in a position that was still dominated by white athletes, was the game's most valuable player. John Elway, the then-hapless Denver QB, was a frustrated also-ran. (He would win the Big Game later.)

The ABC station's *usual* programming schedule, I soon discovered, was a mess of cornball and/or ultraviolent local-news stories, home shopping, and paid programming about the Snak-Master, mail-order cosmetics, emergency CPR training, Deal-a-Meal weight-loss programs, and motivational audio tapes. There was the usual line up of execrable sit coms and soaps (and believe me, I knew them all), Peter Jennings' smarmy newscasting, and something called *Starsearch*, which featured a drooling Ed McMahon overseeing a sort of manic amateur hour from hell. There was even, thank God, some sports.

Like all the males in my family, I am a dedicated if not obsessive sports fan. I'm not ashamed to say I used the b/w to watch college football games on Saturday afternoons in those days. But there were other, darker moments—times when I couldn't face my work, or my wife, or the world. You know for certain you have hit bottom when you tune into *Pro Bowlers' Tour* on a bleak Saturday morning and listen to ABC's Chris Schenkel tell you about the Firestone Des Moines Open or the Goodyear Cleveland Invitational. I watched *Pro Bowlers' Tour*, but I hated myself for it.

In those days I refused to buy a better TV, or get cable, because (I said) I couldn't afford it. The real reason was I thought I would watch it *all the time*. TV can make morons of the best of us. I imagined myself with color cable TV: getting no work done, living life in an alpha-state coma, my body gone to hell, career in ruins, friends all lost. I saw books and letters gathering a thick mantle of dust, pizza boxes stacked to the ceiling. Creditors, building supervisors, financial officers pounding on my door, all unheeded. In the midst of it I would sit, bloodshot eyes glued to the screen, a cable-TV zombie. Have you seen those TV ads that warn you television can be addictive? They're the equivalent of the Surgeon General's warnings on cigarettes and alcohol: they're true, they should be scary, but *nobody pays them any attention.*

As it happens, I am not a cable-TV zombie. I do have cable now, a time when cable is the last refuge of the technologically challenged, but that's because there are few other ways to get sports coverage so reliably and regularly. In general, I probably watch more television than most of my friends. I like to regard this as my duty as a cultural critic, even unto *Bachelor in Paradise*. And, to be fair to my stronger self, in this new state of non-deprivation I've discovered some interesting things. Not about the joys of conversation, or the simple pleasure of an evening spent in the company of a good book, but rather about sports radio.

The first radio sports broadcast—like, say, the first military use of the airplane—is an event much scored by myth-making acids. The way it's usually told, Harold Arlin, a plodding daytime foreman at KDKA in Pittsburgh, just *decided* one day to haul a carbon microphone and power generator over to Forbes Field, where the Pirates were hosting their cross-state rivals, the Phillies. Arlin, who was 26 years old, paid his way into the park, took up a seat directly behind home plate, and simply started talking play-by-play. It was August 5, 1921, and the first sports broadcast was invented, sprouting whole from the forehead of Harold Arlin. Who heard him? What did he sound like? We'll never know for sure. The record says the Pirates won, eight runs to five.

In the next ten years and beyond, radio proved itself surprisingly well suited to the visual medium of sports. This is surely in part because the natural idiom of the fan is gab, and gab was just what the first sportscasters did best. Like all fans, they indulged themselves with aggressive disputes of plays, questioning of coaches' judgment, displays of historical knowledge. Talk, talk, talk—what would sports be without the communal discussion, the bull session, the great conversation of devotion? The first radio sportscasters satisfied the back-brain dream of all fans, that once, for a while, *everyone else will shut up and let them talk*. There was also the imperative of the story line, the drive to narrate, to be the camp fire focus. Who among us, after all, does not imagine that he could tell the game story better than anyone else?

Indeed, some of the first radio men talked about what they had not even seen, for early radio sports relied heavily on studio "recreations," imaginative talk-throughs of telegraph reports of game action. These announcers— among whom one could find, in those days, young Ronald "Dutch" Reagan—thought nothing of inventing actions and plays, sometimes adding a string of non-existent foul balls to their patter when the telegraph signal had been severed. Even at the park itself, accuracy was not always a virtue in announcer chatter. NBC Radio's Bill Stern, for one, was well known for his mis-calls during college-football broadcasts in the 1930s. Stern, who sported not only artificial hair but an artificial leg, was famous for losing sight of Yale halfbacks' numbers as they pounded down the field against Columbia. "If we have a man with the ball on his way to a touchdown," he once told a rookie spotter, "and we discover at the five-yard line that we have the wrong man, *we will have him lateral to the right man.*" I think this must account for the popularity of the last-minute lateral in sandlot football.

Once, when Stern had the bad grace to criticize a fellow radioman, Clem McCarthy, for calling the wrong winner during a Kentucky Derby broadcast, McCarthy shot back: "Well, you can't lateral a horse."

These and other tales are the primitive mythology of radio sports, which found its heroes in unlikely places. There was Mel Allen (Melvin Allen Israel), a bookish Southerner whose mellifluous tones on CBS radio were synonymous with the fate of the New York Yankees from 1939 to 1964. Allen had a sure-fire signature line—*How a-bout that?*—which he developed during a 1949 rip of four home runs by Joe DiMaggio, whom he idiosyncratically and memorably dubbed "The Yankee Clipper" and "Joltin' Joe"—the latter moniker tracking a cultural course all the way into a Simon & Garfunkel song. Allen's myth-making tones and the centrality of Yankee fortunes made his voice arguably the most famous one in America during the 1940s and '50s. (Aficionados call him, simply, The Voice.) He also, unlike Stern and others of the first generation, managed a successful transition from radio to television: in later years he telecast Yankee games, World Series, and was to be heard late into his life doing the baseball magazine show called *This Week in Baseball*, known to fans as *TWIB*.

The other great in early sports radio was Mississippi-born Walter Lanier "Red" Barber, who for years broadcast Dodger exploits out of Brooklyn's Ebbets Field. The contrast with Allen was, and is, much discussed, for the two men plot the opposite poles of radio propriety. On the one hand, the hollering, rollicking Allen, a man dedicated to obliterating dead air with his barrages of partisan, over-excited patter. On the other, Barber's quieter, gentler and more balanced narration, long on detail and short on intemperate outbursts. ("That Barber," a Brooklyn taxi driver is supposed to have said one day in the 1940s, "he's too fair.")

Most of the early radio heroes were locals, tied to the fortunes of a single team their entire careers. There was Byrum Saam in Philadelphia; the irrepressible Bob ("The Gunner") Price, a Pittsburgh institution, given to diving out of hotel windows on a wager; Harry Caray in St. Louis, who originated the "Holy cow!" tag later adopted by Phil Rizzuto; and Curt Gowdy, voice of the Boston Red Sox, later a television star. There was, finally, J.H. "Dizzy" Dean—though Dean is perhaps better remembered for his Hall-of-Fame performances with the 1930s-vintage St. Louis Cardinals, the storied Gas House Gang.

Dean, like Barber and Allen, was a southerner, but from down-home Arkansas and possessing no education beyond the second grade. Nevertheless, Dean's drawling shtick struck a note that sports broadcasting has always loved, and he too slid (or, in Dean vernacular, "slud") easily from radio to television. Of course, it was precisely the rough-edged ungrammatical, cornpone of Dean's 1950s TV broadcasts ("Somebody's complaining about my *syntax?* I didn't know they was taxing that too!") that kept network executives from getting enthusiastically behind televised baseball games.

Like silent-screen stars attempting to keep pace with the talkies, not all the radio wizards could master the peculiar demands of the TV sportscast. For most, it was as simple as this: in radio, the announcer is everything, master of his fate. ("In radio," said veteran Ernie Harwell, "nothing happens until I say so.") In television, he is no more than another prop under a producer's iron control. Lindsey Nelson, one of the radio-TV success stories, put it this way: "I love radio—you're totally in charge. To me, broadcasting baseball all season that way is a delight. You just let yourself roam. And you're the entire show—you paint the picture. If you get in trouble, you can get out of trouble just as easily—and because there's no picture, *nobody knows it*... You have much less freedom in TV. You're at the mercy of what the producer and director show. In language, you have to be more selective. And always, your destiny is in someone else's hands." Not surprisingly for the great talkers of baseball radio, the diamond game made the contrast especially acute. "I guess I notice it so sharply," Nelson concluded, "because there's no radio sport better than baseball to do stream-of-consciousness—the slow pace, the time to improvise. It's an English major's dream."

What is most remarkable about the early history of sports broadcasting, and hardest to recall now, is that radio continued to dominate long into the television age. The thin beam of gab was not shoved aside by the magic of pictures right away. Television was well into its adolescence, in the late 1950s and even early 1960s, before its malevolent masterminds began to sense just how much there was to be had from sports TV. Partly this was owing to technical limitations: a three-camera studio could give you *Jack Benny* or *The Honeymooners* (both really just transplanted radio shows with minimal sets) but the same three cameras, scattered ineffectually around a baseball park, was no improvement on Red Barber's masterful narration. "Baseball was made to look slow and dull," said one veteran broadcaster recently, "because TV was not ready to do justice to baseball. It was like watching grass grow or paint dry."

There were other factors. According to the critic Ron Powers, whose history of early sports television *Supertube*

(1984) is still the best source on the rise of network power in sports, the men in control of television's early destiny were more than a little contemptuous of the American sports audience. They were, almost without exception, golf and polo men, and the drawling, brawling aura of baseball and boxing and wrestling was not for them. It is perhaps no surprise that the first major sport beamed out on television was one born of Ivy League tradition: college football, which had yet to acquire its reputation for recruiting violations, drug money, and free Corvettes from the Booster Club. Like rugby in Britain, football was a brutal game played by gentlemen, while baseball was a gentle game played by rednecks.

Let us not forget, as we consider these somewhat old-school issues about television, how media are changing the fan experience now.

I'm a late adopter: I have a cell phone, but it's a flip phone that might have belonged to somebody cool in 2001 or so. It takes bad pictures, which I share with people using email, if you can believe that. I'm okay with all this, but I also realize it is some distance behind the times. At every game I attend, the fans around me are glued to their smartphone screens—sometimes to the detriment of their fan experience and, in rare cases when a screaming foul ball comes our way, their bodies. But obviously tweeting about games, and taking multiple selfies during them, is just another way of *watching a game*. I used to carry a transistor radio to live games so that I could hear the commentary on what I myself was watching in real time. Sending Twitter updates to your friends and followers is only the latest iteration of the deep wisdom we can see revealed here. There is no such thing as a game without media. The game of baseball is, as a fancy theorist might put it, mediated *a priori*.

However you put it: yes, it is.

Off

IN THE '50S AND '60S, college football was depicted as a titanic battle of crew-cut young giants with pure hearts and school spirit, letterman sweaters and penny loafers in their lockers. So ran the mythology—in its way, as effective as the election-year propaganda of a Roger Ailes. Roone Arledge, the man who almost single-handedly invented sports TV, carved out his niche at ABC by constructing college-football telecasts that were masterpieces of visual manipulation: long shots of ivy-strewn campuses, tan cheerleaders flinging their bodies in collegiate glee, fans carousing in paroxysms of good cheer and fight song, sophomore cornerbacks giving up their bodies joyfully for the ball.

Arledge's style of "total package" sports broadcast set the standard for TV sports through the 1960s, and ABC quickly crushed every other major sport to its money-making bosom. And make money they certainly did. Some sports, like hockey and soccer, resisted the demands of the tube; others, like football, seemed born for them. It was not long before the television producer was controlling the pace of the game, calling commercial time-outs and dictating kickoff times. In exchange, the suddenly popular professional National Football League was waging a war of escalation over the sale of television rights.

New leagues (the AFL, the WFL, the ABA) were created just
to fan the fires of television money-making. New networks
(ESPN, SportsChannel, USA), and new technologies (cable,
pay-per-view), were created just to broadcast the new sports
that had been created for them.

Baseball suffered through neglect and the nature of the
game, not given to the kind of violent visual dissection that
makes football fans so happy. It is hard to recall today that
baseball's demise was confidently predicted in the early
1970s, by sources as diverse in tone and integrity as *Time*
magazine, the *Wall Street Journal*, and Howard Cosell. A
certain kind of nerd will know, as I do, that in the spin-off
universe of Gene Roddenberry's *Star Trek* imagination, baseball has been relegated to the dustbin of history, along with
poverty, hunger, and racial prejudice. The game suffered a
severe decline in popularity, culminating in the final World
Series, played in 2042 before a crowd of 300 and won by legendary player Buck Bokai. By the time of the 24th century,
the game is the marginal geeky preoccupation of a few dedicated nostalgists, including Deep Space Nine commander
Benjamin Sisko (Avery Brooks), who organizes an unlikely
holosuite game against a crew of boasting Vulcans in 2375.

Baseball survived the threat of pro football and other telegenic sports by becoming more telegenic itself, adding more
cameras to game coverage and taking the instant replay to
new heights of absurdity. Though purists balk at the new
tele-consciousness of players and fans, the game could not
have done otherwise. The cycle of TV rights and TV profits,
a dollar-producing turbine set on high speed, was up and
running. Major League sports are now dead in the water
without television contracts, and network competition means
that profit-margins are just about as wide as those lucrative
ad contracts from NFL Sundays, the World Series, the NBA
finals, Bowl Games, and the Final Four. To see where the
unholy alliance of sports and TV has brought us, one has

only to tune in, once a year, to the Super Bowl. Keep a vomit bowl at the ready.

Against a background of such all-consuming TV domi= nance, radio now seems an unlikely medium for sports—the medium of the past, of the early days. We are taught that *serious* sports fans must have massive dish antennae, six-foot screens, and cable. Sports radio, with its thin broadcast schedule and early-era technology, starts looking pretty feeble by comparison. Radio? Who needs radio? I've got 49 channels of 24-hour-a-day action here. I've got NCAA women's fastpitch at two in the afternoon! Australian rules football at five! Fat guys throwing darts from seven to nine! One game of baseball a day on radio? Please. Don't make me laugh.

But the argument founders. To nobody's astonishment, the quality of this programming is inversely proportional to its quantity. Now that I see what cable actually offers, I can prove what I only suspected when I had one thin channel beaming in: the more there is, the worse it gets. And yet, because the visual medium is so seductive, whatever the subject, sports fans may actually find themselves watching things they would have sneered at a few years ago. Monster trucks roaring over mounds of dirt! Has-been football players shooting skeets! Competitive croquet from Long Island!

This lowering of personal standards, the murder of moderation, leads to a second effect: fan burnout. Immersed in inclusive coverage, drowned in all that professionally created imagery, today's TV-sports fan has lost the ability to tell good from bad. It's not couch potatoes we need to worry about, but rather couch potatoes who can't tell the difference between the NBA playoffs and the under-16 synchro-swimming trials from Port St. Lucie. Dimmed by plenty, overcome by an embarrassment of visual riches, switching restlessly from game to game, the cable TV sports fan has lost the ability to *turn the TV off.*

And it is precisely here that radio comes—or comes back—into its own, where the magic of sound actually outstrips the flood of information pouring from its audio-visual rival. Here is the fertility of imagination, the enchantment of inner vision, the power of the invisible. Radio pulls its audience with true drama, the unseen game more exciting for being unseen. It works the tired muscles of the imagination.

This is not true of all sports of course. Most sane people would still rather watch a basketball game than listen to one; a basketball radio broadcast consists mainly of updates on the score. Football and hockey are borderline radio. But baseball is a sports radio natural, a game where medium meets message with joyous results. Consider the slow rhythm of balls and strikes from, say, Toronto's legendary CJCL team of Tom Cheek and Jerry Howarth. The station is now better known as The Fan 590, which means that "CJCL" has become yet another stealthy marker of yore, like old alphabetic telephone exchanges—from MUrray Hill 5 (the Ricardos' number in *I Love Lucy*) to HUdson 9 (my old Winnipeg neighbourhood) or BUtterfield 8 (yes, that's why John O'Hara's 1935 novel sported the title: the central character, Gloria Wandrous, is a call girl with an answering service).

There's a baseball reference in the glorious 1960 Elizabeth Taylor film adaptation of that novel, as it happens. In the drunken voice of Laurence Harvey, playing a married suitor called Weston Liggett, it suggests that the only place big enough to hold a reunion of Miss Wandrous' various boyfriends is ... Yankee Stadium.

Hmm. But let's stay with the family-rating charms of Tom and Jerry for preference. You heard these two medium-masters, and the neurons of imagination and mental representation, the circuitry of the mind's eye, fired through your brain like scatter-shot tracer bullets. Big explosions of spastic bio-electronics. These are the splashing fireworks of inner seeing. There are no instant replays here, no flashy stats graphics, only the moseying words of the old-pro announcers, the rising voices of long balls, and the arcana of old baseball vocabulary.

"Baseball is the last theatre of the mind," Cheek told me long ago, "and so baseball and radio are a natural marriage." Cheek was a veteran of more than 40 years behind the mike, now taken from the world (he died in 2005, aged 66) but residing in memory on the Blue Jays' list of renowned figures inside the SkyDome, alongside Hall-of-Famer Roberto Alomar, Carlos Delgado, Joe Carter, and others. His number on that wall, 4306, represents the unbroken streak of Jays broadcasts he delivered to a grateful public. Cheek, whose doughy face he liked to describe as "made for radio," grew up in Pensacola, Florida, where his daily stick-ball routine included elaborate play-by-play descriptions that drove the other kids crazy. His was the classic story of a childhood dream come true—the dirty kid with only a wooden spoon to talk into, hired, decades later, into a dream job: 162 games of action, seen from the best seats in the house. Along the way, he broadcast everything from Yankee League college football to wrestling matches and bowling. In his final perch in the Telemedia Network broadcast booth inside Toronto's SkyDome, he was in fan heaven.

Cheek and partner Howarth ambled through the summer lineup of Jays games with the effortless grace of Fred Astaire and Ginger Rogers, making the hard look easy. Trading their elaborate courtesies like a couple of Victorian clubmen, they were the heroes of my radio world. Like all lifelong fans, their knowledge of baseball trivia was encyclopedic and bizarre. For someone like me, who can sometimes barely remember a World Series a few years on, this is astounding. They remembered double plays turned a decade ago, lineup changes from the 1970s, clubhouse quips from three seasons back.

Impressed by Curt Gowdy's cozy Red Sox broadcasts while working in Burlington, Vermont, during the '70s ("He always seemed like he was talking just to me"), Cheek developed a warm, even presence on the airwaves. He grew up on radio—on Mel Allen and Bob Price, and the rest. Yet he's more Barber than Allen, and doesn't go in much for the shouting, slangy noise of the old-time heroes. "It's not my style to have signature lines," he said to me when he was the age I am now, which is to say a few ticks past the half-century. "I never went through a period of thinking, 'Now, how am I going to call a home run?'; I don't spend my time trying to come up with nicknames for the players. Whatever the moment dictates, I call."

The calls were unfailingly good, with Cheek's vibrant, twangy voice a power source he modulated at will. He set the scenes and "painted word pictures," while the more stats-minded and in-depth Howarth complemented the broad strokes with detail. The talk! Inside and outside, sliding and curving, dropping and rising, bouncing and chopping—the words of baseball radio jumped out at us like lively Haitian baseballs, peppered with technical language and down-home slang, filled with diamond wit and ballyard bravado. It was a joy to listen to these gabmeisters, to hear the lifting excitement of a ball hit hard, the ranging fielder, the stumble onto the warning track, the clearing of the wall. Baseball on radio is pure summer joy, three hours spent in outs and innings, in the company of those voices and ourselves.

Even a merely fair broadcast can have moments of inadvertent joy. The hapless TBS network, lacking the polish of ESPN, once ran a graphic identifying their on-field commentator as "Carl" Ripken, Jr. A blogger, summarizing the list of TBS outrages, noted "the miracle that is Tyler Naquin becoming the 'first outfielder to start a postseason game for the Indians since 1948'. I suppose that makes a lot of sense now as to why the Indians haven't won a World Series

since that year, what with outfielders being fairly important in baseball and everything. Were there a qualifier like
'rookie outfielder' or 'outfielder with exactly one 'q' and
one 'y' in his name' then it would have made more sense."[21]
The Clevelanders would lose another World Series in 2016,
despite fielding the standard three starting outfielders in
every one of the seven games.

It wasn't all error over at TBS. Ron Darling, my personal
favourite among current word-slingers, peppered his talk
with Latin phrases more common in a seminar room or court
of law: certain decisions made by Cleveland manager Terry
Francona were deemed *ad hoc*, and the relief pitching bullpen
of the side was, during Game Three of the 2016 ALCS against
the Blue Jays, a matter of "Andrew Miller *et al.*" keeping the
Jays' bats quiet. During Game Two of the same series, with
J. A. Happ on the bump for Toronto, Dennis Eckersley and
Brian Anderson offered this telegraphic exchange that will
be parseable only by fans. Eckersley: "Happ is painting right
there." Anderson: "Martin sticks the landing, and a backwards K for Happ."

For those in need of translation: Happ was working the
low-outside corner on the Cleveland batters, getting the
umpire's call with his pinpoint control, with an assist from
catcher Russell Martin, who is a sly artist at the catching
movement that looks merely firm and sure, but in fact brings
the glove slightly farther into the strike zone. Landing stuck
like an Olympic gymnast equals the catcher holding the ball
solidly even as he moves it into the zone. Which equals strike
three looking. Which equals punch out. *Grab some pine, meat!*
(The last with a nod to Giants announcer Mike Krukow.)

"Baseball is more than a game," Cheek said, as baseball
people always do. "It's a lifestyle. It's a long season, it's every
day, it's continuity, and it's simple arithmetic. It's also mobile.
You can take Tom and Jerry to the lake, on the bus, to the
office, out in the garden, anywhere. You might be doing a

lot of things, but there's no reason you can't have your Blue Jays." Surely this was the real magic of baseball radio, and even now holds in those places where you should be looking at your phone. I remember driving from Toronto to New Haven one September in the late 1980s, the Jays closing in on the American League pennant, and the rental car's antenna picked up the fading Tom and Jerry as we skidded through the rainy streets of Batavia, New York. I parked the car, got some coffee, and sat there with the rain pounding on the roof, straining to hear the wavering beam of talk as it skipped across Lake Ontario—a huddled caveman listening to big stories from far away.

When I lived in Britain and worked for a literary quarterly, we used to paste up the galleys while listening to BBC4 broadcasts of Test cricket, another great radio game. Those broadcasts lasted six hours at a stretch, and the veteran announcers, John Arlott and Fred Trueman, filled in the frequent gaps in the action with disquisitions on local politics, the profusion of hedgehogs in the Home Counties, fashion commentary, even recipes. Norman Webster, former editor of the *Globe and Mail* and the Montreal *Gazette*, once told me that, when he was London correspondent for the *Globe*, he and his wife drove all the way from London to Cornwall listening to cricket on the radio. He was, as I would have been, riveted—so much so that he didn't notice she was bored to tears.

You can't do this kind of thing with television. TV sports are fascistic, totalitarian—and not just in terms of the sheer dollar amounts they control. The medium itself is authoritarian. You must sit there, watching. You could just listen to the announcer's voices, but they're not giving much away, saying things like "Look at that one!" You have to *watch* a TV, that's what it's for. It works its will on you. Nothing is left to your imagination—how could it be? Missed a play? Here's an instant replay. Missed it again? Here it is again. Here it is three more times. Want to compare that play with one last week? Here it is. Here, look at it again. JUST SIT THERE. WE'LL LET YOU KNOW WHAT'S INTERESTING. DON'T MOVE!

Television gets the call right, with instant replay now part of baseball; but it destroys the imagination, and so it usurps the human element in sports. Consider *slow-motion* instant replays. What are these but stylized, melodramatic versions of the play, the play laid over with a thick wash of manufactured drama? Slowing the motion provides the illusion of greater significance or accuracy—but it's instant, disposable mythology. It is the sports-TV equivalent of hyper-realist art, visual propaganda that undermines the reality of the action or subject depicted. The play is no longer the thing; it is the replay.

Radio imposes no demands on the game. Nor can it dictate the responses of the fan. Like all great tribal myth-making, sports radio is oral, a matter of storytelling and narrative power. Its force comes from the suggestiveness of words and the allusiveness of the described but not seen. Its power depends on the reality of the game itself, a game played and judged by real people *somewhere else*. That's why baseball, that most mythological of North American sports, is the perfect game for the medium of radio, that locus of elemental magic. When we listen, the feelings of subtle joy and solidarity are the feelings of being gathered to hear tales of people braver and more talented than ourselves. The game is filled with pregnant moments—the 3-2 delivery, the sailing long hit, the catcher's throw to second—and lulls and depressions, which can explode into sudden, dramatic action. Baseball, the storyteller's dream game—the summer game—belongs on radio, the medium of the mouth and ears and mind.

Television should be the perfect medium for sports, the medium that makes staying home better than being at the game. But TV flattens the games out, makes them stagey and forced. Not surprisingly, today's players, so media-minded, are starting to modify their play to TV's demands. They get special haircuts before big games. College sport, once the preserve of true amateurs, is no more or less than a junior league for the pros, with huge television contracts dictating not only play but league structure. The Notre Dame football team, for example, for years had its own network deal to show all home games. Because they're a TV popularity lock, the Penn State football team once had a guaranteed invitation to a Bowl game, whatever their regular season record. (This was before the appalling 2011 Jerry Sandusky sexual abuse scandal.) And worst of all, TV all but owns major team sport these days, underwriting huge portions of annual budgets with the sale of broadcast rights—47 percent in the case of baseball. One major reason the National Hockey League looked like it might not survive the 1990s was that its television revenues were so miniscule—just $5-million a year, compared to the more than $200-million raked in by pro basketball and football. Apparent salvation came in 2011 with a ten-year, multi-billion-dollar deal with NBC, but so far the actual numbers have been disappointing, despite a season that seems to last almost the entire calendar year, with playoff games extending well into the hot weeks of June.

Well, good luck to hockey. Meanwhile, let us not be Luddite about it, but it is merely the case that some technical advances just put us further in the hole. So I've got the big TV, and the cable. But on summer evenings and weekend afternoons, it's the radio that's turned on. And the mind as well as the teams are at play.

Message

MARSHALL MCLUHAN, PIONEERING CANADIAN MEDIA theorist, thought baseball was doomed in the television age.

"Just where to begin to examine the transformation of American attitudes since TV is a most arbitrary affair, as can be seen in a change so great as the abrupt decline of baseball," he argued.[22] "The removal of the Brooklyn Dodgers to Los Angeles was a portent in itself. Baseball moved West in an attempt to retain an audience after TV struck." This was actually fairly common thinking at the time, though not always expressed in such terms as these:

> The characteristic mode of the baseball game is that it features one-thing-at-a-time. It is a lineal, expansive game which, like golf, is perfectly adapted to the outlook of an individualist and inner-directed society. Timing and waiting are of the essence, with the entire field in suspense waiting upon the performance of a single player. By contrast, football, basketball, and ice hockey are games in which many events occur simultaneously, with the entire team involved at the same time.

McLuhan thought, further, that television was an essential arbiter of this distinction:

With the advent of TV, such isolation of the individual performance as occurs in baseball became unacceptable. Interest in baseball declined, and its stars, quite as much as movie stars, found that fame had some very cramping dimensions. Baseball had been, like the movies, a hot medium featuring individual virtuosity and stellar performers.

Contrary to our own recent experience, with the explosion of statistical analysis, McLuhan judged that stats belonged to a dying cultural era:

> The real ball fan is a store of statistical information about previous explosions of batters and pitchers in numerous games. Nothing could indicate more clearly the peculiar satisfaction provided by a game that belonged to the industrial metropolis of ceaselessly exploding populations, stocks and bonds, and production and sales records. Baseball belonged to the age of the first onset of the hot press and the movie medium.

Not the presumptuous past tense there! So, in conclusion: baseball "will always remain a symbol of the era of the hot mommas, jazz babies, of sheiks and shebas, of vamps and gold-diggers and the fast buck. Baseball, in a word, is a hot game that got cooled off in the new TV climate, as did most of the hot politicians and hot issues of the earlier decades."

Now, it is too easy to mock this as high-toned mandarin nonsense, because there is a lot of that in McLuhan. But what is really interesting is not what the analysis gets wrong, but why it seems so right—and therefore so remarkable that it is wrong.

Baseball was slow in responding to the internal demands of television, it's true, with sad graphics and no reliable capacity for instant replay, an essential feature of the medium. Crucially, early televised games did not have the technology necessary for on-screen panels that would display the key statistics of the game: runs, hits, errors, balls and strikes, men on base, and the inning. These details, visible to any fan in the stadium, and repeated regularly by experienced radio game-callers. Without them, *you cannot make sense of the game*. At any given moment, any possible action is (you might say) semantically determined by this context of meaning. Syntactic execution—the proverbial play we've never seen before—is only possible against a background of semantic stability.

Likewise with the replay, which has now inflected the game at most levels, especially at the modern Big League stadiums, which feature massive television screens. Television has been brought inside the park. So has the video review of some plays, albeit with a distinctive baseball flavour (see "Time," below). Some will object that this makes it less of a park, but media do not pause to heed objections like that. At the same time, the television version of the game has grown ever more slick and entertaining, with throwback single broadcasters like Vin Scully—last member of an old school, retired in 2016—replaced by teams of two, or even three commentators. These handsome voices analyze every nuance of the game before us, including statistical notes only a full-time researcher could have on hand.

This is so true that some fans now prefer baseball on television, something that McLuhan's views would have considered impossible. The television game can never give you the holistic view of the field you get at the park, of course. There is too much focus on close-ups and cutaways, and the standard "waiting" shot that isolated the fielding battery as they deal with the batter—a necessary but drastically incomplete view of the game. But a televised baseball game is fully compatible as a medium with a radio broadcast or an in-person viewing. McLuhan seems to forget his own lesson here: media do not, except in rare cases, destroy their predecessors. Instead, new media wrap around existing ones like new rings on a tree trunk.

Who would have thought, meanwhile, that a heavy statistical approach to the game, once the preserve of local nerds and the busy brains of the SABR crowd, would produce not just a winning strategy but a bestselling book and a movie starring Brad Pitt and Jonah Hill? Michael Lewis' *Moneyball: The Art of Winning an Unfair Game* (2003) gripped the imagination of fans everywhere. The film version (2011) somewhat distorted Lewis' story of the 2002 Oakland Athletics under manager Billy Beane—but then, what did anyone expect? It now ranks among the most popular of baseball films.

On the subject of stars, one could agree with McLuhan that the hot individualism of baseball players, like that of fading movie stars, has cooled with television, but the argument is slight. Stars are no less visible now than they were a half-century ago, though it is true that many of them are famous for reasons that seem obscure or non-existent. The full irony of our moment might be the spectacle of a celebrity with no discernible history or artistic or athletic achievement making what we still call, in the dying moments of newspapers, "front-page news."

In sports, the relative normality of baseball players' bodies, as against those armoured stormtroopers of football and hockey, has actually cemented fan connection. We feel, quite insanely when the feats and percentiles are considered, that they play a game that we can more or less also play. (Mostly less.) Football players need to take their helmets off before we even know what they look like—something which television has of course facilitated but with no relative difference in star power. You might not realize that the guy standing next to you in a bar is a Major League baseball player; but you might also not realize that the white football player standing next to you at the same bar is the guy you see on Sunday and thought was black. (This is not a theoretical example: the talented (white) New York Jets cornerback Jason Sehorn, who wore sleeves when he played, was often "mistaken" for black.)

The hot/cool distinction is itself untenable, and not merely because of the bogus version proffered by that guy in a movie line in Woody Allen's *Annie Hall* (1997). Viewers will remember McLuhan's cameo, drawn from behind a poster, to rebuke the preening intellectual dandy: "I heard what you were saying! You know nothing of my work! You mean my whole fallacy is wrong. How you got to teach a course in anything is totally amazing!" Despite the satisfactory drubbing, the "fallacy" in question is opaque. What is the hot/cool business anyway?

The clearest version of the distinction is that a hot medium is ordered and sequential, and comes with an implicit degree of high engagement from its users, while a cool medium is lower in intensity because it allows, or insists that, the viewer fill in the mediated space. Traditional examples of hot media would therefore be newspapers and radio; of cool media, television, telephone, and comic books. This has nothing to do with cool in the sense of hipness—though sunglasses, cool in the fashion manner, are also a perfect cool medium because they hide the hot, information-rich eyes, offering a blank screen onto which we must project our sense of the other.

So did the hot medium of baseball get cooled off in the television age, or did it just heat itself up? Neither. I prefer to think that baseball proved *the game is greater than the sum of its media*. Some of us still read box scores, even sometimes on paper. The radio still works. Sure, players tweet. The game continues. We look and listen.

Watch

WHICH IS ALL VERY INTERESTING, but here's the thing. Sometimes, the game means so much to me that I can't even watch it. It's too excruciating, and baseball is worse than other sports for this, for the same reasons it's so watchable otherwise. The ridiculous difficulty of making anything happen. The struggle to reach base, to advance the runner, to get your man home and not strand him — dying, in the parlance — as a man left on base.

I get up and walk away from the television. I almost hope the team I love should lose, just to experience the relief of not having to care about it anymore, to keep my hair where it belongs, rooted in my scalp.

"This is too hard," my friend Catherine said during the 1992 Blue Jays World Series run. She was not a baseball fan, just a random sentient being, and *she* couldn't bear to look.

What insane endgame is this, where the game turns itself inside out when you care too much? I don't know what to call it. If this is love, it is of a deranged and destructive order, beyond all reason, coiled painfully in its own desire.

Yes, love. Slow-torture love, the love of the damned. You can leave the room, or the game, or the bar — but the contest continues its agonizing course whether you like it or not. Half-shut your eyes, peek through your shaking fingers, look off to the side—it is still happening, my friend. Accept the inevitable. You are in fan lockdown, the final painful stage of devotion.

Alas, there is no cure for what ails you. Lucretius, Ovid, and Shakespeare all pined for a salve, uselessly, and now modern neuroscience has added its peculiar version of cosmetic psychochemistry to the range of options. Maybe there is a version of the eternal sunshine of the spotless mind, a drug or procedure that would address our symptoms just as it does those of depression, anxiety, or fear.

But the trouble is that any offered prescription would strip us of too much selfhood to make it acceptable. We cannot surrender ourselves so far, or commit such comprehensive erasures, which begin to resemble Hamlet's self-slaughter or (if you prefer) Homer Simpson's re-insertion of the crayon to the brain.[23] Painful though it is, how could we ever *not* be the fan that we are? Baseball: you can't live with it, and you can't live without it.

Don't look now.

Slang

EVERYBODY HAS THEIR OWN LIST of favourite baseball terms, formal and slang. I am partial to these:

Defensive indifference: A runner is not credited with a steal if he takes a base when the fielding team judges there is no advantage in attempting to throw him out. It's only stealing if the owner of the base cares whether you take it. But you know what? Indifference at one point in a game can prove to be all too casual later on: any advanced runner may score, and sometimes this "allowed steal" turns out to be a game-changer. Indifference in itself is no crime; but tactics are forever overtaken by events. That's what we mean by life.

Compare Field Marshall Helmuth von Moltke, that master military planner: "No battle plan survives contact with the enemy." Or maybe you prefer boxer and ear-biter Mike Tyson's version of the same wise dictum: "Everybody has a plan until they get punched in the mouth."

Balk: The much-disputed rule that uses a word otherwise employed to describe a horse stalling at a fence or someone refusing an advance. "Balk" is actually rooted in the words for the hindrance itself, a bank of ploughed-up earth, later transferred to the act of stopping short in front of it. Baseball's use of the term was first noted in 1845, and we still don't understand it. In brief, a balk is any of a series of movements whereby the pitcher has apparently committed himself to a pitch and yet does not deliver it. These might include attempting a pick-off throw while moving towards home, or (!) dropping the ball while standing on the pitching rubber.

It is also the case that the pitcher, no matter what his particular windup and delivery techniques, must come to a stop before delivering his pitch when there are runners on base. Observers have long noticed that the balk rule thus contains depths of scientific and philosophical significance. What constitutes a complete stop? During the 1987 season the matter came to a head, and revealed a surprising difference between the two major leagues. In the American League, president Bobby Brown said that "a stop" was merely a change in direction, because theoretically, "when you change directions with your hands, you have to stop."

Science historian Adam Schulman immediately noticed that this principle is in fact Aristotle's.[24] In his *Physics*, the Greek philosopher argues that motion cannot be both continuous and eternal. The universe is finite, and so there must eventually be reversals of direction in any motion. When that occurs, there is an instant of motionlessness, however brief.

Over in the Senior Circuit, though, ancient Greek theoretical physics had been abandoned in favour of modern Galilean notions. A motion with an apparent stop, such as a ball thrown into the air, was in fact in continuous motion. There were not two motions (up and down) separated by a moment of motionlessness. A change of trajectory does not entail that the moving body has ever stopped.

Aristotelians rely on logic for their arguments about stopping. That's because the stop may not be discernible by observation. Baseball has, on the whole, favoured seeing over reasoning, and so the Official Play Rules Committee says this: "A complete stop should not be construed as occurring because of a change in direction of the hands and arms."

American League Aristotelians pushed back with a revision that changed "complete stop" to "complete and discernible stop." The difference is massive: the logical implication is that there could be a complete stop that is *in*discernible, and so the (logically) correct call gets (empirically) missed.

Note for geeks: this is an application of the truth-function rule of conjunction, which states that both terms separated by "and" must hold for a claim to be true. It's worth noticing that flight attendants, who are widely mocked for speaking of the aircraft "coming to a complete and final stop" are actually being good logicians. The plane might stop completely, but not finally, somewhere short of the gate. Happens all the time. Remain seated until the seatbelt light goes off, people!

In effect, the American Leaguers implied that if you're going to be empiricists, you have to be consistent ones. You have to admit the limits of observation—and the umpire's exercise of it. Logic remains superior, as usual. Television commentators, meanwhile, armed with slow-motion replays, who delight in pointing out balk calls that the umpires have missed, lie somewhere in between.

The hard truth? Almost anything can count as a balk if the umpire is in an ornery mood. A pitcher I know, throwing a game in chilly conditions one April day on Randall's Island, up near East Harlem, *shivered* while she was in the prescribed pause between stretch and throw. *Balk!* cried the ump. No runners were on base, but the call resulted in a ball. The batter was at 3-2, and so that meant a walk.

She's still mad about it. She thinks the balk call is about umpires "power-tripping." Could be, could be. Certainly we know that some pitchers with kooky, triple-bob motions never get called. At that point, it's like travelling in NBA basketball or holding in the NFL: you could call it on *virtually every* drive to the hoop or offensive down. But then what?

Five-run homer: A dismissive term for a batter who is trying too hard, in quest of the impossible *coup de grâce*. No home run can ever score more than four runs. Duh. Don't try so hard (a topic to which we will return).

Fence-swinger: Someone who swings for the fences; i.e., tries hard and might just succeed, but probably not. Can be dismissive, not always. Swinging for the fences can count as heroic. But again, don't try so hard.

Warning-track power: What a lot of fence-swingers alas possess. Always dismissive.

Four-strikeout inning: By contrast, there *can* be an inning with four strikeouts. The weird rule about a swinging third strike is that the batter is given an opportunity to get to first base anyway. The catcher must field the ball cleanly, and if the runner attempts to dash to first, either tag him or throw him out at first to complete the retirement.

This is very confusing to new viewers of the game. Sometimes, rarely, the runner makes it safely to first. He was struck out but is not out. The pitcher, if he has recorded three strikeouts already, might then strike out the next batter, ending the inning with a fourth strikeout.

Ground-rule triple: The common "ground-rule double," where a ball bounces out of play before being fielded, is technically not a matter of ground rules. It is a dead-ball award of two bases, akin to a ball thrown out of play resulting in a single awarded base. The rare ground-rule triple is awarded when a defensive player attempts to use his hat to alter the path of the ball, either in the air or on fair ground. The batter and any on-base runners are given three bags. I am not making this up.

Uncle Charlie: The curveball, nemesis of all those who would vie for seats in the show. Also hook, hammer, yakker, yack attack, deuce, or number two. The big bending hook goes twelve to six, like the face of a clock. You're out, my friend. Grab some bench.

Cheese: Still in use as a favoured term for the fastball, otherwise known as the heater or the gas. You might get served some *alto queso*—the high, hard cheese. Some coaches even like to specify the flavour: *Bring the cheddar, kid!* (It's usually cheddar.)

Chin music: What you hear when the high cheese comes in tight, humming its way past your head. Only incompetent or evil pitchers throw at your head or, worse, behind it, where the instinctive backwards flinch would put your temple squarely in the crosshairs of the pitch. Good chin music is a tune in every pitcher's repertoire.

Cement-mixer: A pitch, typically a slider, that is meant to break hard, buckling the legs of a waving batter, but spins sideways and hangs. Boom! You know what happens next: the pitcher turns around, takes off his hat, and scratches his head, because the ball is now a bleacher souvenir.

Southpaw: A left-handed pitcher, allegedly so called because baseball stadiums are conventionally built with the third-base line pointing north, to limit sun in the fielders' eyes. Major League Baseball Rule 1.04 states: "It is desirable that the line from home base through the pitchers plate to second base shall run East Northeast." Thus a left-handed pitcher, standing on the mound and facing home, would have his business hand on the south side. But the term predates any evidence of convention in stadium orientation, which is optional anyway, according to the rule. Also used in boxing, maybe the only other sport where being a lefty is a comprehensive advantage.

Baltimore chop: Not a cut of meat, but the hard swing that sends a ball directly down in front of the plate, bouncing high over the pitcher's head for a base hit. Allegedly associated with Baltimore, who installed cement below the field in front of home to facilitate the play. Hard to believe, but maybe true, especially in the dead-ball era. For a while, when turf-covered concrete surfaces were legion in baseball, the chop could be served up almost anywhere.

Texas leaguer: A high blooper that falls into the no-man's-land region between the infield and the outfield, resulting in a hit. The link to Texas is obscure. Sportswriter John Marshall:

"The Texas League theories range from a team in the Texas League that specialized in the use of the bloop single as an offensive weapon; to the effects of strong Gulf Stream winds on outfield flies in the Texas League; to the debut of Ollie Pickering, either in the majors or the Texas League, who came to bat and proceeded to run off a string of seven straight bloop hits."[25] Also known, excellently, as a *gork shot*.

Seeing-eye single: The one that gets through the defence and will, if you are blessed with enough luck to hit a few, get you to the next level in baseball. Crash Davis, in *Bull Durham*, places this semi-conscious hit in its proper cosmic position: "Know what the difference between hitting .250 and .300 is? It's 25 hits. Twenty-five hits in 500 at bats is 50 points, okay? There's six months in a season, that's about 25 weeks. That means if you get just one extra flare a week—just one—a gorp ... you get a groundball, you get a groundball with eyes ... you get a dying quail, just one more dying quail a week ... and you're in Yankee Stadium."

Crooked number: The good kind of crooked, which is to say any number greater than zero or one; what you want to hang on the scoreboard in a single inning.

Can of corn: An easy fly ball, said to be based on the old general-store practice of fetching down said item from a tall shelf using a pole. Out of fashion in the 1980s—some players specifically warned *Los Angeles Times* writer Scott Ostler away from it in a 1986 article, but you'll hear it now even from the young guys on TBS and Sportsnet.[26]

Wilson Pickett: How did he get here? In the same article, Ostler notes that a fielder's glove, usually called his leather or rag, might be labelled a *skillet* if he can't make routine catches, the ball bouncing off it like dried peas hitting a frying pan. This makes me think of my high-school football coach, who used to chide me for dropping passes by shouting, "*Kingwell!* Son, you have *boards* for hands! *Boards!*"

Then Ostler adds what would turn out to be a tragic note: "If a player is a skillful fielder, he can *pickett* (pick it).

Bill Buckner once named his first baseman's glove Wilson Pickett." For those not of a certain age, that's the legendary soul and R&B man (1941-2006) who gave the world, among other things, "Mustang Sally" and "In the Midnight Hour." This baseball-slang article was written in May of 1986. Bill Buckner's most notorious act as a Major Leaguer, his daylight midnight hour, an error that would overshadow every achievement of more than two decades in the Bigs, would happen in October of the same year.

You know the play. October 25, 1986. The Red Sox are facing the Mets at Shea Stadium in Game Six of the World Series, implausibly leading three games to two. Tied three-all, the game goes into extra innings, and then the Bostons score two in the top of the tenth. Three outs and they are World Series champions, busting at long last the Curse of the Bambino! Boston, and the world, are holding their collective breath.

In the bottom of the inning, Sox manager John McNamara elects not to replace Buckner at first base, even though the veteran is hobbled by leg damage that makes him scuttle around the diamond like an arthritic old lady. Calvin Schiraldi is on the mound and retires Wally Backman and Keith Hernandez on routine flies to left and centre, respectively. Say it again: *the Red Sox are one out away from the title*.

Legend has it that a programming error briefly flashed "Congratulations Boston Red Sox, 1986 World Champions" onto the stadium scoreboard. Schiraldi gets the yips and allows two Mets to get on base, then gives up a run after facing the crafty Gary Carter. Sox 5, Mets 4. McNamara replaces Schiraldi with Bob Stanley, who sets up against Mookie Wilson, the coolest Met ever until Curtis Granderson. Stanley works Wilson to two strikes — Sox one *strike* away from the title! — but a wild pitch allows another run to score. Tie game, 5-5.

And then the dribbler that would echo as loudly as the Shot Heard Around the World. Stanley serves up a clunky pitch and Wilson pushes it feebly down the first-base line.

119

Buckner, crabbing over from his cover position, bends to field the easy ball and end the inning.

But no. Right through the wickets, rolling with maddening casualness into shallow right, goes Wilson's slow dribbler. New York's Ray Knight comes around third and scores without a play. The Mets walk it off, Bill "No Legs" Buckner is the goat. Where is your Wilson Pickett now, son? Wickets, not pickets.

Vin Scully, calling the game, said this: "So the winning run is at second base, with two outs, three and two to Mookie Wilson. Little roller up along first ... behind the bag! It gets through Buckner! Here comes Knight, and the Mets win it!" Scully then remained silent for almost three minutes of riotous cheering—a technique of Zen broadcasting genius that he would make into a trademark. With the series tied at three games each, the Boston side was entirely deflated. Game Seven was, in historical terms, an afterthought. Mets starter Ron Darling, the Hero of Yale College, gave up three runs in the second, the Sox added two more in the top of the eighth, but the New York team had an answer every time. Final score 8-5; series over; the Curse continues.

Boston would break that curse, of course, in 2004, and then snag the big trophy again in 2007 *and* 2013. But the Massachusetts town is one that thrives on Black Irish pessimism and a perverse talent for finding the dark moment in every sunny day. In certain Beantown bars you can still cause a stir just by saying, a little too loudly, "1986." Try it. "Did you just fuckin' say 1986 to me?" Actually, don't try it. MLB Network ranked the Buckner game in the top three of the half-century between 1960 and 2010.

Buckner, for his part, was reviled and denounced; he received death threats and appalling personal insults on a regular basis—imagine all that in an era before social media, the effort involved. And though there was an official "forgiveness" moment at Fenway Park in 2008, when he threw out the ceremonial first pitch and received a four-minute standing ovation, his botched play will live forever in the minds of some Red Sox fans.

Another tiny tragic detail. Buckner, looking over replays of the error afterwards, noted that his glove, a loose outfield-style number unlike the traditional first baseman's "trapper," closed as he dragged it across the dirt toward the ball. There was no pocket, hence no pickett. The gap is everything.

Linda Ronstadt: How did *she* get here? Well, it's a little dated but I heard a sportscaster use the term just the other day, here in the playoff month of October 2016. One of the sultry singer's biggest hits was her 1977 version of the Roy Orbison ballad "Blue Bayou" (1963). Yes, that 90-mph high fastball was a Ronstadt, or a Linda. It, ahem, blew by you.

Goodbye Mr. Spalding!: There are so many terms for the home run, from tater to dinger to long ball (as in "Chicks dig the long ball"), so many ways to say downtown, outta here, bleacher feature, big fly, and "Get out, ball," that a fan has to choose one as a gold standard. This is my favourite, though I am well aware that since 1977 the supplier of Major League baseballs has been Rawlings, not Spalding. "Goodbye Mr. Rawlings!" just doesn't sound as good.

Seed: A sharp line drive or, alternately, a hard and accurate throw. Also pea, bolt, rocket, or frozen rope. In Spanish *linea*, though I have never personally heard that one.

Blown save: Just a routine phrase for a relief pitcher who enters the game in a save position and then fails to execute. But it feels like a death sentence from the underworld of failure. Blown. Save.

Mendoza Line: Likewise this famous threshold of failure. Mario (Aizpuru) Mendoza, born in 1950, is forever associated with struggles at the plate. Though Mendoza ended his Major League career with a batting average of .215, his difficulties in clearing .200 during the Seattle Mariners' 1979 season led teammates Tom Paciorek and Bruce Bochte to link that mark of just-one-success-in-five to his surname.

Kansas City's George Brett, who flirted with the mythical .400 mark the next year, reportedly said that "The first thing I look for in the Sunday papers is who is below the Mendoza line." Various ESPN broadcasters, sources now say, popularized the term.

There is, naturally, a long thesaurus of terms for light or inconsistent hitters. The "tapperitis hitter" suffers from the fatal condition of only hitting tappers. Some batters "can't hit a balloon" or "can't hit a bull in the ass with a shovel." Some noodle-armed would-be sluggers are "buttercup hitters," "banjo hitters," "ukulele hitters," or "Punch and Judy hitters," while others just hit below their weight. A few have holes in their bats or are ten o'clock hitters — leaving their best in BP, like singers who peak during the soundcheck. More contemporary is the hitter who is "stuck on the Interstate," that is, hitting .180 and looking on the scoreboard like I 80.

I can report from my own idiosyncratic experience that the first time I heard the term Mendoza Line was in a dialogue exchange on the television show *Beverly Hills 90210*, when a teacher uses the term to describe a minimum grade standard, and Minnesota transplant Brandon Walsh (played by my countryman Jason Priestley, who probably knows more about hockey than baseball) is the only student who gets the reference.

Not surprisingly, Mendoza Line variants can be found in other sports and in other walks of life, including politics (getting just one delegate in a primary, used of Rudy Giuliani by Keith Olbermann in 1988) and the movies (earning less than $2,000 on average at theatres on a film's opening weekend). There is, so far as I know, no Mendoza Line in philosophy, which is probably just as well. Nobody wants to quantify things like lack of comprehension or botched coherence in argument.

Or do they?

Aiming

THE SUMMER OF 1986, I was working as an editorial writer at the *Globe and Mail*. The Blue Jays were contending, and the game's summer progress was a daily buzz through the sprawling, old-school open-plan newsroom. Little fabric-covered separators would come the year after, creating the standard cubicle-farm office space that Douglas Coupland lampooned as "veal-fattening pens." A mid-season feature about the team and its players coughed up one of those nice conjunctions of wisdom that shape one's sense of the game. Three different coaches, asked for their most essential wisdom, provided variants on "Don't think too much out there."

Don't think seems like an imperative unlikely to generate success, but it is a longstanding mantra in sports, and maybe especially baseball, the game of expectant waiting. The great Yogi Berra offered his version of the wisdom as a kind of confession: "I can't think and hit at the same time." Which makes it sound like a shortcoming, on the order of failing to walk while chewing bubble gum. But what if not-thinking is a *gift*, a liberation from troublesome effort? Maybe the ideal condition for hitting is a mind clear of all conscious thought? And perhaps that fielder fields best whose busy thought-centres are open, empty, waiting without specific expectation but vast reserves of muscle memory, habit, and a knowledge beyond knowing? Repetition, and difference.

Compare Crash Davis, in *Bull Durham*, as usual chiding the young fireballer Ebby Calvin "Nuke" LaLoosh: "You just got lesson number one: don't think; it can only hurt the ball club."

It has to be noted, before we explore non-thinking further, that Berra complicates matters with his perfect mix of paradox and inventive mathematics. "Baseball is ninety percent mental," he said, clearly having thought about it. "The other half is physical."

Yes, of course. But I want to make the point about mental instability in a different way. There is a passage from J. D. Salinger's *Seymour: An Introduction* that has become a sort of classic of its kind. The scene is in Manhattan, at the magic moment of dusk.

Two boys are playing marbles while a third, a brother of one of the players, is watching, then commenting on the play. "'Could you try not aiming so much?' he asked me, still standing there. 'If you hit him when you aim, it'll just be luck.' He was speaking, communicating, and yet not breaking the spell. I then broke it. Quite deliberately. 'How can it be luck if I aim?' I said back to him, not loud but with rather more irritation in my voice than I was actually feeling. He didn't say anything for a moment but simply stood balanced on the curb, looking at me, I knew imperfectly, with love. 'Because it will be,' he said. 'You'll be glad if you hit his marble—Ira's marble—won't you? Won't you be glad? And if you're glad when you hit somebody's marble, then you sort of secretly didn't expect too much to do it. So there'd have to be some luck in it, there'd have to be slightly quite a lot of accident in it.'"[27]

The scene illuminates, in Salinger's typical fashion, that the perfection of a truly transcendent or transfinite performance involves no luck or accident. One can almost hear, in a time-travel moment, the voice of Yoda indicting the failure of Luke Skywalker to raise his X-Wing fighter from the Dagobah swamp: "Try not. Do, or do not. There is no try." There are other, less mystical forms of not-trying of course. Homer Simpson to Bart and Lisa: "Kids, you tried your best and you failed miserably. The lesson is, never try." The difference is that Seymour's not-aiming, and Yoda's not-trying, are themselves forms of *action*.

In other words, we go beyond our sense that it would be a *good thing* or a *happy thing* if something happened, some outcome was achieved, to a *certainty* that it always has happened, is happening, and will happen. When the Zen archer draws her bow, the arrow is, in a sense, *always already* in the target. The mere enactment of its flight is the least of the truths concerning bow, arrow, and target. Now compare the archer to the very best quarterback, tennis player, or hockey forward: even in finite games, there is ever this hint of the transcendent.[28]

Aiming is a more complicated act that we usually assume. I don't mean the technical difficulties associated with deliberate aiming, as when a sniper factors a handful of complex variables—distance, elevation, windspeed, bullet trajectory, humidity, and so on—into the explosive execution of the deadly logic of "one shot, one kill." I mean instead the ability to forget oneself sufficiently so that the ball flows smoothly from the arm and hand and makes its true way to the waiting glove.

Playing for the hapless *Globe and Mail* fastpitch side in the mid-1980s, I came to realize that my throwing arm was erratic to the point of disaster. The hint of my debility had come in a summer pick-up game the year before. Playing drawn in at shortstop, I charged a slow dribbler from one of the less formidable batters on the other side, scooped up the ball cleanly and in one *beautiful smooth motion* I sailed it about twelve feet above the first baseman's head. My muscle memory had suffered some kind of internal breakdown, dissolving my once-reliable put-out throw into a three-ring circus of wild tosses and extra bases. In the manner of these things, I was relegated to left field, in the weeds, where my off-line throws could be soaked up by agile cut-off men.

The following year, in an actual competitive league, albeit one filled with pikers and stiffs, I was attempting to play short again. The catcher's girlfriend, a charitable, sporty sort, offered to catch during warm-ups. I kept throwing the ball at her, but jerking the last part of the motion in a bizarre way, sending the little orb wide or high or both. She eventually got frustrated with me and shouted, "Dammit, can't you just *aim?*"

It struck me even in that moment that this was a signal instance of the Salinger-Seymour conundrum. I was trying to aim, but I couldn't. Then I was trying too hard to correct the first failure. And then I was becoming self-conscious about my bad arm, and introducing fatal hesitations and hitches.

Pitchers are often told by coaches not to aim. But how are they supposed to do that when the target they seek is the corner of a strike zone no more than about six feet square? Batters are told not to hit the ball, but rather to throw their hands *through* it. What? This should be impossible—the striking face of a cylindrical bat on a round ball coming at you at 90-plus miles an hour is ridiculously tiny. And yet, the best of them can do this, they can execute this impossible feat. Somewhere in here, the normal realms of the mental and the physical have been decisively transcended. The impossible has been made possible.

How do we know? It just happened, my friend. *Boom*: strikeout! *Boom*: home run!

I thought about a couple of minor sports tragedies that had jumped out at me from the pages of *Sports Illustrated*. The first was Australian golfer Ian Baker-Finch. He won the Open Championship, usually known as the British Open, in 1991, flashing one of the sweetest swings on the tour. Then, in a slow crumbling of his game, in particular his on-course confidence, tinkering with his swing, he pulled it completely undone. He dropped in rankings and slipped from his tentative toehold on elite status. Soon, by the mid-1990s, he could not play competitively at all, even though he hit flawlessly in practice and casual rounds.

"I lost my confidence," Baker-Finch told a reporter from *Golf Today*. "I got to the point where I didn't even want to be out on the golf course because I was playing so poorly. I would try my hardest but when I came out to play, I managed to find a way to miss the cut time and time again. It became a habit."[29]

A couple of things are notable in this confession. The first is his mention of trying, indeed "trying his hardest," to play better. This stands revealed as a comprehensive self-defeat. Trying harder only reinforces the series of psychological blocks that are making for the physical failure to execute. That is why some baseball coaches will caution their athletes to *try easier* — a paradoxical command on the road to true wisdom about the nature of trying.

The second feature is Baker-Finch's accurate diagnosis that his failure had become a *habit*. This is the essence of the issue. Aristotle long ago argued for the central role of habit in creating and executing human excellence. Habitual repetition of difficult actions is the only way to make them reliably available, and, in that pinnacle of achievement, to make them look easy. Bad habits are likewise action-governing, and failure can become as automatic as success under the right — which is to say, the wrong — circumstances of reinforcement.

The other case comes from the world of baseball. Mackey Sasser was a successful catcher with the New York Mets, as well as several other teams. He had a good if unspectacular career between 1987 and 1995. After two years as a backup for Hall of Fame backstop Gary Carter—until Andre Dawson in 2010, the only player in the Hall depicted with a Montreal Expos cap, Carter's former team—Sasser went full-time in 1990 and had a good year, hitting .307. But a plate collision with Atlanta's Jim Presley left him shaken and with a strange new quirk. From then on, when attempting to throw the ball back to the pitcher after a deal, Sasser double-clutched his throw. In fact, if you watch old footage of Mets games from that season, it is a sort of triple- or quadruple-clutch, with several false starts eventually issuing in a toss back to the mound. Sasser had no explanation for this, and he was not otherwise hampered. When a runner attempted to steal from first, for example, his put-out throws were clean and accurate.

The obvious conclusion was that, in those cases, Sasser *had no time to think*. Behind the plate, however, negotiating the regular business of the battery, something crept into his mind at a level somewhere below consciousness but nevertheless affecting action. Bup, bup, bup—throw. Bup, bup, bup—throw. Sasser made it through a few more seasons with the Giants, Padres, and Mariners, but his peak had been reached. Upon retirement he took a job as a community-college coach in Alabama, but the weird tic followed him there: he was unable to throw batting-practice balls to his young players. In this sense, Sasser's block was deeper than Baker-Finch's, which clearly derived mainly from performance anxiety. Sasser sought psychotherapeutic help and was eventually able to dismantle the block.[30] The ultimate source of these action-destroying hiccups remains mysterious, however. There is a brain-lock engaged, which prevents the special, semi-conscious effort necessary for action without effort; trying becomes the enemy of doing. Here, the mind is its own worst enemy.

Both of these tales serve to remind us of the force of habit, but also of the limits of trying. In many cases, especially in sports, skilful action is a matter of automaticity, not effort. This is strongly reminiscent once more of Lao Tzu's doctrine of *wu wei*, the paradoxical action without action. *Trying not to try* is another way of articulating this key paradox, the step beyond, we might say, the transitional stage of trying easier.[31] To know the *tao*, or the way, is not to acquire and master knowledge; it is, rather, to let go of the need for control and so arrive at a state of automatic, apparently effortless action that is indistinguishable from the spontaneous.

"Stop thinking, and end your problems," Lao Tzu counsels. "Act without expectation."

Also: "Manifest plainness, embrace simplicity, reduce selfishness, have few desires."

Also: "The softest things in the world overcome the hardest things in the world. Through this I know the advantage of taking no action."

Also: "By letting go, it all gets done. The world is won by those who let it go! But when you try and try, the world is then beyond the winning."

When you throw the ball to first, do not think; just do. The ball is an egg, as Crash Davis said; don't crush it. Throw it. There is no effort, there is only success. The ball was always in the first baseman's glove.

Easier said than done, of course. Or, if you're feeling puckish: *Nice try, Lao Tzu!* New appreciation of automaticity in skilful action gives added resonance to this ancient poetic wisdom, however. Cognitive science has shown convincingly that actions undertaken without conscious effort are often far more successful than those subject to thought. Excellence, Aristotle's notion of virtue, is indeed a matter of habituation.

Which leads to another piece of ancient wisdom that is still relevant every day. Question: How do you get to The Show? Answer: How else? Practice, practice, practice.

(PS: It doesn't matter what The Show is.)

Sportspace

IN PHYSICS, *SPACETIME* IS ANY mathematical model that combines space and time into a single, interwoven continuum. Baseball does that, and while it is not itself a mathematical model, it is surely the most number-enshrouded sport we know. I don't just mean the obvious geometry of its layout, but also the vast and expanding web of numbers that encompass its universe of meaning—averages, ratios, percentages, and, not least, the da-da-dum marching rhythms of all those threes and combinations of threes (strikes, outs, bases, players, and innings). These non-material functions and relations define baseball's gameworld as necessarily as any player or play.

There is space in games as there is in life, space defined and controlled, fought over and hard-won, created and nullified instantly, measured and celebrated by the passage of objects called balls, accomplishments called passes, triumphs called goals. Game-space is life space, metonymic and synecdochic, where nations battle (England v. West Indies) and cities tangle (Pittsburgh taking on New Orleans), where the turf is horse-racing culture and the pitch is all that's cricket and the gridiron is a whole world of collective aggression. Game-space is also crucially *more than* life, an abstract critique of life advanced between the lines, within the boundary, inside the gridiron. Games are relationships; they create artificial situations that, at their best and worst, reflect critically on the social possibilities of life.

But game-space is so much a part of us that we do not often take the time to separate it off from life, to contain it conceptually—contenting ourselves, instead, to contain it physically within the monumental architecture of spectacle, the domes, stadiums, coliseums, parks, and grounds of our social imagination. To enter these spaces is to participate in the game's critical possibilities, but also, paradoxically, to limit them. To succeed as more than diversion, to realize its possibilities, game-space must be both completely other than life and yet a crucial part of life. How can it be so, when failure lurks at every turn—and with every new astronomical contract, every report of off-field criminality or on-field racism? Begin with the inner spaces of game-space.

Accepting Marshall McLuhan's distinction, game-space is, in professional team sports—the sports of social critique—either *territorial* or *linear*. It is, in other words, either rectangular or irregular, either measured and standard or idiosyncratic and conventional. Territorial games pit teams of equal number against each other in a battle of space control. Balls are advanced as tokens of ground won, strategic advantage gained. Goals await: the sheer advancement of the token beyond a certain line or plane (rugby tries, where the ball must be placed on the ground, football touchdowns where it must "break the plane" of the goal line); or the deposit of the token in a designated, defended space (the soccer or hockey goal, the basket). And the ball is not merely a token, but also a prize, deeply bound up with the conquest of space in the game. Game ball. Spiking the ball. Writing a winning score on the ball, and placing it in the trophy cabinet.

In territorial games the ball is also frequently the medium of movement. It can pass magically over the heads of toiling players bound to earth, advancing their territorial cause in great elegant leaps. One begins to understand the absolute territorial dominance enjoyed by the Notre Dame football team, whose innovation of the forward pass must have made their opponents taste instant despair. How could they—clay-footed mortals—compete with this death from above? Were they not now hapless infantrymen beset by aerial bombardment, out of their league, out of luck?

Territorial games, though circumscribed by defined space, work, at the tactical level, by the creation of space *within* the field. The field's limitations must be exploited, its spaces manipulated for advantage: the sideline pass pattern in football, the opening of holes in the defending line, the detection of seams in the zone defence—tiny unprotected spaces that open for a sub-second, only to close dramatically in an instant with the arrival of vengeful defenders. The quarterback, waiting for receivers to find the seams, has his own spatial worries. He surveys the forward field from a pocket of blocking teammates, keeping at bay, for at best a few seconds, the encroaching defenders. The pocket collapses—he is sacked. Or it holds, and his gaze picks out of the crowded game-space a receiver who is, or will be, open or sometimes even wide open. The spiralling ball describes an arc, a curved line of power, from one clearing, the pocket, to another, the open receiver in the seam. Success is measured in connecting open spaces, and the magic of football's forward pass is the magic of opening up small pockets of peace in a crowded battlefield of bodies.

Football is only the least fluid and most measured of the territorial games, the contest stopped after every move while new options are considered and reconsidered for the next. Moves are measured, motion is set, the game is laborious and sometimes tedious, but broken by explosions of movement and conflict. Yet even the more fluid territorial games like soccer and basketball turn on the creation of space: the pass to the open man, getting around a defender, placing the ball accurately and according to one's desires. Advantage is created, as in football, by drawing the defender into commitments that leave areas of the field unprotected, however momentarily, and thus open for exploitation. Skill in attacking consists in the ability to draw the defender and manipulate the resulting spaces; skill in defending is a matter of closing spaces quickly or preventing their creation altogether.

The field of territorial games is fixed, usually by statute; it is also usually rectangular and regular, measured by yard lines or offside boxes. All this is given: the field exists, immutable and consistent, before we step onto it as players. The field is the scene of the game, the circumscription of conflict. Moving off the field—going out of bounds, into touch, beyond the boundary—steals my status as a player, a participant in the game. The ball, beyond the boundary, is no longer a token of conflict. The question of whether the receiver's feet were in bounds when he caught the forward pass, now the subject of apparently interminable review by the television monitor, is really a question of whether in that instant he is still a player, the ball still part of the game—or have they become mere furniture, indistinguishable from the rest of that surprisingly large milling crowd of spares, coaches, trainers, and hangers-on who throng the sidelines of every football game?

But these limitations, however powerful, are only the beginning of the game's spatial nature. For within the set boundaries, the moves are not fixed. In fluid territorial games, players have enormous freedom of movement. They may have assigned positions, but, with the exception of the oddball goalie (if there is one) these are tactical and do not represent limitations of the game itself. A defenseman may score in hockey, a forward may block his shot, and no coach will ruffle. To prevent spatial chaos in territorial games there are frequently subtle and complicated offside rules—in hockey, rugby, soccer, and even static football. These rules limit the manipulation of the game-space in the interests of the game itself. I cannot move in advance of the ball, or cross the blue line ahead of the puck, or enter the penalty area ahead of the last defender: the conflict of territorial games, in other words, must be head-on.

The rules, like the creation of the field itself, combine to make the game less like life and more like an idealized version of life, more like, indeed, a utopian critique of life. Unfair advantage cannot be taken within game-space. The teams are of equal number — if not talent, but talent is the affair of God (and the general manager). The game is limited in time and space to produce the satisfaction of a result, never forgetting that a draw is a result too. Soccer, perhaps the most basic and certainly most universal of the territorial games, describes in its development a gradual drawing in of game-space, moving from its medieval English form of village-to-village conflict ranging over miles and days, marked by violence and cheating and irresolute cessation of hostilities, to its present, limited form. Here, inside the limited green space, conflict is still basic but now highly stylized, most obviously in the essential rule that no one but the goalkeeper may employ his hands, unless the ball goes, as they say, "into touch" — and thus out of the game.

What use is a game, after all, that is merely life by other means? The game can only reflect on life when its limits are clear, when it is clearly not-life in a definite respect. That game conflict spills over into life — in, say, the Honduras Soccer War or England's hooligan skirmishes — might be evidence of many things: a pathological inability to separate game from life, a continuation of deep hostility in a wider context, perhaps the profound effectiveness of the game's social critique. Contest reveals character, but so does response to conflict.

But conflict is the essence of some sporting contests, those confrontations that are not games and do not engage teams, but which are essential meetings of self with other. These are struggles for recognition and dominance that characterize the combative sports of fencing, boxing, wrestling, and others like them. Here, space is not often of strategic interest, but defines the area in which one can run but cannot hide: the ring (another synecdoche there, as in the title of boxing's famous journal), the circle, the square. These combat spaces act, like the territories of game-space, to confine and stylize the conflict, to set artificial limits that pose questions of an essential nature—who is strongest, fastest, most cunning—within a controlled space. And, just as two lawyers arguing does not always mean (though it sometimes can) that they disagree, two boxers fighting does not always indicate a hatred or even dislike. Indeed, the brute nature of their conflict sometimes engenders a deep mutual respect: the recognition that after conflict—the struggle to the death—there is rest, and recognition.

In a few cases, the conflict of combat is itself about space, as, say, one thundering sumo wrestler attempts to push, throw, or knock another from the magic, sacred circle. More often it is about finding open spaces in personal defence, chinks in the armour of the boxer's dancing gloves—which pick off incoming punches to blunt their force—or the fencer's parrying épée. In wrestling, defended by John Irving's Garp as the most basic and essential of human sports, the object is even simpler: bring your opponent to the ground without aid of equipment or tool. This task, the planned destruction of the upright posture, that essential human achievement, is a return to the primitive both in method and result. Once standing, I am felled; once independent, I am dominated. I lie on my back, looking up at my conqueror; no longer do I survey the world from atop my six-foot tower, master (as we say) of all that I survey. I am returned to the earth, with a thud and against my will.

This toppling of the upright posture plays a role in boxing as well, though its achievement is not, in contrast to wrestling, the only way to win the contest. A knock-down brings a standing count, as the combatant is allowed to rise and collect himself; a knock-out is what happens when he cannot rise in the time (usually ten seconds) allowed him. It is not the opponent's body that pins me to the floor but the force of his blows, the violent punches to the head that will render me unconscious, or jelly-legged, or simply too dispirited to stand up for more.

Destroying uprightness is also the essence of another violent confrontation, football tackling, that tiny instance of hand-to-hand combat within the larger spaces of territorial advancement. Bringing the man down is decisive, it stops play, which must begin again from this new site of man's fall. But here the conflict is not so controlled, or so focussed on the essential confrontation of ego and alter. There may be many tacklers, sometimes four or five, and they care not so much for bringing me to my knees as for stopping my forward progress. But taking the evolutionary view, can we not say that these two notions are the same?

Linear

TERRITORIAL AND COMBATIVE GAMES ARE not the only arbi-
ters of game-space, nor the only or even best locus of social
critique in the world of games. Territorial achievements and
combat successes are, even when stylized and limited in space,
to many minds still too much like life to offer much critical
reflection. They may, in fact, reinforce dominant values of
aggression and collective triumph, the values of warrior cultures and imperial nations. Linear games are fewer but their
influence is sometimes wider, especially in defining national
character at its best, what a people wants itself to be but often
isn't. In this sense the baseball diamond is a field of dreams in a
way the gridiron will never be, and the cricket pitch says more
about English cultural mythology and its attendant attitudes
concerning elegance and village life than the public school,
and therefore upper-class, game of rugby ever can.

Linear games are not territorial: there is no context for
space, no obvious notion of ground won. The teams do not
face each other as teams, but instead engage in a complex,
related series of individual efforts and confrontations. A
player may find himself on the field of play with no allies —
or perhaps just one, his partner batsman or next batter in
the order. Success is measured in ritualized simulacra of

progress: not attainment of goals, but movement along set lines in an elegant choreography of motions.

The ball, though now apparently less important because no longer a sign of territorial triumph, actually takes on a new, necromantic power in linear games. It becomes a charged orb of menace and guile. It moves—curves and slides through space, swings in on a spin bowl—or it takes a bad bounce (a bounce with evil intent). It passes beyond a fielder's reach, skips past an outstretched glove, or, in the most final of linear movements, leaves the field of play altogether: goes beyond the boundary, out of the park. In linear games, as opposed to territorial ones, to send the ball out of the game-space is to succeed wildly, not to fail or merely to stall play while it is brought back in. The ball remains a token of game progress, but it takes on new technological roles: the ball as tool, not merely as marker. Roger Angell has reminded us that only the pitcher can, in the game of baseball, continue to regard the ball as an ally; it does things *for* him, but *to* everyone else. His tool, his weapon. The pitcher's success depends on an ability to control the ball's flight, to make it travel in lines that are not straight, in thaumaturgical arcs.

All else in baseball is straight lines. The field is a diamond placed within two diverging foul lines, imagined in theory to extend to infinity. The diamond is fixed but the field is not, for the space opened up by the lines may be contained in idiosyncratic ways. No two baseball fields have the same dimensions, and part of the game's charm lies in just this eschewal of rigidity. Fenway Park's Green Monster, the massive fence in left field, compensates for urban encroachment on the field of play. No football field with such variance would remain a football field; and, by extension though less firmly by definition, no baseball field struck to rigidly controlled dimensions would satisfy the spirit of baseball. Space is fluid here because the available space is infinite.

Likewise with the cricket pitch, whose precise boundaries are never drawn, not even (as now in baseball) measured.

The game arises as though naturally, Edenically, from village green and country-house sward. The game is the sum of a set of relationships, not of rules and defined spaces. Linear games require, and embody, more culture than territorial games: their value-sets are more complex, less codifiable, more determined by social norms and conventions. It is only here that one can even attempt to argue, though perhaps with only limited success, for the presence of civility in sport.

Bartlett Giammatti suggests, in his short classic *Take Time for Paradise* (1990), that baseball is a narrative of Romantic implications, an endlessly repeated and never-wavering quest to leave home and return home safely, against all odds, on a mythic patch of paradise. Here, in a little chunk of Eden, the enforced fairness of the rules, and the more natural civility of the conventions of the game, make it effective as both critique and ideal. The game, though circumscribed by the city, is not the city: not the getting and spending for which cities evolve, nor the jostling and rudeness of city life; but instead an instant of peace, a moment of attention to larger-than-life events that take place, inevitably, in a park.

This plea for civility in baseball is, however Quixotic in light of what now goes on there, one that makes no sense in the context of football. Michael Oakeshott's parallel claim, in *Rationalism in Politics* (1962), that cricket is a practice whose integrity resides in its tradition, including, centrally, its tradition of manners (not its rules, that is, but its norms), meets a more favourable, though nowadays ever more threatened, reception. It is because linear games do not measure success simply with the attainment of territory that their social depth is more pronounced, and their possibilities of social critique that much more marked. They separate their green game-spaces, little Edens even when the turf is artificial, off from the rest of life.

There is nevertheless also here an issue of space creation. In baseball, balls are hit into the hole near the shortstop or to the gap between outfielders. The categorical imperative of baseball is, as the wise Stengel had it, to "Hit 'em where they ain't." To protect themselves from the onslaught of gap-seeking balls, fielders will cover ground to track down balls and so prevent hits. Occasionally they may be foiled by a seeing-eye grounder, a ball that skips through an open space seemingly of its own volition, or by a bloop single that drops providentially into a square of open space between centre-fielder, second baseman, and shortstop.

Cricketers also seek gaps in the fielding, responding to shifts of the fielding players. In contrast to baseball, the language of cricket names positions, rather than players, when fielding is discussed. A shortstop is always a shortstop, no matter how close he is shading to second base, or even playing shallow right field in a defensive shift for a dead-pull hitter. If he flubs a line drive, it is still E6, even though it was committed over near the right foul line (see "Score," above). But the cricketer occupying *silly mid-on* may become the cricketer at *square leg* at the whim of bowler or captain. The space of the cricket pitch is thus divided conceptually into a finite number of fielding positions, not all of them played at once, and with no firm boundaries between—but between is where the ball must go if a batsman is to score.

There are other issues of space creation. Both baseball batter and cricket batsman have safe spaces and dangerous ones. Vulnerability and security follow closely on one another, and one may be caught in the wrong place at the wrong time: run down between bases, or run out on the way back to the crease. ("There are no dragons in baseball," says Giamatti, "only shortstops, but they can emerge from nowhere to cut one down.") This may be owing to a teammate's ineptitude, bad judgment, or the basic exigencies of play. Success cannot be gained without risk—no runs are scored if I do not leave my crease or venture onto the basepath—but defeat can be swift. The ball returns with a vengeance, agent of my defeat: if it touches me, I am out; if it reaches the base or wicket before me, I am likewise dismissed. I cover space as a mortal while the ball flies over it, a winged harpy of destruction. It is a wonder that I get any runs or hits at all.

Reflecting on the difficulty of linear games is always to reflect on their spaces, on distances that must be traversed. For example: in the room where I am writing this I have on the wall a reproduction of a baseball painting by John Dobbs. It is called "Stretching at First" and shows a baseball scene so familiar as to be iconic. The perspective, about ten feet directly down the first-base line in right field, shows a batter who, running full tilt, has placed his right foot on first base. The fielder, glove extended, is stretched to full extension while holding his left foot on the bag. The ball is not visible, though an umpire's head protrudes from the side of the frame.

In this frozen instant lies the essence of baseball space, the paradigmatic linearity of the game. Think of the converging vectors: pitcher's fastball delivery to the batter; batter's sharp grounder to, say, third base; the quick throw over to first; the batter, meanwhile, covering the line from home to first at best speed. Batter and ball, who have parted so explosively a moment before at home, now meet again in the crucial convergence at first. Safe or out? The umpire's gaze is directed at the batter's foot touching the base, his ear concentrating for the sound of the fatal ball thumping into the fielder's extended glove. The ball remains, though visible neither to him nor to us, the scene's spherical choreographer, its magic pill. Space separates and converges, and the game advances its slow ballet of lines.

What gives this confrontation its peculiar perfection? It is often remarked that the distance between the bases in baseball (ninety feet) is arbitrary, based on no relevant authority except the dubious Doubleday. But the fact is misleading, for while the distance—the space to be covered—is indeed conventional, in that it has no grounding metaphysical rationale, it is *not* arbitrary. There is something, in other words, given the average speed of athletic, running humans, the quickness of a thrown baseball, and the space created by the foul lines, that makes this contest one with meaning. Add five feet to the baseline, and batters would rarely beat out grounders for singles; subtract five, and they would perhaps do it all too often. Whatever the result, the game would no longer enjoy its delicate equilibrium of checks and balances—and so would cease to be the game. Its space would be destroyed, and without its space baseball is not baseball.

It is possible that linear games are superior to territorial and combative ones precisely in their ability to give game-space more meaning in this fashion. Certainly it is true that watching linear games requires a degree of concentration and reflection unnecessary in the appreciation of the territorial. It also requires time, for the essence of both cricket and baseball is that the game is not measured by a clock, only by a set of tasks—getting the required number of men out. In Test cricket, that may take three or more days. And so anti-clock-wise is the game of baseball that, as Giamatti reminds us, the players and the game proceed in that eccentric direction.

What this brings to our attention, and what the irregular contours of diamond and pitch finally emphasize, is that understanding game-space is not always a matter of conquering space, of gaining territory, or of defeating the other. Teamwork and aggression, the grammar of attacking and defending, do not tell us all we want to know about space. And to that extent anyway, space manipulated in that manner does not exhaust the meaning and the critical possibilities of the game. Ground is not always there to be won; opponents are not always to be brought down; life is not always to be conquered. The quest to reach home, or simply to create a small patch of regulated, civil endeavour—a piece of paradise, if you like, or just a piece of relative stillness on a greensward set amid the hurly-burly of life—is life's task too.

Parks

THERE IS WRIGLEY, WHERE ALFONSO Soriano flirted with us and the other left-field fans between innings, an elegant young god in his glory days.

And Fenway, where I saw so many games over so many years that I can still recall just walking up and getting tickets back in 1987, when the park was only ever half-full. I went with grad-school friends, including Matthew Parfitt, who got us obstructed-view seats behind a massive rivet-studded iron girder. When we moved to better seats, we were so self-conscious about it that, when some people came to squeeze past us into the row beyond, we panicked and thought they were there to kick us out. Back to the obstructed view we went.

Or going there on the spur of the moment with Mark Gaffney, my Edinburgh University pal who hailed from a donut-shop family of evangelicals near Manchester-by-the-Sea, Massachusetts. We'd drive in from out of town, getting Italian sausage sandwiches with fried onions and peppers on Yawkey Way. Being there with my brother Steve and my (then) young niece Aidan, in the "family" section—no alcohol or swearing allowed—and Steve getting busted for trying to bring a plastic cup of Sam Adams into the restricted area.

There is the old Jacobs Field, which Clevelanders told me never to call The Jake, and the cab driver, who took me away from there and back to old Alcazar Hotel in Cleveland Heights, marvelling at the very fact of Jim Thome, who played for six different teams and later entered the Hall of Fame. He squeezed me for every detail of a routine midsummer game. Who hit? Who pitched? Home runs? Errors? But it always came back to Thome. "He has surely made a name for himself," the cabbie said, and I think of it often. *He has surely made a name for himself.* Yes, he has.

Yankee Stadium, the old one, where they played Sinatra's "New York, New York" over and over as you tried to exit through the vast assemblage of concrete tunnels beneath the seats. My former Yale student Brennan, a thin man of insatiable appetite, ordered and consumed a whole box of Krispy Kreme doughnuts one night in the box seats. Another game, high in the rafters, with Rich Cohen, that excellent sportswriter, when a Yankees fan, speaking into his phone, pretended to call in a sniper shot on my position when I cheered for a Blue Jays run. Or another game still, with my friend Leanne, a designer and artist, former competitive swimmer, who just loved the aesthetics of the game, the bodies in motion. Sport for sport's sake.

In Seattle, where Steve bought a hoodie to stave off the cold, and in Chicago, on the South Side, where Molly did the same. Good clam chowder to warm you up at Safeco, but nothing good except hot dogs dragged through the garden at the White Sox venue. Though who can complain about that?

Other Major League parks. Cincinnati's Three Rivers, where I had a long discussion with a colleague about Bill Clinton and what counts as sex, when I really just wanted to watch the game. Baltimore's Camden Yards, maybe the most perfect park in the whole system. Pittsburgh, Arlington, Oakland, St. Louis, San Francisco—I have never been there, and I want to visit them all, the new Nationals park in DC, the tropical vibes of Los Angeles and San Diego, the chilly confines of Minnesota and the ugly indoor enclosure of Tropicana Field.

Actually, scratch that: I have no interest in ever visiting the Trop.

The SkyDome, of course, my home park. A concrete oven in the summer, fans being slowly, humidly cooked like old meat, sweating in their seats. A strange twilit bunker when the roof is closed, the air crepuscular and hard to pierce. But then, when, according to rules nobody understands, the roof is opened during a game—the simple joy of it, the sky revealed, the air immediately freshened. And yes, when the place is full of its capacity of 50,000 fans, the *noise*, the *vibe*. It gets crazy, and sometimes ugly, and usually drunken. The fans know no civility: they will swear in the foulest terms in front of little kids and head-shaking older fans. There is no polite Toronto here, just a raving mass of manspreading, overstuffed hooligans. On good days, we like it; on bad ones, the beer cans and insults come raining down. Shamefully. I try to go on Saturday or Sunday afternoons, to minimize exposure to bad behaviour, but this is not a faultless strategy. The bros get drunk early on the weekend.

Unlike almost everyone else, I preferred the old Exhibition Stadium, that vast chilly yard which witnessed home openers so cold there was snow on the field. I went to one of these, with my pal Tim Baker, and we shivered through nine unremarkable innings by sneaking squirts from the leather wineskin Tim has slipped under his shirt, like an old-timey shepherd or member of the Mackenzie-Papineau Battalion in the Spanish Civil War.

Minor league parks: Nat Bailey in Vancouver, the park within a park, where the beer is cheap and you can sit right behind the umpire and see just how off his calls might be. The Red Sox AA park in New Britain, where you can have a picnic on the grass before the game, maybe with a bottle of Sachem's Picnic wine from the vineyard over in New

Preston. My friends John and Cornelia going for hot dogs and, literary types that they were, writing people's names on the wieners with the ballpark mustard dispenser. Drunk fans taunting the young prospects, who knew they were better than the stadium duffers but could not know if they were destined for The Show.

A nice park in Spokane, where a foul ball came right at my head. I ducked, and it hit the woman behind me, knocking out two of her teeth. My fault?

The old stadiums in Calgary, Edmonton, Ottawa, and Winnipeg. Northland baseball. My father running for a home-run ball that had cleared the fence during an old Winnipeg Whips game, just as we were approaching the stadium. He sprinted after it like nothing I'd ever seen from him, but a young, quicker man got there first. I didn't care. I can still conjure the image of that youthful iteration of him, so lately crippled by blindness and immobility, legging it out for the ball, windbreaker flapping out sideways in the southern Manitoba breeze. Go Dad!

The old Doubleday Field in Cooperstown, boxy and small, where I sat inning after inning as a couple of beer-league teams enjoyed their 15 minutes—well, two and a half hours—on some hallowed diamond real estate.

Taking Aunt Linny and a bunch of us from Cady House to a Swamp Bats game in Keene, New Hampshire. Summer-league ball, not quite A-level. Cape Codders, college students, a few decent prospects. A hot, buggy night, and Linny being difficult about the bleachers, and the hot dogs, and the ice cream. But is there a better team name in the whole universe of baseball than Swamp Bats?

Not even summer league, just semi-pro—the dregs of organized baseball. The Toronto Maple Leafs, not the hockey team, play at a little scrub park in the city called Christie Pits. In August of 1933, this park was the scene of a race riot that started with a baseball game. The side from Harbord

Playground, mostly Jewish, was facing a white-bread Catholic team based at St. Peter's Church, about eight blocks away. In game one of the series, some small swastika signs had been noticed, displayed with nasty intent by the St. Peter's supporters. This was 1933, and Hitler had just taken power in Germany, beginning the project of Holocaust genocide the world would know all too well within a few decades. There was a class dimension too, since the Harbord team represented Jewish and Italian families from south of Bloor Street, notably less prosperous, and more recently arrived in Canada, than the Catholic families from the Annex and Seaton Village.

The second game, on August 16, witnessed a number of provocative signs, including a blanket festooned with a swastika. After the final out of the game—a quarter-final contest, if anyone is keeping score—a squad of Jewish and Italian boys rushed the wielders of the sign and the fight was on. The riot spread and ramified, lasting almost six hours. Here is how the *Toronto Daily Star* reported the *mêlée* (Willowvale Park is the official name of the Pits):

> While groups of Jewish and Gentile youths wielded fists and clubs in a series of violent scraps for possession of a white flag bearing a swastika symbol at Willowvale Park last night, a crowd of more than 10,000 citizens, excited by cries of "Heil Hitler" became suddenly a disorderly mob and surged wildly about the park and surrounding streets, trying to gain a view of the actual combatants, which soon developed in violence and intensity of racial feeling into one of the worst free-for-alls ever seen in the city.

No one was killed but, as the *Star* reporter goes on to tell, there were dozens of injuries:

> Scores were injured, many requiring medical and hospital attention... Heads were opened, eyes blackened and bodies thumped

149

and battered as literally dozens of persons, young or old, many of them non-combatant spectators, were injured more or less seriously by a variety of ugly weapons in the hands of wild-eyed and irresponsible young hoodlums, both Jewish and Gentile.[32]

It may be hard to imagine a riot in staid Toronto, let alone one that pitted Fascists against Jews after a baseball game, but this is on the historical record. Some even credit this moment as the beginning of multicultural Toronto, the wonderful, semi-anarchic mix of nationalities and ethnic groups that so many of us now cherish.[33]

I try to recall this ugly incident when I go to Christie Pits now, to see the Leafs contest their semi-skilled semi-pro rivals in what is known as the Inter-County League: teams from Guelph, Hamilton, London, and St. Catharines (all Ontario). I also recall, without trying, the times when my mother asked to spend a Sunday afternoon there. Visiting from the West Coast, she had no more pressing desire. The whole city of Toronto was before her, and what she wanted most was a few hours sitting on the grass at the Pits, a park she had walked through every day as a high-school student on her way to class, and watch the young men contesting the beautiful game of baseball.

Small parks encompass big lessons. Any park, with that magic square of ninety-foot spans arrayed around the plate and the mound, contains the universe of baseball. You can have stands for 50,000 people or no stands at all; you can have a dugout that is just a hardscrabble tuck in the chain-link fencing with a cooler of Gatorade at one end; you can have a park that exists in a declivity made by an old quarry, a literal pit; you can have a park where people come with folding chairs and their own sandwiches, maybe considering the luxury of a bag of popcorn or soft-serve ice-cream cone, chocolate and vanilla swirled together—you can have all that, and it will still be what it is, the eternal site of the game.

Throwing

MY COLLEGE FRIEND LAURIE BELL, who was a very good soft-ball player, is not shy about her political views. When, on a long-ago summer night, we played a pick-up game on a corner of the University of Toronto's front campus, she was enraged when a male player mocked his friend's style by say-ing, "Shit, man, you throw like a *woman*." She stopped play, verbally dressed him down, and delivered a spontaneous but obviously well-oiled miniature lecture on feminism and rou-tine forms of misogyny. We were all suitably chastened. It was 1983, and we university boys were just being made to learn about what we didn't know. There was in those days no such phrase as *being woke*, but I guess we were groping towards that state.

More striking now is the nuance of saying "woman," instead of "girl," which would have been more canonical. I mean, one of the things we were being taught by our non-male and non-cisgender friends (another concept that did not then obtain in everyday life) was that "woman" was the preferred term, a mark of respect. My uncle, for instance, would have been considered a dinosaur for his habit of refer-ring to any female human other than his mother and mother-in-law as a "girl."

And *throwing like a girl* is the nub of the matter.

What does it mean to throw this way, in allegedly girl-ish fashion? Well, you might say it's obvious: stiff-armed, unnatural, sending the ball careening off at a right angle, as hapless female singers or actors sometimes do when forced into the ordeal of the ceremonial first pitch. The shoulder and wrist do not break, and so the ball gets a sort of chicken-wing launch that betrays insecurity and awkwardness.

But of course lots of boys—and men—throw just like that; and many girls, or women, throw with greater power and accuracy than the average man. Mo'ne Davis, the Little League all-star from Philadelphia, was the first girl to throw a no-hitter in 2011. At age 13, her fastball was clocked at over 70 miles an hour—equivalent, in reaction time, to 93 miles an hour on a full-sized diamond. Believe me when I say that it is unlikely you or I could hit a fastball thrown that hard. Does she throw like a girl? Well, let's say that is how a girl throws.

The philosopher Iris Marion Young explored the hidden dimensions contained in the everyday insult of throwing like a girl.[34] Young approaches the question phenomeno-logically, which is to say by examining everyday actions in terms of the complex relations among body, consciousness, and world. This apparently narrow subject—does it *matter* why girls throw like girls?—acquires a deeper significance the more we consider the matter. What is it to throw at all? A girl-throw is, on the standard sexist logic, presumptively a failed throw; it cannot help but illuminate what counts as a successful throw.

We can identify four related issues in the presumed girl-throw fail. They are: (a) ambiguous transcendence; (b) inhibited intentionality; (c) discontinuous unity; and (d) an imperative of sexual "comportment." These terms may be unfamiliar, but the ideas and experiences are very common.

The transcendence is ambiguous because, in the act of throwing, the "girl" is clouded by thoughts—in particular by doubts and misgivings concerning the throw. The girl-throw lacks the unselfconscious ease of the "natural" throw, the way a practiced thrower can execute the passage of ball from one place to another. This transcendence, so seemingly routine on the baseball field, is actually, of course, a very high-level achievement. It is a physical act which lies deeply embedded in time (the hours of practice) and space (the almost-instinctive, second-nature of the judgment of distance and velocity). We are all capable of this transcendence, but in practice it is rare. The remarkable thing is not that people throw badly, it is that anyone throws well.

Likewise, then, the inhibited intentionality. Intentionality is the manner in which we smoothly execute motions and judgments in the world. It is not a matter of explicit intention ("I mean to clean the yard after work") but, rather, the necessary semi-conscious projection of mind into any possible action. I step across a stream by means of stones and fallen logs. My intentionality is fully engaged in taking the steps, and I succeed best by not thinking too much about it; if I pause to consider a step, I am lost, a fallen man.

Intentionality is inhibited, then, when the conscious mind obtrudes in automatic or nearly automatic movements. My friend Chris, for example, though he is a professor highly skilled at phenomenological investigation, has a hard time with escalators. He sees the rolling steps and cannot decide to put his foot on any of them. But the point is that there should be no decision here at all: to negotiate an escalator, you simply look at a moving step and *step onto it*.

Except there is nothing simple about this at all. To achieve a state where intentionality is uninhibited is not easy, and the girl-throw once more shows us how this is so. A skilled thrower throws to the target, and hits it. That is just what skill means: the state of uninhibited intention. But even the most skilled throwers air mail the ball sometimes, or bounce it in the dirt. Why? Well, they were hurried on the play, or double-clutched before the toss—that mini-choke moment of millisecond second-guessing. These are miniature forms of panic, and panic is where inhibition sneaks back into the frame. You do not quell doubt by reason; you quell it by not feeling it in the first place.

Discontinuous unity is another dimension of the same failure. For many of us, girls or not, our sense of embodied self is not smooth or tightly knit. We are not comfortable in our own skins, at least when it comes to physical achievements. We may be blessed with spiritual or intellectual continuity, but that may be shattered by a routine physical challenge. Like what? Like throwing a ball. The smoothly thrown ball, as we can all appreciate, is a graceful deployment of the whole body, acting as one motion. We can break the motion down into its component parts: the leg-lift, the step, the arm-cock, the forward pull, the turn over, the release, the follow-through. But this is *analysis*, necessarily abstracted from the throw as it is experienced. The throw, when we do it right, is a single, continuous action.

Once again, though, we note the hidden levels of difficulty here. Golfers speak of a *hole* in their swing, meaning some little breach of continuity that keeps them slicing or hooking against their will. Highly paid coaches may be sought, to break down the swing and re-build it in more continuous form. What holds for the golf swing also holds for the ball-throw, or the bat-swing, or the fly-fishing cast. The motion, to be successful, must feel as if it has no discrete parts. There must be no discontinuity.

I am a fly fisherman myself, and I know that learning how to cast that relatively heavy line with light rods cost me many hours of failure. They were happy ones, in retrospect, no matter how frustrating. Because eventually we may achieve continuity, and therefore success, by knitting up the pieces of our body in motion, and deploying the cast—or the throw—without thought. It is still the case, as my fishing buddies would be the first to point out, that I will send a cast into the oblivions of slack-heavy failure whenever I think too much about what I am doing.[35]

It is a peculiar fact of human life that one of the most powerful causes of inhibited and discontinuous action is *observance*. Even the most practised among us can become self-conscious when aware that we are being watched, and this fact is subject to amplifier effects: more spectators, or spectators whom we know, co-workers and friends, can all make the condition considerably worse. I might have thrown the ball perfectly several hundred times while practising on my own; take me out to the ballgame for the ceremonial first pitch, with the crowd and my buddies watching, though, and I am all too likely to flub it.

Worries about success are themselves a barrier to success: performance anxiety. Paradoxically, those who have lower expectations of success, whether imposed by self or others, sometimes manage to outperform the more likely candidates.

This fact is, interestingly, gendered in the opposite direction of the girl-throw insult. I have been told many times by fishing guides and tutors that women make better fly casters than men, primarily because they accept that they don't know what they are doing at first and are willing to learn. Men tend to think that the fly cast is just an analogue of the basic ball-throw, which is a fatal error. The fly cast is killed by the broken-wrist motion typical of throwing and, though it can just barely survive an incorrigible side-arm tendency like the one my brother Sean and I exhibit, it reaches perfection only in a looping flick that is more like a whiplash than a throw.

And here we must confront the main issue of the girl-throw insult. There is not just one kind of phenomenology, because there is not just one kind of bodily being-in-the-world. The world of a woman is distinct from that of a man, even though they share the upright posture and presumptive freedom of movement enjoyed by the able-bodied. But musculature and frame differ between the sexes; even more significantly, we are taught to hold ourselves differently, a teaching that is largely unconscious and therefore retains the veil of "naturalness." In fact, our sense of bodily deployment is highly contingent, ingested through painting and films, media and advertising, and the actions of all the grown-up humans around us. Humans are deeply imitative creatures. While that primate quality helps us along the road to success, as Aristotle taught, it also reproduces aspects of our shared lifeworld that are harmful and retrograde.

Think, for example, of a scene in the Disney blockbuster *Frozen* (2014), when the once-inhibited—and literally frigid, since everything she touches turns to ice—Elsa breaks out of her adolescent inhibition and executes a "sexy walk" song sequence. In the subtle animation, she instantly seems womanly and curvaceous, rolling her hips in a provocative runway strut. The accompanying song, "Let It Go," is all about freedom from constraint, and it is true that Elsa's transformation, including a thigh-slit dress and cosmetic makeover, seems to be entirely self-directed. And yet, opinion was naturally divided over whether Elsa was a powerful feminist role model or another sad retreat into sexualized girlishness. Sure, there is nobody actually ogling her at the moment, but who or what is she being sexy for?

I can't settle that question here. I'm not sure it can be decided at all, in fact, since the two sides of the debate are both correct. Deployment of the body for sexual purposes is part of what it means to be embodied, and so long as there is sexual dimorphism (plus its many variants), there will always be ways of presenting a body to enhance its erotic appeal. At the same time, we are right to be skeptical of forms of bodily enhancement that seem always to award active roles, athletic prowess among them, to males, and then reserve submissive and receptive roles for females.[36]

Even basic posture is a loaded feature of gendered life. We all know the leans and tilts of flirtatious behaviour, or the light-in-the-loafers comportment that is, somehow, suspect because it's insufficiently masculine. At baseball games, or on subways, we witness the phenomenon of *manspreading* — taking up more space than you deserve by flinging the knees wide, presumably to allow room for a heavy genital package.[37] Come on, man: your junk just doesn't need that wide a trunk. (Some transit authorities agree: it is now a ticketable offence on subways in New York and elsewhere.) Meanwhile, a friend of mine, a hugely successful visual and performance artist, complained not long ago about how, when visiting her family, objective successes like major museum shows were overwhelmed by questions about her finances and love life. Among them, this: "Maybe if you didn't hold your body like a teenager, you could get a date." Body normativity comes in many forms.

It is so much more complicated than active = male and female = passive; or at least it should be. Attending baseball games now, it feels like not very much has changed since those days in the early 1980s, when we thought that sex- or gender-based insults were destined for the dustbin of history. The ballpark is still a largely male preserve. There are no tickets here for manspreading, as far as I know, let alone for stupid, sexist remarks. At its worst, baseball continues to give sanction to an idea of insult that finds female anatomy at once a joke ("She can't throw") and a mere provocation ("She's so hot"). At its best, which isn't much better because it won't acknowledge its own homoerotic biases, baseball expresses a sneaking admiration for male beauty in its transcendent, uninhibited, continuous form. I mean throwing well, which is assumed to mean throwing like a boy.

But we should always remember that just about anybody, indeed most of us, throw like girls. Which is really to say, not like girls at all. Mostly, most of us just can't throw. Blaming that on girlishness, or even associating the two features of life, is the worst kind of failure—a failure of imagination.

Playtime

CONSIDER, IN THIS AGE OF social media and smarter-than-us search engines, the notion of your *temporal online trace*.

Online trace creates a kind of extended personality or consciousness, in both organizations and persons. We all know this, but the implications of it are not entirely clear. In an older model of extended consciousness, my consciousness might extend physically: beyond the limits of my body, say, by means of things such as a cane that helps me see, or with communications media that allow my voice to traverse large distances, and so on. These extensions are obviously spatial.[38]

But now we also have new forms of temporal extensions of consciousness; earlier versions of ourselves trail after us and, in many cases, can be very hard to eradicate, supposing you wanted to do that. We are in transition concerning the very nature of individuality. More and more, reflecting on what it means to be who we are, games and play illuminate in surprising ways. The created narratives of sports, especially ones rife with contingencies and failures, force us to examine our own narrative efforts.

The *aesthetic hypothesis* holds that the way to live a good life, a happy life, is to consider that life as a work of art, and

159

to see that the aesthetic dimension of one's consciousness, where pleasure is taken from beauty and harmony, is the primary one. This position might seem strange, because we tend to think of aesthetic values as secondary or even tertiary to other kinds of values: ethical ones, political ones, family-based or kinship values, and so on. But those aesthetic values, properly conceived, are at the very heart of human experience; they are, more importantly, the locus of the most important and lasting meanings of which human consciousness is capable.

The "art of play" is a doubled phrase. That is, the "of" here is a grammatical double genitive: there is the art of play that is learning how to play or thinking about what it is to play; but there is also the kind of play that is particular to art—not just visual art but aesthetic values in general. We are, in turn, playing with that doubleness—the art of play, the play of art—in what baseball teaches.

Lesson one: playing is *time out of time*.[39] Baseball, the most timeless of mortal games, cannot help but put time into question. As the humourist Scott Feschuk has noted, baseball even deploys the now-ubiquitous convention of video-review challenge in its own leisurely fashion. "Managers still get to stall before deciding whether to challenge a play. Even the way the umps mosey over to the headsets is infuriating," he wrote. "We get it, baseball— you're soooo different and special. 'Our game is eternal! We don't have a clock! We let David Ortiz undress and re-dress between pitches!' That's great, but some of us have dinner reservations and/or the desire not to miss an important stage in our children's lives, like their first step or the entirety of puberty."[40]

Television aside, the idea of the temporal shift has a long and cluttered history in philosophy and in other traditions, particularly religious ones: the concept of the Sabbath, or sacred day, the time that is different, time that is not secular. In Greek we find a distinction between ruled time, *chronos*, and a disruptive, possibly eternal experience of unruly time: *kairos*. Chronological time is measured, horizontal, workaday. Kairotic time is boundless, vertical, infinite.[41]

Play takes place within, and allows, that temporal shift. It is the entry into a non-secular time. In everyday life, the most common experience of time, shown among other things in the persistence of memory, is of a kind of dominance. That is, we are burdened by time. We have to *spend* time, we fear that we may *waste* time, we have to *save* time. Everywhere in the secular realm, we are expected to be on time, sometimes we have to make time, or make up time, and so on. Time may not always be money, but it is routinely transactional.

Salvador Dali's 1931 painting *The Persistence of Memory* gives a graphic (and surreal) expression to a specific experience of time and memory. It captures the uncanny texture of having one's personhood constituted, or underwritten, by the variable faculty of memory across temporal ranges: having to, among other things, reconstitute one's personal identity each morning by recalling the night before and the constructed continuity of all the previous nights, mornings, and days in between. But this image also conveys the larger sense that measured time, the time of the melting, creepy clock, is everywhere in our lives; and how we must structure our lives relentlessly according to that secular time. This is the time of, let us say, *appointment*, of always having to be somewhere, and to be there on time.

Now it is obviously true that some things are just impossible, things such as efficiency but also higher-order human goods such as cooperation and shared projects, without such appointed time. We cannot get together and do things unless we have an agreed time at which they will happen. But the idea of play as a diacritical refusal of that transactional time, something that shifts away from it, is powerful and persistent. Not surprisingly, play and its associated playtime — the time out of time — has existed in every culture and tradition that we know of.

Pieter Bruegel's *Children's Games* (1560), is a depiction of play, but it is not just a social document. Social historians have examined this famous painting and found at least 35 games actually being played, with some estimates as high as 80. It is a beautiful example of a kind of social history, but the most important thing about this scene as depicted is that these people are not working. They are outside of the workaday; they are in a different time. They are likewise visible to each in a public space, owned by everyone and no one, never subject to transaction and the use values of the secular.

Play can be analyzed as a form of socialization. Socialization is not as simple as it sounds, however, because the playful bite *that is not a real bite* is not just a matter of socializing. It is also a matter of communicating: it communicates the kind of irony of which non-human animals are capable. That is, the wolf is able to send the message, "This is play. I am biting you without really biting you." The bite is "just a friendly nip," a playful bite; that message goes along with the bite itself. This kind of play can also establish position, so that when the play results in the performance of submission, then the dominant play-fighter asserts position without actually having to fight the submissive.

Humans do it too. I have two brothers, and I have the scars to show it. The cuts, the bruises, the broken arm. I won't tell the story of it here, as it still kind of pains me to think about my brother breaking my arm; but he did. Was it playful? Yes, I can say that now. And it happened during a game of one-on-one basketball, so it involved play in that sense too. Because we have higher-order consciousness and are always learning how to create skills that will be transferable to other parts of life, human play is multidimensional. Studies show, for example, that sibling behaviour creates skills and competencies for relationships, for work, and so on. I'm not sure what I learned by having my arm broken by my brother, other than that it was an uncalled, flagrant foul in a game whose convention is that you call your own fouls, but no doubt I am more socialized as a result.

"Baseball is fathers and sons," Donald Hall says. "Football is brothers beating each other up in the backyard."

Play can be, further, a kind of thinking: free-ranging creative imagining. We sometimes call this process "brain-storming," or "idea-floating," or "blueskying." By playing around with things, by having a non-directed encounter with each other, we can actually do better and achieve more than if we were constrained by an actual direction. Whether this actually works, or is just an excuse to goof around and ignore deadlines, probably depends on what kind of office you work in.

Humans engage, as do other animals, in sexual foreplay. Sexual foreplay can include, in my conception here, flirting and other forms of behaviour that allow us to act in ways that may or may not lead to further acts of procreation that sustain our position in the natural environment. From a strictly biological point of view, foreplay is unnecessary and, indeed, there are many people who go along with that theory if they can find partners who are willing to tolerate them. It's not biologically necessary to procreation that there should be anything other than unadorned intercourse, and frankly not even that; but typically, we take pleasure from these behaviours because they allow us to establish relationships and ongoing intimacy as well as to procreate.

There is no procreation in baseball, but there is intimacy, relationships, and an intricate web of human desire. Unlike the forms of play that prevail in human life more generally, baseball's mechanisms are all a form of fiction—a matter of pretending. How is this possible, and why does it seem to matter so much?

Pretend

HOWEVER REVEALING, ALL OF THESE notions of play still fail to see the big picture. They do not embrace what I want to call the *transcendental aspect of play*. To see what I mean, let us look briefly at some analysis of what goes on in certain kinds of play, crucially in the play of pretending. This follows, in outline, the work of Donald Winnicott and other Freudian-influenced child psychologists. In this psychoanalytical view, what is important about play is not just its ability to socialize, or to instrumentally serve other desired ends, whether in the services of ideas, procreation, or intimacy; what is important is to pretend *on purpose but without purpose*.

I said earlier that the animals are enacting their own limited form of irony with the bite that is not a real bite. Humans are capable of much more complex forms and layers of pretending, ironizing means. Consider a little girl giving a piece of cookie to her teddy bear. There are at least two levels of meaning here. The bear is not a real bear, and she is not really feeding it because, in being not a real bear, it cannot ingest the morsel of food. If you asked the girl what she is doing, she would say, "I'm feeding my bear." The pretended deflections from the real state of affairs allow us to create levels of consciousness, and the ability to make this kind of distinction, between real and pretend, even as we decide to ignore it in the service of play. This strange contract of consciousness with itself—to create something unreal, and then treat it precisely as real—is at the heart of our appreciation of higher-order forms of pretending such as literature and, given their total lack of utility, sports. We observe here the layered "as if" consciousness, or the suspension of disbelief.

Notice that feeding the bear doesn't have a purpose, indeed can have no purpose, since it is not a real bear and it is not eating. The bear will be just as nourished, or non-nourished, before and after the feeding session. What, then, is the point of doing it? It is precisely to enact this simultaneous is/is-not consciousness of pretending. If you were to ask why the girl is making these motions, given that the bear is not a bear and cannot eat—the questions only a psychologist or a spoilsport would imagine asking—she might respond, perhaps impatiently, "Because the bear is hungry!" It is not the place of the non-pretender to end the double consciousness; only the pretender has that privilege, and responsibility.

Under the right circumstances, a pointed finger becomes the gun. But notice that there is, once again, more than one level at work in such play. With a pretend gun, I can nevertheless shoot real enemies. Warning: this is not recommended. If you were to go down the street going BANG! BANG! BANG! with a pretend gun, "shooting" people you really don't like, even strangers, that is considered assault under the Common Law of this country. Yes, it's true: you can be arrested on the charge of assault for pretend-shooting someone, and a defence hinging on the fact that the gun was only a pretend gun may or may not help you. Of course, you can also be arrested for really shooting someone, but I feel compelled to issue this fair warning against pretend-shooting: the play of pretending takes you out of the mundane realities of the everyday world, perhaps, but others are still in that world, and may judge you according to its standards.

So: one can (a) pretend to shoot real enemies by aiming a pretend gun at them (the cocked finger); and one can (b) really shoot real enemies with a real gun. But there are at least four other logical possibilities in play here, and they illustrate the levels and complexity of any and all pretending. In addition, then, one can (c) pretend to shoot real enemies with a real gun, by not firing it but instead shouting (say), "Bang, bang, you're dead." This, too, constitutes an assault under the law, perhaps even more obviously than the "real" shot from the pretend gun. One can also (d) pretend to shoot pretend enemies with a real gun, as when, for instance, I am joking around with my (real) gun and "playfully" point it at a friend.

Not a good idea, as gun-accident statistics demonstrate. And though it is a little hard to imagine the circumstance that would call for it, except within the details of a complicated game, it is logically possible that one can (e) pretend-shoot pretend enemies with a pretend gun. Why? To confuse another player in the game? To complete some *ruse de guerre*? I don't know, but logic demands the option—though it also throws open a host of possible second- and third-order pretending possibilities within a given game. And, finally, in what is very likely the most common case of pretending when it comes to guns and play, the paradigm case that implies all the others, one can (f) shoot pretend enemies with a pretend gun.

When my brothers and I took up our imagined spaceman and cowboy adventures as children, we were almost certainly performing the last of these forms of deflection from the real (not a real gun, not a real enemy). We would shoot a pretend enemy with a pretend weapon, and he would pretend-die. We might, if the appropriate toys were on hand, substitute a fake gun—a gun made of plastic, resembling a real gun, or fantastic science-fiction-style gun, also made of plastic but not resembling a real gun—in place of the hand with pointed finger. But I want to say that the hand-as-gun gesture is actually essential to the performance of pretending, because here we perform the basic deflection of meaning without anything except the imagined similarity between the index finger and the gun's barrel, the fist's sense of gripping something, the raised thumb's ability to recall a cocked trigger on a single-action revolver.

There are many lurking limits to this kind of play, as my references to the force of law indicate, but of course the obvious limit is reality itself. This makes it clear that the space in which this common, but in fact profound, kind of play is possible is at the edge of the real — going beyond it. The kind of play evident in pretending is all about the world of the game *not being real*, a conceptual move away from the presumed limits of reality. Those limits can be painful, as I have suggested. When the pretend pistols go up against the actual police force, that is almost a bad thing. In all seriousness, I cannot say you should do it.

Baseball, like all sports, is a form of pretend. Of course, it is physically and emotionally real. The players actually perform their movements on an actual field. But the field itself is a notional space, a space set off from the real. The actions performed on the field are real, but they do not really count as actions in the world we mostly inhabit. Thus a fight in hockey is tolerated, even sanctioned by convention, but it escalates into assault and battery if taken too far. Just how far that is — the limits of the pretend-space — is not always clear. But we know the limit is there, and that knowledge likewise underwrites the transcendent status of the field of play.

By the same token, our caring about the outcomes of games is a form of pretend. We know, with part of our rational minds, that it does not matter who wins a baseball game. And yet, it matters — sometimes so deeply as to generate much genuine emotion. And if we wonder how non-real things can arouse real emotions, we need only recall Aristotle's analysis of *catharsis*, the psychologically beneficial venting of painful feelings under controlled conditions such as the theatre. Whatever else it is or is not, baseball is theatre and we fans can experience as much fear and pity at the park as some people can in a darkened auditorium.

Infinite

GAMES AND PLAY ARE NOT identical categories. Games are organized forms of play; they have elements that might not be playful. *Finite* games are games that come to some kind of conclusion, and the conclusion governs how the game is played and what the game means. In philosophical terms this outcome would be the *telos*, or final cause of the game—its meaning-bestowing purpose. To accept this point, you don't have to be Vince Lombardi and say, "Winning isn't everything, it's the only thing." You need not be quite that strict about the *telos* to recognize that a finite game has an outcome. We play until we reach some kind of conclusion.

In certain kinds of finite games called sports, especially the category of territorial finite games that includes hockey, football, and soccer, we *create a game-space* in order to give the contest shape and help achieve the outcome. That is, we construct a very particular kind of constrained arena or forum, a deployment of bounded space which also operates according to a logic of bounded time, set off from ordinary spaces and times. But this constrained time, though distinct from the pervasive time of the world outside the sport—it can be started and stopped, for example, or extended into overtime, even into that pinnacle of sporting drama, *sudden-death double overtime*, a concept with the power to terrify a character in one of Paul Quarrington's novels—is still clock-regulated. It does not yet achieve the temporal shift of transcendental play.

So, for example, in a hockey game there are three periods of 20 minutes; in a football game, there are four quarters of 15 minutes, and so on. Even though this game-time can be counted down dramatically, stopped and started, its actions even captured and studied in slow-motion replays which effectively slow time below the experiential threshold, it is still working according to the logic of the outside, chronological time. The gametime is, as it were, a way of bringing that outside time into the constrained space and *squeezing* it for dramatic effect. That fact is important because it will show that these games are unstable with respect to realizing the transcendental possibilities of play.

By creating a constrained space, we strive to force a heightened outcome. That is what the field of sport does. There are often arguments, within the game's logic, about how exactly the space is arranged. Consider the hockey rink. There are ongoing disputes about whether there should be a red line, whether you can have rink-long passes, or whether they should be shorter passes. There is an icing rule, which prevents the puck from being moved without certain kinds of control. Most significantly, there are the blue lines, which create the possibility of offside calls. As I already argued, the offside concept is essential to territorial games because it creates a limit, such that all attacks on the goal shall be square and just. There would be no need for an offside rule if this notion of fair territorial confrontation were not itself generated by the idea of the game's constraints.

We want the outcome to have a certain kind of character. So you are forbidden from hanging around down in your opponent's end when the puck is behind you: hockey's offside rule dictates that you cannot advance into the opponent's end ahead of the puck. In soccer, by contrast, there is also an offside rule but there is no painted line, only the imaginary line that goes through the body of the final defender in front of the goaltender. Hence the possibility, in soccer, of the "offside trap," where the attacker is left hanging without the ball by the defenders running upfield. This risky tactic offers a neat nuance of the offside rule's inner meaning of maintaining fairness, trapping an attacker with a kind of *jiu-jitsu* counter-move.

Fascinating for baseball fans is that this non-territorial game puts us in a different relationship with time. Time in baseball is not told in minutes and hours; it is told in outs and innings. A baseball game can take as little time as an hour and as much time as 8, 10, 12 hours. In fact, theoretically, a baseball game can go on forever. If the score is high and nobody ever gets a winning run in extra innings, there is nothing in the rules of baseball to stop the game from never ending. Meanwhile, the foul lines in baseball, before the invention of outfield fences, which vary from park to park, were considered to extend to infinity. Baseball is thus a game that encompasses the entire earth and can last forever. No wonder philosophers like it so much.

We can also consider more specific kinds of contests, violent but still technically playful sporting tussles such as the confrontation between individuals in boxing. We create the ring; this rope-bounded square can then become a metaphor or a synecdoche for any constrained conflict. You will find it in political rhetoric: to enter the ring, to throw your hat in the ring, to call in your second, and so on. The idea is that this is a conflict and the ring is not just a physical space anymore, it is a metaphorical space. Tennis has a similar quality, though here, as David Foster Wallace argued, your opponent is not actually the person on the other side of the net. Your opponent is mostly yourself for, unlike boxing, tennis is not a game of direct conflict but a game performed within geometric vectors, a constrained confrontation with space itself. Can I bend my return such that it *both* passes the out-stretched racquet of my opponent *and* manages to strike the earth within the tight confines of the court? Yes, I will want to anticipate my opponent's moves, or get him moving the wrong way; but unless I can execute the required manipulation of space, there is no point.

Now, I think, we are getting to the heart of finite games. I said before that they are unstable, and in part that is because they can never quite resist the infinite elements that keep creeping in—the elements of transcendent play. Consider an image of a football field, marked according to the conventions of its finiteness. But what does a football game actually look like? The field seen from 90 vertical degrees is an abstraction. A football game *looks* like the beautiful moment when a thrown pass hits a downfield receiver in midstride. You can draw up a play, the coach can give the players their assignments, but when they execute the play there is something absolutely incalculable about the success of a thrown pass.

We might say, loosely, that the quarterback "calculates" the distance from his position in the pocket to where the receiver will be, but in fact he does nothing of the sort, as we have seen. In philosophical terms, he is not engaged in Cartesian geometry, he is engaged in lifeworld phenomenology. When you are a good quarterback, you don't measure distances, you exercise skillful judgment and *throw to the spot you know the receiver will occupy*. That is what it means to be good at this sport, to execute the play you might have learned from the diagram. This interesting incalculability lingers at the centre of what looks like the most finite, constrained, drawn-up game.

This is the beauty of any finite game, ultimately: not the contest itself, and certainly not the field, but the moments of pure connection created from within the constraints. That is when you can say, with some plausibility, football is *poetry in motion.* That is when you have an aesthetic appreciation of the game. We might call this aesthetic dimension the whiff of the transcendent, or the non-finite, in this particular finite game. There is unsettling violence at the heart of this same game, which makes appreciation of it an uneasy business.

At least since Plato and Aristotle, people have believed that the importance of games was that they created a kind of competitive wisdom: *agon*, the competition-born wisdom of play. The Athenian gymnasium was for things other than play: it was for socializing, establishing position, finding lovers, advancing political outcomes, and so on. But the most important thing, philosophically, about the gymnasium was that struggle itself was wisdom-producing. To wrestle — to wrestle in nakedness, as the Greeks did — was to bring yourself to the other in order to learn about yourself. Some people think that this claim about wisdom is just a lot of high-toned hooey, but the idea persists: games, especially competitive sports, are thought to build character. Perhaps. But at the margins of thought, this character argument runs into trouble.

There are many ways in which the outcome of games and other playful things are instrumentalized. Exercise can elide into self-punishment. Entertainment, the kind of play that is not athletic, can become a site of competition. People out for an evening of fun are having such a good time that they will be able to say, tomorrow, "I got so wasted!" "How wasted did you get?" "More wasted than he did!" It is interesting how conceptually close these two things are — disciplining the body and competing to make the body suffer through intoxication. They are both ways of putting otherwise playful elements of our existence and physicality into a competitive frame.

We might then link this apparently odd similarity to the insight that many kinds of play and games are subject to the creation of status or position. Golf, for example, which can be in many ways a beautiful game, is inseparable from its status-conferring features, the deployment of capital and its benefits. To have a golf membership, to play golf, to talk golf, to make business deals on the golf course: all these things are unrelated to the game itself, yet attach themselves so inextricably that golf becomes a handy metaphor for privilege.

Other kinds of marginal problems occur when elements that do not seem intrinsic to the play enter into the game and become ineradicable over time. What are the conventions of plonking a hated batter? How high or far is it okay to flip your bat after a home run? Is it sporting to sucker-punch a hated bat-flipping player after plonking him at the plate — some months after the original incident? How you answer these questions usually says more about where you live than about the nature of the game itself.

Finally, in a related tangle of marginal outcomes, notice how many of the things we now call play are not only sedentary, they do not have any aspect of somatic or psychological interplay to them. For many children and young adults, "playing together" might mean a mediated contact by means of a screen and two video-game controllers. The players need not even be in the same room in order to play together in this sense. There is a phenomenon described in child psychology known as *parallel play*: this is where you might get two girls with teddy bears, say, both feeding them but not doing it together — and yet they are nevertheless aware of each other as they both engage in play. Such shared semi-solitude is considered an important moment in psychological development. Combined video-gaming is parallel play of a different kind: the two players are not relating to each other at all, even though they are playing the same game. It will come as no surprise to hear that when you do a Google image search of the word "play," the computer icon for "start" — the right-facing triangle — is by far the most common image to generate hits.

With those kinds of limitations on finite games in view, but also bearing in mind the hint of the transcendental that I identified before, that kind of Zen-like arrow, what can we say in conclusion about the art of play?

Infinite games offer the obvious point of contrast to instrumental degradations of play. In such games, there are many possible nodes of temporary outcome, momentary points of contact where the players reach a momentary conclusion or victory, but the point of an infinite game is *that it shall continue*. Thus, a good move in an infinite game is a move that keeps the game going, whereas, naturally, a move in a finite game is one that gets you closer to the end. We play infinite games in a different way than finite ones because we play them not to win. There are no winners, nor is there an end. In fact, we play infinite games in a manner that extends right back to the earliest forms of pretending: we do it, in one very straightforward sense, because it is *fun*. But an infinite game is more than just fun — or perhaps I should say that fun is more philosophically significant than we sometimes think.

An infinite game is a game that has no purpose beyond itself. But the purpose within itself is precisely to expand the realm of human possibility. (I'll have more to say later about the Kantian notion of beauty, the experience of *purposiveness without purpose*.) An infinite game is governed by the norms of *poiesis*, in the original Greek sense of creativity itself. In English we hear this etymological root when we talk about poems and poetry, but *poiesis* in Greek just means "making." *Poiesis* does not necessarily mean the making of things; it can be the making of moves, of gestures, of ideas.

Dancing is thus a kind of infinite game. There are of course forms of constrained dancing. You can go to a conservatory to learn your prescribed steps, maybe even in order to execute them later in a ballroom-dancing competition; but when we dance at a nightclub we dance because it has no purpose beyond itself — or, at least, the purposes in play (flirting, showing off, being part of a group) — do not usually prescribe my dance moves. On the contrary. We dance because dancing is its own reward. Art-making, of objects or installations to be enjoyed just for what they are, is likewise a form of such infinite gaming. It is actually quite a curious fact about humans that we make art, that there is such thing as the art world. Though there is an economics of buying and purchasing art, even of producing and enjoying art, art's value lies precisely in the fact that these objects are not necessary even as we realize, in our experience of them, that the aesthetic is among the most profound aspects of ourselves, of our human possibilities.

More important here is the openness, the gestural, intimate quality of art. You do not have to be Georgia O'Keefe to see that art is an infinite game. Philosophy and poetry are also infinite games in this sense of undirected, non-utilitarian purposiveness. Baseball stands unique in this array, it seems to me, as the technically finite game with infinite possibilities, the closest a competitive sport comes to the status of art — not least because, as I shall argue, it is the most beautiful of team sports.

But first, there are some paradoxes to consider.

Paradox

YOU CAN IMAGINE THAT, AS a professional philosopher—that paradoxical title!—I am often asked to explain the point of what I do. People are usually too polite to demand this explanation in a direct way. Instead, they say something like, "So you teach *philosophy?* What do you tell your students they are going to do with it?" There is, as I have noted more than once, a particular intonation of that verb "do" that I have come to dread. "What are you going to *do* with that? What is it going to *do?*" "I don't know," I want to reply. "Is *doing* so important? My students are becoming philosophers; that is quite something all by itself." But it can be hard to make this intrinsic-value argument to an often confrontational non-philosopher.

This generates a version of what we could call the Paradox of Philosophy, which is not really restricted to philosophy. You only come to value philosophy, or any other "useless" thing, when you are already doing it, because seeing the value of philosophy is itself part of what doing philosophy demonstrates; but you cannot give non-philosophical reasons for why philosophy is worth doing because the reasons philosophy is worth doing are all philosophical. It follows that you can only do philosophy if you are already doing it.

Indeed, we can go farther: this paradoxical quality of the undertaking is part of what makes philosophy an infinite game. All of its reasons for being valuable are contained within itself. It cannot be instrumentalized; it cannot be reduced to some other scale of value. Of course, one always can say, "Well, you should take philosophy because then you will do well on the LSAT and get into law school and make a lot of money." You can say that, and it might even be true. But that is not why you should do philosophy. You should do philosophy because philosophy is worth doing. And I invite you to find out why.

If you are a good teacher of philosophy, you seduce people into seeing themselves philosophically, and then they might just see that philosophy is worth doing. In fact, I am of the view that this structure or possibility of seduction is found in all the best aspects, the most playful aspects, of our lives; and this is so because they refuse to be judged by the scale of everyday standards of use-value and necessity. We can therefore say that the most playful kind of games, the highest forms of play, are those which touch the divine. I mean the divine that Aristotle speaks about in the last book of the *Nicomachean Ethics*: that which in us, as mortals, is closest to immortality.

Baseball generates its own paradoxes, and exerts its own particular seductions. Why should it matter to me that these players, on this day, are engaged in this odd contest? It should not, and yet it does. If you love the game, that is more than sufficient; if you do not, no amount of argument will shift the balance — a fact known to anyone who has taken a skeptic to a baseball game. As Homer Simpson realizes when Duff beer is suddenly unavailable at Isotope Stadium, baseball without love is just boring. It can also seem endless, infinite in the bad sense. But baseball contests eventually end, at least most of the time; sometimes they are suspended by weather, abandoned, or put out of their misery by way of a mercy rule. And yet, even the concluded games are told in actions and passages we have enacted or witnessed, not measured in minutes and seconds told by a mechanism indifferent to the action.

And so we return to the themes of time and consciousness. What is immortality, after all? Our bodies perish but we are all capable of immortality nevertheless. The immortality I have in mind depends on no supernatural order, and makes no claims about infinite mortal existence; it is, instead, the contemplation of that which is beyond the workaday. Immortality is the entry into that time which is not regulated, which is not constrained, which is open and forever. That happens here and now, not in some other heavenly place, but it happens only when we suspend the normal understandings of here and now: when we no longer tell time, even in outs and innings, but instead experience ourselves as out of time, lost in a game without end.

The philosopher Wittgenstein advised us to think about time on the analogy of the visual field. At any moment, your visual field may be constrained by what is around you. Even in an open field you will be constrained by the field of your vision and the horizon. But vision has no theoretical end; it extends infinitely. We have to move our bodies physically toward the horizon but theoretically that horizon is unlimited. Life itself is like this in similarly having no limit within our experience of it.

This is never easy. As adults, we all too often misplace our ability to drop out of time, so powerful are its mundane demands. But if you can conceive of life and temporality the way I am suggesting, then not only are you immortal, you are playing infinitely. You are doing what the poet Blake famously did when he wrote, in "Auguries of Innocence," from *Songs of Innocence and Experience*, these lines: "To see the world in a grain of sand / And a heaven in a wild flower, / Hold infinity in the palm of your hand, / And eternity in an hour."

If it's a pitcher's duel, that glimpse of eternity may take two hours, or three for a slugfest. Extras are always possible, as are weather delays. *El tiempo!* How long will we be here? I couldn't possibly say. Not even god can say.

Game on.

Character

THE WORLD OF PROFESSIONAL SPORT moves ever on, to the next game and eventually the next season, so it's surprising that fans and players were still citing a minor incident from a May 30, 2007, game between the New York Yankees and the Toronto Blue Jays when the Yankees' Alex Rodriguez retired in August of 2016. Except that it reflects on the character of an otherwise great player, and so on the deeper issue of character's relation to sports.

The burning question: did Rodriguez *cheat* when he yelled something—he says "Hah!," others say "Mine!"—as he ran between shortstop John McDonald and third baseman Howie Clark, causing Clark to duck and miss the routine put out?

First, some obvious distinctions. Whatever Rodriguez did, it was not cheating in the flagrant sense of using performance-enhancing drugs, as his teammate Jason Giambi admitted to doing the week before—and for which he himself would later be punished, after lying about the matter. The drug issue, which irrevocably spoiled that summer's bid by San Francisco outfielder Barry Bonds to crack Hank Aaron's all-time home-run record, still hangs over baseball like a toxic stench. The shouting incident was a minor eruption of bad odour by comparison. Nor was the shout even an obvious violation of the rules of Major League Baseball. There is a rule against interference with a fielder, but the intent of the rule is clearly aimed at the physical variety. (And we say nothing about the charges of off-field cheating that continued to dog Rodriguez, suave patron of Toronto pole-dancing bars and other recreational activities.)

No, if there was an offence here it was not to the *rules* of baseball, but to its *norms* — those unspoken guidelines that are not set down in any rulebook precisely because they are not hard and fast. Various opposing players and managers, not just Blue Jays, called the move "bush league" and "cheap," signifying its lack of class. Rodriguez's own manager, the gentlemanly Joe Torre, nine-time All-Star and former MVP, told reporters he thought his player had made a mistake. The Yankees won the game, avoiding a sweep by the Jays and notching a win during an otherwise dismal run of losses, but even that, Torre implied, did not justify the move.

The clearest summoned expression of disapproval was that Rodriguez was not treating his opponents with due respect. His disingenuous little smile after the play, a complacent smirk caught by broadcast cameras, was for many the final insult. For many viewers, that facial expression confirmed everything we know and hated about the Ranger-turned-Yankee. What a punk!

Now, I agree completely with that judgment; but then, I'm a Blue Jays fan. The controversy raises a deeper issue, though, which is whether deception is ever allowed in sport. In war, as we know, the *ruse de guerre* is a standard and even honoured device of engagement, from booby traps to faked insignia or swapped naval ensigns. Without Greek guile, the Homeric epics are just so much slaughter. Even in law, trickery is allowed as long as it serves the interests of justice: DNA samples may be surreptitiously collected by offering a suspect gum or a cup of coffee. To what extent should the staged antagonism of sport, the spectacle of struggle, resemble the real cut and thrust found in these adversarial human theatres?

One stake of this age-old debate was planted firmly by Charles W. Eliot, the legendary president of Harvard University. The curveball, Eliot argued, should be banned from baseball because, like a lie, it was a falsehood delivered with deliberate intent to deceive. *Say it ain't so!* Unfortunately for truth-lovers like Eliot, but fortunately for fans, that was in 1894 and even then most people thought he was bonkers. (He was, however, spot on about the bloody carnage that was college football, his era's equivalent of the Ultimate Fighting Championship.)

So, assuming we think curveballs are okay—also sliders, sinkers, slurves, and splitters, not to mention change-ups and knuckleballs—what is not? Well, for one thing, spitballs. Applying goo to alter the ball's natural spin, or roughing it with a hidden file or piece of sandpaper is beyond the pale. So is stealing the catcher's signals while on base and conveying them to your teammate at the plate. At first glance, it is not clear why the latter is so bad even if the former obviously is. The pitcher-catcher battery is clearly working together to fool the batter. Doesn't the batter have a right to countermeasures? Apparently not, at least not with the aid of a teammate—a batter's job is to outguess the battery, but by himself—and stealing signals will earn you official censure, a manager's tirade, and probably a fastball to the ribs the next time you're up.

The norms in sport are ones of balance as well as civility. Ideally, baseball, like any game, should present the best possible displays of skill and grace. If the batter knows too much about what's coming, the little chess game between him and the pitcher is ruined. By the same token, if deception were endemic to every single play, sports would soon descend into the hellish region of Stephen Potter's hilarious *Gamesmanship* books, those manuals for wrong-footing opponents in every walk of life by way of elaborate ploys, limps, put-downs, and miniature humiliations (more on this in a later section).

Paradoxically, we actually tolerate overt deceit in the controlled-catharsis environment of sport more than we do in life, where deceit is usually covert. No-look passes in basketball, play-action fakes in football, and googlies in cricket are all considered fair, if slightly devious, play. Even hiding the ball, that sandlot staple, is still sometimes to be seen on professional baseball diamonds. But such playful sleight of hand has to be mutually accepted, witty, and good for the game. If I am fooled by it, I should feel outplayed, not cheated.

A fine distinction, yes, but a necessary one. Charles Eliot's curveball prohibition was kooky, but his attitude was right. In sport, he said, there is too often "an unwholesome desire for victory by whatever means"; when that is true, there is no difference between sport and life. He would hate it here in the 'roid-riddled age of false testimony and gangster quarterbacks; but he'd be perversely gratified to know it is still possible to violate the unspoken norms of sport. And I'm pretty sure he'd agree that Alex Rodriguez is a punk. Among other things.

Baseball, like all great philosophy, teaches us how and when to change the world; also, and maybe more importantly, how and when not to. It allows us to understand the challenges of virtue and the rewards of happiness. Football tells us much about technology, basketball about the unfairness of the genetic lottery, soccer is "the beautiful game," and hockey, as already mentioned, offers a multivalent metaphor for life in Canada. Baseball is of course the most philosophical of games; it teaches us what Aristotle was at pains to describe in the *Nicomachean Ethics*; namely, the true nature of the ethical life.

Aristotle's ethical theory is the first and greatest version of what philosophers call virtue ethics. The basic insight of this kind of theory is that *character* and *action* are in dynamic relation, a functional feedback loop: my discernible qualities as a person, my virtues, will shape how I respond to situations; and the actions I perform will, in sum, create the character I possess. Virtue ethics is distinct from rule-following ethical schemes, including both deontological, or duty-based, theories such as Kant's (where possible actions are assessed for their morality via the rational universalization test of the categorical imperative) and consequentialist theories such as Mill's utilitarianism (whereby actions and/or rules are tested according to their ability to maximize the happiness of the greatest number).

The signal advantage of virtue ethics is that it situates ethical action in a rich field of practical detail, taking full measure of the complex relationship among persons and their circumstances, friends, community, and purposes. Our lives are the sum total of what we do, and thus a whole life, not this or that commission or omission, is the proper subject of ethical judgment. Aristotle argues that we orient ourselves to the natural *telos*, or end, of *eudaimonia*: a word usually translated as "happiness," but understood to mean not mere positive feeling but an ethical state of doing and faring well, becoming all we might be, flourishing.

Baseball reflects all of this. There, on the quadrant of action called fair, we face issues of character and luck. Fielders get chances, and make plays; but errors will also be made, and recorded. The game is difficult, success rare. A hitter will be considered exceptionally good if he fails just six times out of ten. (Cf. Stengel: "They don't pay me to win every game, just two out of three.") Luck plays a large, sometimes overwhelming role: to be happy, we need both skill and good fortune. The standard of flourishing is contained within the game itself, but must be realized in our actions: no matter our intentions and other states of mind, we are not good players if we don't play well.

And, as suggested before, *practice practice practice* really is the only way to ready ourselves for challenges not yet arrived. In any baseball game, as in any life, there are situations that have never arisen before. General rules will not help us; they can at best set the parameters within which infinite possibility is offered. We must be poised and ready to scoop the grounder and throw to first. We cultivate a disposition to act, by imitation and habit, so that doing well becomes almost second nature. In fact, without imitation there can be no initiation into the practice, because this is something that must be learned by the body and not the mind.

We begin by imitating the best and most virtuous, the exemplars of success in the practice. "A kid copies what is good" Ted Williams told *The Sporting News* in 1994. "I remember the first time I saw Lefty O'Doul, and he was as far away as those palms. And I saw the guy come to bat in batting practice. I was looking through a knothole, and I said, 'Geez, does that guy look good!' And it was Lefty O'Doul, one of the greatest hitters ever." That is how it begins. So that when The Kid, the Splendid Splinter, realizes his own ambition of surpassing O'Doul and is *recognized* as the Greatest Hitter Ever, we know that the game has created, and then realized, its own conditions of self-transcendence.

But we must ask: do these ethical resonances really function in the modern culture of the game? What notion of human flourishing is present when athletes use performance-enhancing drugs, steroid treatments, and muscle-building supplements such as androstenedione? What form of virtue is exhibited when multi-million-dollar salaries, rather than contributions to the game, dominate our sports pages? Can the free spirit of the game survive the noted fan obsession with the rigidity of statistics and the "money ball" approach, all of which seem to reduce poetry to mathematics?

More generally, what kind of society have we become when happiness is, for us, not the pursuit of virtuous *eudaimonia*—with its sense of commitment to good character, friendship, justice and a thriving civic association—but the increasingly desperate attempt to be "better than well"? What role does virtue have when happiness means consumerism, individual gain, and even technological bioenhancement—for those who can afford it?

Virtue ethics, modified for our own form of life, can help answer. Just as baseball, as a game, retains critical norms of virtue despite current realities, so the idea of human flourishing retains norms of practical judgment that we can, and must, apply to our current pluralistic ethical realities. *Eudaimonia* and its attendant relations to civic virtue, luck, and justice are notions we can update usefully for our own context. We lack Aristotle's relatively simple, small, and like-minded ethical world. The result is not irrelevance but, instead, a situation where his insights are, if anything, more important than ever.

Baseball reminds us, in moments of reflection, how life might be guided, how we must shape character to dispose to action.

Nation

TORONTO'S TRANSFORMATION OCCURRED LATE INTO the night, after Game Six of the 1992 World Series. The game was in Atlanta and went into 11 nail-biting innings. When it finally ended, Toronto did what all championship cities do: it erupted into a massive street celebration. People spilled from their houses and from the SkyDome, more recently branded with the usual corporate arrogance after a rapacious media company, where the game had been shown on the huge JumboTron television. They thronged the city's main downtown thoroughfare, Yonge Street, and began hugging and kissing each other with abandon. Some people later compared it to V-E Day, in 1945, when there was a similar outpouring of public joy and a dismantling of the usual dour inhibitions of the Toronto public, though the comparison seems a little off-scale, if not outrageous.

A more proximate comparison, to my mind, was to the race riots of the previous May. Prompted by the violence in Los Angeles and the death of a young black man shot by a white Toronto policeman, blacks and Latinos in Toronto had made the same area, around Yonge Street, a temporary war zone. Now, in October, black kids and white kids were embracing openly. The sense of shared accomplishment seemed to wipe out not only the usual differences in a racially and culturally diverse city, but also, somehow, the history of failure that had marked Toronto's recent years. Toronto is, by most civic standards, an urban success. It is clean, pretty affordable, fun, and relatively peaceful. But it wasn't perfect, especially for a sports fan. Our baseball team seemed to fold in late-season choking sprees, suddenly forgetting how to play the game. Our hockey team was a long-standing joke. And, in a bid to host the Olympics we had been beaten, significantly, by Atlanta. In its ongoing quest to be taken seriously as a city, Toronto had stumbled, if not fallen.

The Blue Jays had become a repository of civic values, their progress in the American League a kind of city-wide barometer of aspiration and success. Their victory, when it came, was a victory for the entire city. More to the point, it was a victory for the entire country of Canada. How else to explain the massive public support the team enjoyed, setting consecutive Major League attendance records as soon as the new stadium was opened? How else to explain the fact that, though I live in Toronto and think of the Jays as "my" team, my friends and family in Vancouver and Montreal speak of them with the same air of ownership, using the same possessive "our" to describe victories and losses? The first World Series victory demonstrated something that is impossible outside of Canada: that a baseball team can become a truly national institution, a genuine focus for national self-image.

But, like the hangover that follows a victory celebration, this national status is an ambivalent property. It both defines and undermines the Canadian effort to establish a national identity. And it does so in a way peculiar to Canada in its status as an economic and political colony of the United States. As so often, the place of Canada as an adjunct to American culture offers it a special critical ability not found within that culture. This status, which challenges and ultimately must redefine American self-understanding concerning baseball, shows how the idea of a national team can be revitalized. Canadian ambivalence may, in other words, prove to be the critical self-definition that we have been searching for all along: our marginal position the more powerful for being marginal.

Not a new idea: failure at power might be construed as success at critique. And yes, maybe inevitably, I will invoke the philosopher Hegel's so-called "dialectic of lordship and bondage" in what follows. You can feel free to skip that part.

It is common to argue that games are a showcase and a vessel of cultural value. They can emphasize, and so help to define, the best aspects of our self-image: fairness, honest competition, good sportsmanship. Or they can provide controlled outlets for those aspects of ourselves we regard with less pleasure: the violence, the competitiveness, which we try to keep between the lines, stylized and balletic. Games are an effective critique of life precisely by being unlike life, by offering something outside the hurly-burly that can stand in for and interpret those things we otherwise cannot see so clearly. They are not always *idealized* versions of life, as some would have it, but they are always different—not life by other means, but something separated off from life to reflect back on it critically.

That, at least, is the hopeful picture. One could argue, with equal plausibility, that when a game spirals out of economic control—as baseball has done more than once—it loses its critical abilities entirely, even while remaining utterly unlike life as most of us live it. Where else can a not-even-exceptional 25-year-old earn $15 million a year for throwing and catching a ball? And it is a depressing truth that some of the everyday world's worst features, like routine discrimination of people based on non-essential traits of skin colour, genitals, or preference, are more than alive in sports. In a cruel but familiar irony, the very things that elevate some individuals above the multitude—physical gifts and chances—give

the possessors of those gifts a sense of comprehensive entitlement, as if athletic talent were a free pass to behave any
way you please. This is, to say the least of it, a gross and yet
persistent error.

In Canada, the game that has carried our self-image
most effectively is of course hockey. We view it as a metaphor for our sense of ourselves as hardy survivors. Hockey
reminds us that we are the kind of people who team up to
cross frozen expanses and, triumphantly, achieve desired
goals. Canadians also pride themselves, less fancifully, on
our ability to play the game. We take solace in the fact that
the majority of NHL players are still Canadian. Of course,
claims to global dominance have been rocked now and
then, especially (and for the first time) during the epic 1972
Canada-Russia series.

The novelist Mordecai Richler once wrote that this
first series, in which the Russians surprised the complacent Canadian team, marked a cultural watershed. Though
Canada won the series, it was in spectacular, last-minute
fashion, after a tough slog, and not therefore the cakewalk
it should have been. "We already knew that our politicians
lied, that our bodies would be betrayed by age," Richler said
then. "But we had not suspected that our hockey players
were anything but the very best... After the series, nothing
was ever the same again in Canada. Beer didn't taste as good.
The Rockies seemed smaller, the northern lights dimmer."

Baseball has not historically played this kind of role in
Canadian culture, for obvious reasons. The summer is too
short to make the game a natural obsession. Speaking as
someone who shivered through several home openers at
Toronto's old Exhibition Stadium, I can attest to this climatic
argument. And because we don't play the game obsessively
as children, it doesn't take hold of our hearts and minds
as adults. In a way, it simply can't. The images of baseball
fantasy, the cherished scenes from "the heartland," of raw

recruits and ballyards emerging naturally from the plains, are through and through American. Though one of the prominent practitioners of this baseball myth-making, W.P. Kinsella, was a Canadian, his imagery was, as we know, all of Iowan cornfields and simple farming folk looking for diamond truth.

We can't seem to tap into the tradition of baseball because that tradition is so relentlessly American, so culturally specific—a specificity most evident, perhaps, in the visual propaganda of the photo collection *Baseball in America* (1991), which gives iconic baseball images the status of Soviet labour posters, or the somewhat punishing Ken Burns documentary (1994), which mythologizes the game almost to a conceptual breaking point: if you are not a fan after watching it, please surrender your eagle-embossed passport! For these reasons, and perhaps others, I'm not sure that baseball will ever occupy a place in the Canadian psyche to rival its dominance in Boston or Chicago.

And yet, increasingly over the past three decades, the Toronto Blue Jays have generated almost unprecedented popular support in Canada. This is doubly surprising to Torontonians, who are used to having the rest of the country regard them with ill-tempered scorn—an attitude we tend to repay in spades with urban arrogance, gentle condescension, and rudeness. In this sense, Toronto is the Paris of Canada—though obviously very much *mutatis mutandis!* The place of the Blue Jays in the national consciousness is also surprising because the first base of support for the team was distinctively urban, and founded on a sad old Torontonian desire to be "world-class." This adjective has become a one-word joke, a compact put-down of the grasping and ultimately provincial attitude that drives cities to excesses of civic ambition. It was a disease that afflicted Toronto in large measure, and it was possible even up to a few years ago to hear people, especially politicians and businesspeople, using the adjective seriously. There is little doubt that the construction of the SkyDome—an arrogant and thrusting structure that came into being over the objections of urban planners and housing advocates—was a world-class civic achievement.

The logical extension of this was the team itself, which in 1992 boasted the largest payroll in Major League baseball at the time, almost $43 million—a payroll, moreover, almost three times the size of the $14.85 million floated by Canada's then-extant other Major League team, the Montreal Expos, who ranked 24th among major clubs.[42] The Toronto fans flocked to the high-priced highrise to see highly paid foreign mercenaries compete against the best of the American League. If they didn't really understand the subtleties of the game, as many players and broadcasters complained, they at least understood its economics. Pouring hard-earned cash into the Blue Jay coffers was bound, sooner or later, to produce a winner.

And then nobody could deny that Toronto was a world-class city, or say that its baseball team was doomed to near-greatness, failure in the critical moment. They could complain that the SkyDome was a concrete monstrosity, a place where the spirit of baseball wouldn't be caught dead. They could scream, as I saw one apoplectic Yankee fan doing at a game not long ago, that they don't even play "Take Me Out to the Ballgame" during the seventh-inning stretch. It is dominated instead by a crew of idiotically perky aerobics instructors and a dimwit Blue Jays workout—and *then* they play the classic tune. They could laugh at the fans who leap to their feet at the crack of a routine fly-out nowhere near the fence. But nobody could say (could they?) that Toronto was any longer a provincial city—that it wasn't, in a word, world-class.

I won't dwell on the pitfalls and pathos of this attitude, which are considerable, because the larger story is even more interesting. Along the way, something happened:

baseball took ahold of the Canadian consciousness. Or rather, I should say, the Blue Jays did; because it's painfully clear that many of the fans who jumped aboard the Blue Jay bandwagon last year are fair-weather supporters—the kind I suppose you can get when you have a domed stadium. They have little interest in, and less serious knowledge of, baseball as such. Most of them never attended a game at gusty Exhibition Stadium, which drew average crowds of less than 25,000. Now they routinely sell out the massive SkyDome, with its 50,000 plus capacity.

In theory I have nothing to say against these fans. Who could? They provide a base of mass support who attend games and follow the team with a kind of coincidental interest, an interest motivated by the desire to feel included. For them, the Jays provided, as the sportswriter Stephen Brunt wrote, all the excitement of romantic infatuation. "The franchise history is summed up in a swift, smooth climb to respectability," he said, "a few tragic near-misses without a collapse in between, a short tease and then total satisfaction. The Blue Jays have delivered emotionally for their millions of supplicants, and the relationship between the team and the people remains as fresh and delirious and topsy-turvy as first love. Someday it won't be like that. Someday, the Blue-Jay-fans-not-baseball-fans will understand that winning the World Series can be a once-in-a-lifetime thing. They'll know the dull ache of a going-nowhere season, of rebuilding projects that don't pan out, of watching others celebrate and knowing the thrill won't be theirs anytime soon. A whole lot of them will likely fall by the wayside, drawn to some other diversion."[43]

No doubt this is true. Early success can give you unrealistic expectations. It will be some time before the true fan of baseball's tragedy—the erstwhile George V. Higgins Red Sox fan, whose life was organized around disappointment, or the Cubs fan who got panicky when Chicago won, lest he begin to think they can do it[44]—will be found in Toronto. Brunt was speaking, still, mostly of Toronto when he says this. Across the rest of Canada, there are fans who made long road trips into cities along the border just to see the Jays, boosting their attendance records with scores of cross-border baseball shoppers: Detroit, Seattle, Minneapolis, Milwaukee, and Cleveland all reaped the benefits of Canadian mania for the Jays. It is of course impossible to say how many of these fans will be in it for the long haul, how many of them are "true" baseball fans.

We *should* pause to question, after all, why a fan in Vancouver should prove a Jays supporter. The usual indices are apparently meaningless. The nearest Major League team is the Seattle Mariners, a team in a city economically and culturally similar to his own—much more similar, certainly, than Toronto. His Triple A farm team, the Vancouver Canadians, was affiliated first with the Chicago White Sox then with the California Angels—distant cities, yes, but still closer than Toronto. It may seem strange even to make these arguments, but there is something essential about them. If it were not for the presence of the Canada-U.S. border, in short, the Vancouver fan's interest in the Jays would be peculiar, a vestige of some boyhood obsession perhaps, or a long-ago player's heroism. Instead it's something we take entirely for granted, as we do for fans in Saskatoon and Medicine Hat and Flin Flon and Saint John and Halifax.

As I'm writing this, I hear a television broadcast of a Jays game at Safeco Field in Seattle, where blue-clad Jays fans are flooding into the stadium, drowning out the home fans— even though the Mariners have a shot at a wild card playoff slot. And they do the same in Cleveland, Minneapolis, Detroit, and Denver. This is not the same as a Red Sox Nation fan, shut out of access to bandbox Fenway, motoring up to Toronto to catch a game (when home features were not all sold out there too, as they are of late). A Vancouver or Kelowna fan doesn't consider the SkyDome as a missed opportunity. The question doesn't arise. No, for him or her, a fixture in Seattle *is* a home game. Maybe more impressive is the spectacle of a Halifax native cheering on the Jays in Seattle. Now that's a national fan, with several thousand miles on the personal odometer...

The expansion of fans across the country demonstrates that the Blue Jays have become a genuine repository of cultural values in Canada. They are a true national team, something that is functionally impossible for any team playing within the United States—despite the diasporas of Yankees and Red Sox fans from coast to coast. The Jays have done this, moreover, without many high-profile Canadian players (Russell Martin, Michael Saunders, Brett Lawrie briefly), and only a few players who identify themselves positively with the city and the country. Yet it's not irrelevant that there are many Dominican and Puerto Rican players on the Jays roster. They are, after all the closest thing to a neutral property—or, to be cynical, true mercenaries—in the implicit battle between Canada and the U.S. that defines the Jays' place in our national consciousness.

As I'm writing this, Edwin Encarnacion, a Dominican superstar who does not speak English with any great comfort, just hit a home run in Seattle. The mostly Canadian crowd went wild as the shy-smiling slugger rounded the bases in his characteristic "parrot arm" or "Ed-wing" trot. José Bautista, another Dominican-born diamond genius, drew a walk and then stole second. The waves of blue rippled with deafening happiness. Two-zip Blue Jays. This is happening in Seattle! (In the subsequent off-season, both Encarnacion and Bautista would test the free-agent market. When the Jays failed to break the bank for either or both, the quietly charming first-baseman would end up going to hated Cleveland, and a slightly chastened Joey Bats would sign for at least one more year with Toronto.)

The commentators are marvelling at this latest manifestation of trans-national fandom, calling it new. But that 1992 World Series victory was just the ambivalent achievement that Canada was longing for, and whose logic we are still working out. All that dearly bought foreign talent is at once an illustration and a limit-case of Canadian diversity. To say the least, most new arrivals get nothing like the welcome of these Caribbean heroes.

Colony

TO UNDERSTAND THE WEIGHT OF that first World Series victory, and the marvel of its successor the next year, we have to understand the place of Canadian *colonial* self-understanding in a continental context.

This is partly a matter of our national history, which consists, in large measure, of squabbles between imperial powers. It is also, and perhaps more crucially, a matter of economics. It used to be said in English Canada that our culture was roughly equal parts British and American. But the waning British presence in the country, which now includes many more people with no ties to Britain of any kind, has meant that the American influence—an influence chiefly of culture and money—has grown proportionately stronger. Because we depend on American markets for our country's economic health, and because our airwaves and public discourse are dominated to an alarming extent by American products, it is not an exaggeration to say that we stand in the relation of a wealthy de facto colony to the imperial power of the United States.

I do not mean, in saying this, to underestimate the crucial differences between the national cultures—an underestimation that many Americans perform almost without reflection. If they give the matter any thought at all, our

American cousins believe that Canada is really no different in principle, if a bit colder in practice, than any part of the northern United States. They fail to recognize the changing demographics, the distinctive literature, the multicultural ...

But wait, no! I have to stop myself, right here, and veer away from these tired Canadian replies, replies that emphasize differences but only, in their insistence, reinforce the subordinate position of Canada. It is a colonial gesture through and through to emphasize these differences, to insist upon them. If we had a more comfortable national self-image, we wouldn't be *insisting* upon them; instead we would be forcibly exporting them to weaker nations. The self-doubt evident in Canadian insistence on difference links up meaningfully with the civic anxiety about "world-class" achievements discussed a moment ago.

And, as before, this colonial anxiety is carried into our games. If there is room in a country's national self-consciousness for only one bat-and-ball game, there is no doubt that place is reserved in Canada for baseball. Cricket, the quintessential English bat-and-ball game, *is* played in Canada, but only on a very small scale indeed. So baseball is our game — and yet it is not our game, being so obviously American in its culture and traditions. Predictably, the thoroughly Canadian response to this situation — the response of doubtful colonial self-image — is to become insistent about Canadian contributions to the game. Perhaps some of you are familiar with claims that the first game of organized baseball was played in Zorra Township, near London, Ontario, in 1838.[45] Adam Ford, a seven-year-old spectator of the contest between the Zorra team and a side from nearby Beachville, later wrote an account of it, including a drawing of the knocker's stone (home plate) and the five byes (or bases). In 1988, a sesquicentennial recreation of the game was played in the vicinity, an event coinciding with the induction of five players into the Canadian Baseball Hall of Fame.

The trouble with this story, and Dr. Ford's account, is that it wasn't published—in Philadelphia's *Sporting Life* magazine—until 1886, fifty years after the bucolic contest was supposed to have taken place behind Enoch Burdick's carpentry shop. By then Dr. Ford was a hard-drinking middle-aged man and not the most reliable of correspondents. Still, Dr. Ford's account seems to possess at least as much historic credence as the mythic Doubleday accounts of an 1839 game (or was it, perhaps, an 1845 game?) played in Cooperstown.

My concern isn't the historic arguments, though they are fascinating. I'm more interested in what the recreation, and the institution of a Canadian Baseball Hall of Fame itself, tells us about Canadian aspiration concerning baseball. The insertion of the national adjective—what I've come to think of as "the pro-national claim"—is a distinctive colonial tic, a defining gesture of defiant limitation. There is only one Canadian-born player in the nearby Baseball Hall of Fame— Ferguson Jenkins—and no doubt many fans don't know that he is Canadian. The only player enshrined as a Blue Jay, Roberto Alomar, is a Puerto-Rican-born American citizen. (Several other former Jays, among them Paul Molitor and Dave Winfield, are in the Hall but wearing other caps. The defunct Montreal Expos' first representative, Gary Carter (2003), initially wanted to be present wearing a Mets cap instead. Carter relented and later apologized to the Montreal fans who had helped make him a star. The non-existent Expos now boast two further plaques in the Hall: Andre "The Hawk" Dawson (2010) and base-stealing legend Tim Raines (2017), who squeaked by in his last year of eligibility.

You can bet that every Canadian fan of the game knows these details, and will share them with you at only the slightest provocation. More subtly, that there should even exist such a place as the *Canadian* Baseball Hall of Fame is an admission of colonial inferiority and self-doubt. It is the pro-national claim made into an institution, a frozen gesture of cultural weakness.

Trumpeting our national achievements, especially if they take place on the world stage, is part of a threatened culture's insistence on its own merits. Did you know that Babe Ruth hit his first professional home run at Hanlon's Point, on Toronto Island? Did you know that Dr. James Naismith, inventor of basketball, was a Montreal-born doctor? That Alexander Graham Bell was Canadian? Or Peter Jennings? Or John Kenneth Galbraith? Robert MacNeil? Alex Trebek? Donald Sutherland? Oscar Peterson? Joni Mitchell? Paul Anka? Michael J. Fox? Mike Myers? Do a relevant update, and the names would be these: Ryan Reynolds, Ryan Gosling, Seth Rogen, Rachel McAdams, Hayden Christensen, Taylor Kitsch. And, for continuity fans, Kiefer Sutherland, son of Donald. Also: Justin Bieber! Carly Rae Jepsen!

Such reminders of famous sons and daughters, the stock-in-trade of the pro-national claim, communicate far more inferiority and anxiety than solid pride in achievement. They indicate that the Canadian stage is, by definition, a limited one—a scene to transcend. They also provide evidence of what the communications theorist Anthony Wilden has labelled "strategic envelopment": the pervasive, all-encompassing cultural or economic victory of empire, which succeeds so well that it actually defines the terms of possible public discussion.[46] This creates what Wilden calls, using psychological language, "identity double-binds." Under strategic envelopment—as in, say, Marx's analysis of dominant ideology—neither agreement nor disagreement with the dominant values retains any liberating possibilities. All arguments, pro and con, are phraseable only in the discourse of a public sphere defined and controlled by the dominant power.

This has serious versions, driven by asymmetries based on race or gender, and less serious ones. Consider a discussion of Canadian identity. To agree with American assumptions of sameness is merely to capitulate, to participate in my own oppression; but to disagree is to reinforce my subordinate position by using the limited language of insistence, a language of uncertainty. The true victory of imperial domination is that condition in which the slaves not only fail to revolt, but also actively participate in, and embrace, their own subordination. This is a "strategic" victory, one that defines and includes within itself all possible "tactical" responses. Tactics, says Wilden (following the philosopher Sun Tzu), can never defeat strategy; only strategy can defeat strategy.

The triumph of imperialism is just this ability to define the available language of both consent and dissent. The only way out of this colonial double-bind is, in some sense, to transcend the available language: but not, as we might expect, by creating an entirely new language. Instead, it is to use the internal dynamics of the existing language to critical effect. Working, still, under the assumption that sports are vehicles of value, including imperial value, consider an example of colonial reaction to strategic envelopment that has a strong bearing on the place of baseball in Canadian culture. The example I have in mind is West Indian cricket.

There was, and remains, a critical possibility built into the dominance of cricket values, values that are deeply imperialistic. The Indian critic Ashis Nandy argued that "some arguments about colonial, neo-colonial, anti-colonial and post-colonial consciousness can be made better in the language of international cricket than that of political economy."[47]

The values exported in Britain's imperialist adventures were decidedly Victorian, embodied in the dominant amateur player W.G. Grace, cricket's Babe Ruth. A physician by trade, Grace was an "amateur" of cricket, and a gentleman; yet he played the game with a fierceness and guile that often verged on the ungentlemanly. Grace's contradictory nature, says Nandy, made of cricket "a representative Victorian game—at one plane a violent battle which by common consent had to be played like a gentle, ritualized garden party; at another, a new profession which had to be practised as if it was a pastime."[48]

This is what Nandy calls the "intrinsic schizophrenia of traditional cricket,"[49] a kind of inner dynamic that pitted the overtly valued virtues of good sportsmanship against the largely unmentionable, but nevertheless widely recognized and valued virtues of aggression and drive to win. The internal conflicts of traditional cricket were dynamic, but delicately poised within the context of England's class system. It could not survive the process of exportation unaltered, however, for its class-based social balance and peculiar brand of hypocrisy were too delicate for overt challenge.

The challenge came from the colonies, especially Australia, India, and the West Indies. The exportation of cricket contained within it the seeds of its own destruction, just as colonialism more generally would lead to the destruction of empire. "Victorian cricket reversed the process" of exporting aristocratic values, Nandy argues. "It allowed Indians to assess their colonial rulers by western values reflected in the official philosophy of cricket, *and to find the rulers wanting*. The assessment assumed that cricket was not the whole of Englishness but was the moral underside of English life which the English at the turn of the century, even with much of the world at their feet, found difficult to live down."[50] To the extent they could not live down these values, the oppressors gave the oppressed the exact means of their own liberation.

These arguments complicate the accepted interpretation of the colonial appropriation of cricket. Traditional thinking on the topic has it that colonial cricketers were less bound by the strictures of norm-behavior in cricket, and so more fully able to exploit the rules to their advantage.[51] The desire to beat the masters at their own game, a celebrated colonial enterprise, succeeded in changing the game because it made it impossible to win in any fashion other than the aggressive style adopted by the Australian sides of the 1920s or the West Indian teams of the 1970s. On this view, the colonial competitiveness, a competitiveness not sufficiently fettered by the culture of sportsmanship, transformed cricket by chipping away the patina of hypocrisy the Victorian game had given itself. By being good at the game, the colonials forced the masters to play harder and show their true nature. And, like all demonstrations of hypocrisy, this transformation has access to a certain cynical piece of high ground, for our moral culture is such that any exposé of hypocrisy, no matter how self-serving, provides an illusion of ethical bona fides.[52]

But the colonial reception of cricket is not so simple. The Trinidadian Marxist C.L.R. James describes how his own critical character was formed when he became, as a young boy, a kind of perfect model of sportsmanship—an English gentleman in miniature, more perfect than the real thing. This is, at first glance, colonial behaviour at its most obvious. This response to domination is in fact a structural defeat, a double-bind on colonials. The double-bind resides in there being no really effective response within the constraints of imperial domination: *difference* in manners is proof of subordination (the natives aren't even civilized), while *simulation* is proof of submission (the natives have no identity of their own). Both strategies are defeatist, because the parameters of the situation allow no other possibility.

"It was only long years after," James notes, "that I understood the limitation on spirit, vision and self-respect which was imposed on us by the fact that our masters, our curriculum, our code of morals, *everything*, began from the basis that Britain was the source of all light and learning, and our business was to admire wonder, imitate, learn; our criterion of success was to have succeeded in approaching that distant ideal—*to attain it was, of course, impossible.* Both masters and boys accepted it as in the very nature of things."[53]

The triumph of imperialism is that such structural domination gives the masters an ability to interpret any and all behavioural responses in terms that reinforce, and never challenge, the contours of the domination. But with this gloomy awareness comes no respite from the response's attractions. The Canadian diplomat Charles Ritchie notes in his diaries how Elizabeth Bowen once remarked on his manners as being "more English than the English." They were, she said, sufficient to make an upper-class English *chargé d'affaires* "feel like a bloody savage." And one can feel Ritchie's rather perverse pride in this.[54]

Yet, the limitations of the response still contain an interesting critical possibility. What better way—indeed, what *other* way?—to challenge the masters than to illustrate their own ideals more perfectly than they themselves? What more serious challenge to domination than to beat the masters at their own chosen game, not only the game of cricket itself but the civil norms lying beneath cricket?[55] Not only to beat them, that is, but to beat them by being more themselves than they are—to beat them, here, by exploiting what I have called the norms of civility. It is this advantage that makes colonial cricket more than a matter of beating the masters through exploitation of the strict rules of the game.

The ever-present danger—and the option which, in the event, proved more attractive to aggressive colonial cricketers—is a desire to win at any cost, changing the game in a way that destroys its critical possibilities. The colonial killer instinct, which achieves the ultimate goal of winning, here triumphs only at the price of making cricket a game like all other professional, commoditized sports, one without the possibility of social critique: failing by succeeding, rather than succeeding by failing. What looks simultaneously like a valuable expression of national achievement and a salutary exposure of hypocrisy turns out, on reflection, to be a capitulation not only to domination but also to the worst imperatives of hyper-competitive modern sport. Colonialism's unique possibilities are here sacrificed for a false goal. And thus we return to the original analysis of colonial cricket, all critical possibilities lost.

Critique

THIS SITUATION IS STRUCTURALLY SIMILAR to the one facing the non-American baseball fan. The 1992 and 1993 World Series victories provided an example of a truly critical colonial response to strategic cultural envelopment. Whether that critical response will have any lasting effects is anyone's guess. But the unease evident in some baseball executives at the prospect of an all-Canadian World Series—a prospect canvassed at the time in (I almost hate to say it) the Canadian edition of *Sports Illustrated*—is at least superficial evidence of a genuine challenge. Perhaps more to the point, anything that makes the executives of network TV uneasy, as a Montreal-Toronto series clearly does, must be a good thing. Alas, the possibility fails even as a counterfactual, with the Expos franchise now decamped to Washington.

The Toronto Blue Jays World Series victories posed a challenge to American self-understanding concerning baseball because they demonstrated (a) that, for the first time, a team from outside the U.S. could be the best in the game; and also (b) that victory could be gained by calling out the best elements of the game's culture, not flouting them. In other words, the Blue Jays' victories were both tactical and strategic. They won the Series, and that tactical achievement is the necessary precondition of the critique I am interested in. But the critique was really vouchsafed by the *way* in which they won the two Series, and especially in the way the fans responded—namely with a kind of cheerful civility, the joyful largesse of the good winner. This second, non-athletic victory is a strategic cultural win, an avoidance that in some fashion transcends the limitations placed on the colonized by imperial strategic envelopment. Again, as Sun Tzu says, only strategy can defeat strategy.

This description of the Jays and their fans as "good winners" may seem unsurprising, or perhaps trivial—and no longer even accurate, about which more in a moment. For surely there are some good winners and some bad ones, a matter of contingency. But given the imperial/colonial background of the Series victory, the fact that Toronto could assume the role of the good winner is more than usually significant. The good winner role is normally one reserved for the masters, since only those who have nothing really to lose can be expected to lose gracefully. The slaves, typically, are good *losers*: they are resigned and cheerful in defeat, their traditional good humour a kind of defence against the harsh reality of inferiority. When they do manage to win—as in, for example, early Australian and West Indian cricketing victories—they are most often bad winners, ungracious and savage. And often the victory is purchased only at the cost of undermining the game's critical possibilities, its ability to offer a utopian critique of life. Poor losers in general, and colonized ones in particular, reduce games to simply more life, life by other means. When slavish resentment infects the game, the game is no longer all that it can be.

The gracious victory of the colonized is an interesting, and unusual, combination. It is not, of course, anything like a direct bid for power, a serious challenge to the mainstream domination of the imperial power. But it is an effective critique of that power. It offers a reflection of the highest aspirations of that power, aspirations which, as in the systematic hypocrisy of Victorian cricket, are at odds with the reality of the power's exercise. Colonial victory, when gracious, holds up a mirror to the enveloping masters—a mirror in which the reflection must seem, perhaps for the first time, cruelly undistorted. This form of critique, which calls the masters to order in their own stated terms, is something that can best, and perhaps only, come from the margins, precisely the forums where the masters exercise their power.

At the risk—perhaps considerable—of alienating some readers, I am now going to illuminate these points by briefly examining the most influential theoretical discussion of them known to me, that of G.W.F. Hegel. Afterwards I will return to earth, and baseball, by discussing a few examples from the 1992 World Series that were significant. Side note: Hegel died in 1831, seven years before the match between the Zorra and Beachville sides mentioned earlier. We can only say that Hegel understood baseball in a way he understood many things: ahead of his time.

The theoretical notions concern the "dialectic of lordship and bondage," a celebrated passage from Hegel's *Phenomenology of Spirit* (1807). The passage involves an encounter between two self-conscious entities; let's call them, for present purposes, Yank and Canuck. Their struggle for recognition is, says Hegel, a struggle to the death. The outcome of the struggle can be, indeed, the death of one, but more significant is the result where one, the master, dominates but does not kill the other, a slave. The crucial aspect of the encounter, for Hegel, is that it in some sense completes the quest for full self-consciousness that marks the early development of human spirit. Bear with me, now, as I quote Hegel on this point.

Self-consciousness, he says, sees in the encounter with the other that "it at once is, and is not, another consciousness, and equally that this other is for itself only when it supersedes itself as being for itself, and is for itself only in the being-for-self of the other. Each is for the other the middle term, through which each mediates itself with itself and unites with itself; and each is for itself, and for the other, an immediate being on its own account, which at the same time is such only through this mediation. *They recognize themselves as mutually recognizing one another.*"[56]

This structure of mutual recognition defines the encounter, and it colours too the eventual domination of the slave by the master: so much so, in fact, that the master comes to *require* the slave for his own sense of himself. The structure of master and slave is thus, rather unexpectedly, one of mutual reinforcement. While the master clearly has power over the slave, the slave likewise has a power over the master as that person who the master requires to complete his identity *as* master.

The point of this excursus is that the structure of mutual recognition gives the slave an enormous, usually untapped, critical power. The master is as much his slave in these psychological terms as he is the master's slave in economic terms. He can, by reminding the master of the fact of his existence, unsettle the foundations of the master's domination, and hence of his identity. The slave, returning the master's gaze and showing his awareness of the mutual recognition, challenges and even undermines the master's sense of himself. The two are locked in an eternal struggle, a struggle just as much to the death as their original encounter but here deflected and sublimated: no longer open conflict but instead a kind of battle of epistemological will. Whose knowledge of the other will prove more powerful, more unsettling? In this struggle the slave, paradoxically, has the advantage: his being dominated has unexpectedly liberated him to critical possibilities denied to the master himself.

In the same way, colonized peoples stand in a critically privileged relation to their colonizers. They have an ability to *shame* the colonizers by virtue of intimately knowing the hypocrisies of the colonizers' ideal, to show them the precise shape and limits of their acts of imperial domination. This not only undermines the recognition that all masters must demand from all slaves; it also challenges the masters' very sense of themselves. Are we only masters, they will be forced to ask? Do we dominate? What about the other values we cherish? If the colonial challenge can make use of exactly these cherished values, its effectiveness is redoubled, for it emphasizes all the more the gap between self-image (how the masters see themselves) and reality (how they are in fact seen).

The Blue Jays World Series victories provided a vehicle for just this kind of challenge. First, it was crucial that the Jays take on the role of a national team, that they be identified strongly with Canadian, and not just Torontonian, aspiration. It was likewise crucial, of course, that they play good baseball. Losing the World Series, however well, would have changed nothing. Finally, then, it was crucial that the victory be a good one, which is to say one that was gracious, cheerful, and civil. The victory had to be performed in the best baseball terms, while bending those terms back on the dominant American culture of baseball in a critical fashion.

Several examples illustrate how this last condition was in fact met. All may seem trivial at first, but their cumulative effect, properly understood, is not.

The first concerns a comment made by David Justice, the Atlanta outfielder, about his only visit to Toronto before the '92 Series. "I didn't go out much," he said, "because if I got lost and encountered somebody speaking French, I knew I had no chance. So I just kind of stayed in my hotel room." There was no need for worry. In Toronto he would have been more likely to encounter someone speaking Portuguese, Italian, or Cantonese. Possibly Justice was thinking of a visit to Montreal, once a National League city, but I'm not sure that makes the remark any more forgivable. The point is that the remark *was* forgiven, and in a telling fashion; in fact, every mention I saw of it, in the press and on Canadian television, treated it as a joke.

I don't mean they thought Justice was joking, or making an ironic comment about the Major Leaguer's road-game existence. I mean that commentators took it, with great good humour, as yet another example of the expansive and profound ignorance that Americans have about Canada. I could speak endlessly about that ignorance, so benign and so pervasive, but it's not worth the trouble. One thing that is notable about this ignorance is that no amount of complaining by Canadians has yet given Americans what they consider a good reason for doing anything about it.

Consider an interesting parallel. The comedian Scott Thompson of *The Kids in the Hall* (did you know *they* were Canadian?) once did a monologue in which he compared being Canadian to being gay. People in the American mainstream, he suggested, know as much about one as about the other. So thinking it's going to be cold in Toronto in August is not much different from, say, thinking that all gay men like to dress up in women's clothes. Also like Canadians, gay men have a penchant for keeping inventory of homosexuals who made good in the wider world: Socrates, Plato, Leonardo, Walt Whitman, Rock Hudson. Here's a final correspondence: the population of Canada is about 10 per cent of the American population, a figure that gay activists consider an accurate estimate of the number of gays and lesbians in most Western countries, including the United States. One of the things I'm here to tell you is that being Canadian is not just a phase we're going through.

Another incident from the Series, more remarked still, displayed elements of the same ignorance. The celebrated gaffe of the Marine colour guard in Game One, displaying the Canadian flag upside down, provoked a flurry of responses from both sides of the border. Major League Baseball issued a statement apologizing "to the people of

Canada and to all baseball fans," calling the mistake "wholly unintentional." I don't think many people, even the most stridently anti-American of Canadian fans, thought the Marines just decided, intentionally, to insult a whole country on network television. In fact, when it came to joking off this piece of American ignorance, we mostly laughed about the fate of the hapless Marine corporal who hoisted the inverted Maple Leaf. Would he, we wondered, be ordered to clean out the SkyDome with a toothbrush? Would he be doing pushups until the turn of the millennium? Unfailingly, though, formal responses to the slight were gracious, and informal ones (as on t-shirts and posters) were humorous, not angry. This played out yet another of the routine clichés of Canadian reputation: that we are incredibly polite.

In my experience of living in three countries and visiting many others, Canadians as a nation are no more or less polite than most peoples. You find plenty of surly waiters and disgruntled fellow-passengers on the subway, lots of discourteous drivers and unhelpful bureaucrats. The difference lies in the matter of self-regard. Canadians believe, and want others to believe, that there exists a culture of politeness within our country.

This is a complicated proposition, because it's something we both laugh about and cherish. In that sense it has some commonality with many of the national myths of identity, including the one that says we have no national identity. We both believe this and don't believe it; and we do so because it's both true and false. The ground-breaking female sportswriter Alison Gordon, thinking in this mood, wrote a commissioned article for *Sports Illustrated* called "Canada From Eh to Zed": an alphabetical compendium of things that Americans needed to know as the first cross-border World Series began. It contained all the usual suspects. E, Gordon wrote, is for "Excuse me"—what a Canadian says when you step on his foot.[57]

Politeness and self-deprecation are clear badges of colonization, evidence of a peculiar, in-bred desire to rush into a defensive position. From one point of view, this is despicable weakness. It capitulates to domination not only without a murmur of protest but with a smile upon the lips and a gracious remark. It is weakness taken to a high level of self-congratulation, and made, along the way, into a strangely funny joke that undercuts our stronger selves. A *strong* response to American ignorance about Canada would be some kind of vocal protest. Instead of politely accepting the apology about the flag mistake, we should perhaps have returned the favour by dropping the American flag on the SkyDome dirt or having the R.C.M.P. colour guard fly it upside down.

The point is such a response would have been ineffectual. It cannot, structurally, be passed off as something done out of ignorance. For ignorance is impossible here: strategic envelopment means, among other things, cultural envelopment. We know, we have no choice about knowing, how your flag is supposed to fly. Contrarily, ignorance is always a defence for your insults about Canada. Even more, when an angry response does come—let's say you've stumbled into a barroom argument with an angry Canadian at an academic conference—it's probably hard for you to understand what all the fuss is about. Isn't it, after all, more amusing than anything else?

So it's the impossibility of the strong response that makes the weak response strategically effective. Wilden, again following Sun Tzu, argues that frontal assault is unwise when one finds oneself enveloped. The strategic response, the response that transcends the domination of having definition in somebody else's power, is instead some form of guerilla warfare. The celebrated Canadian politeness, a politeness which looks at first blush like submission, is in fact this kind of subversive response to imperial domination. Whether or not we believe in our responses, they treat insult in a particularly effective way, given the uneven balance of power. By setting a high standard of behaviour, we implicitly call attention to deficiencies of behaviour in others.

Perhaps, as in the cricket example, this response makes reference to elements of the self-image cherished by the powerful, and the gap between image and reality. Perhaps it sets a standard envied for its benefits. It used to be the practice of American backpackers to stitch Canadian flags to their bags while travelling in Europe: it brought them friendlier service and reduced the risk of terrorist attack. This wasn't only because Americans were uniformly despised by Europeans; it was also because Canadians, so unfailingly polite and so nice, had an excellent reputation. Ironically, it's a reputation—indeed, it's a national characteristic—that we can only have by virtue precisely of being marginal to a world power like the United States.

It's in that marginal status that our critical possibilities lie—not by way of a direct response to the thousand unconscious slights and insults of Americans, to the increasing saturation of our national life by American products; but rather by way of an oblique, almost paradoxical, response that makes of our weakness a strength.

The last example concerns the adjective "World" itself. For years, it has been common in Canada to hear disparaging remarks about this designation. Then, in '92, it was equally common to hear some satisfaction expressed that the adjective would at last have some relevance: not a world series yet, certainly, but at least an international one. But this also started an interesting debate about the origin of the adjective. Was it just what we in Canada would call the usual American arrogance? Or did it have some other story? CNN, the Atlanta-based news channel, did a story on the topic, asking Canadians in a sports bar what they thought about the now-international series. One image was striking. Prefaced by a joke about Canadian ignorance of baseball, including the obligatory remark that we only understand hockey, the reporter quoted a Canadian bar patron saying the "World" in "World Series" came from the old New York *World* newspaper. Look, said sports anchor Fred Hickman, laughing, they sure have some funny ideas way up north in Toronto.

Well, you could look it up, but my compatriot was in the right. There *is* a connection between a newspaper called the *World* and the first championship series between American League and National League winners. The paper was either among the original sponsors or supplied the trophy. I began to think of this small exchange as emblematic. It wasn't just that the Canadian knew the American history better; that, after all, might have been expected. What was significant was that he was ridiculed for doing so. Talk about strategic envelopment.

The first international World Series made it clear, as the simple existence of the Canadian teams could not, that baseball is no longer America's game. This has been true for some time, given the quality of Japanese play and the presence of Central American players of consistent excellence in the Major Leagues. But it was never so obvious as when Toronto won their first World Series, taking the trophy north of the border for the first time ever, and thus warming the nice, polite hearts of all those Canadians who saw, clearly, that the Blue Jays were a means of expressing their national identity. It remains to be seen whether these fans will consistently find in the Blue Jays a reflection of themselves, and thus find identity in recognition.

It also remains to be seen what long-term effects, if any, the Blue Jays' successes will have on the baseline American culture of baseball. Global demographics are a far more influential feature of the game now, with a Latino inflection — more emotion, some say, more stylishness — that can only grow. What I've called the civility by reference to which Canadian victories can assume their critical position is something threatened both in Canadian culture and in the culture of baseball, and certainly in American discourse considered more generally—I write these words in the fall of 2016, in the midst of both a stellar baseball playoff season and one of the nastiest, most unseemly American presidential elections in history.

And so, despite the rather hopeful arguments of Giamatti and others like him, there seems to be less and less of baseball that recalls the Edenic, paradisial themes of Romance and redemption prized so highly by that able Renaissance scholar. There is more profit-taking and nastiness, more naked greed, than ever before. There is also more naked incivility and boorishness. The Jays are no longer always, in 2015 and 2016, gracious winners. I'm okay with the Bautista bat flip, for example, but I understand why others are not; it was showy and unnecessary. The Jays have developed a reputation for being whiny and arrogant at the same time— in short, the Toronto Maple Leafs of baseball.

The team's new-millennium fans, meanwhile, are even harder to defend. They also seem hell-bent on *the hockeyization of baseball*, with hat-trick (i.e., three-homer) cap tossing from the stands and, less defensibly, the hurling of beer cans, racial insults, and water bottles onto the field, or even directly at opposing players, sometimes from the upper decks of the chaotic SkyDome.[58] According to Nick Swisher, one of the most hated players in the game, and thus a putative authority on the subject, Toronto's baseball fans are widely regarded as the worst in the Bigs.

"I would say they're the worst," Swisher told sports columnist Cathal Kelly. "But I don't want to give them the credit." Okay, but Kelly wanted to know: just how bad is bad? "You would not believe the things you hear out there," Swisher said. "Not just things about you. Things about your family. They'll go on the Internet and find out their names and use them. It's really unbelievable."

Alas, it is not at all unbelievable if you have ever attended one of the beer-soaked bro-parties that Blue Jays night and playoff games have become. Kelly wanted to push the question. "We are, officially, the worst," he wrote. "That it's hard to argue the point has made Torontonians suddenly shy and unsure. Do we deny what's pretty plainly true? Do we embrace our new identity as the drunken cousin who ruins every family gathering? And if neither of those things suit us, whom can we blame instead?"[59]

Exactly, because where is our vaunted Canadian civility now, in all this? Just a smokescreen, a myth, a national delusion tossed in superiority dressing? All of those, plus a secret combination of shame and pride that leads to passivity and evasion of responsibility. Toronto has become, Kelly argued, the Philadelphia of baseball. Worse than Philadelphia! A colony of beer-tossing punks! And while it is naturally unthinkable in the corporate baseball universe to ban or limit beer sales during the playoffs, what about a sense of shared outrage and collective responsibility? Nope. (At the time I was writing this, the Blue Jays had issued a formal apology to the Orioles and Toronto police were still seeking the beer-thrower for possible criminal charges. He later came forward.)

Incivility is a species of what economists call a collective-action problem—a race to the bottom, in other words, exacerbated by alcohol and the diffusion of personal responsibility always evident in mobs. And so this state of affairs can only get worse. The next thing you know, we'll witness condoned one-on-one fights between team enforcers after a brush-back, instead of the confused bench-clearing rumble-dances we witness now, many of them lacking a single decent punch. The 2016 right hook that Rougned Odor landed on José Baustista as delayed-action payback for the bat flip was perhaps the single most solid blow baseball has witnessed since Nolan Ryan. But with all due respect to fans of the sweet science, that rarity is a good thing. Fighting in baseball is, to use an old-fashioned word, unseemly.

The players and the fans are ruled by passions, and passions lately run high. We can't always count on clear thought in the middle of a game, even (or especially) a victory. Instead, the critical effects of this non-American baseball success will be mostly contingent on how well baseball continues to work its global magic: not exporting a national vision as if it were the one size that fits all, but instead embracing the world's contributions to the game from every imaginable location. The game is the world, and already the World Series title is more apt than ever.

As for Canadians? Well, we will no doubt continue to indulge our mixture of griping and self-congratulation, with occasional outbursts of violence marring the oddly persistent reputation for niceness. There may remain some useful aspects of critical perspective here in what my American friends fondly called "The Hat," but we ought to treat the point with suitable nuance. The smiling polite Canadian, meanwhile, is a beast that should be relegated to the *Invisible Mythological Creatures Magic Picture Book*. (Note: this is a real book.[60])

Anyway, politeness was never the point; civility was. The first is a matter of mere comportment, and can therefore conceal many hateful attitudes and hateful crimes—a point long noticed by the oppressed. In contrast, the latter is recognition that the most important move in any game is the one that lets the game continue. This is the most minimal, also the most central, of the norms that foster and enjoin civility. And for these norms, the game is a better teacher than any national culture, dominant or otherwise, could ever be.

José Bautista, commenting on the much-anticipated "grudge re-match" division playoff series with Texas in the fall of 2016, said this: "We're baseball players, not UFC fighters." Well, yes. Then, in Game One, the Jays proceeded to thump the Rangers 10-1, including an unnecessary but satisfying three-run homer from Bautista in the ninth, incidentally tying Joe Carter's postseason mark for dingers. No bat flips, no fights, no trash talk.

As Robbie Alomar said, hitting a home run right after being forced to dive to the ground on an inside pitch: "That's how you do it."

Yes. Yes, it is.

Nostalgia

THE MOST FAMOUS, THE *ORIGINAL*, nostalgic was Odysseus, who left home and suffered the sickness of home-loss—*nostos algos*—that gave the world an iconic image, and word, for a long, treacherous voyage. Odysseus makes it home, like a batted-around victim of base on balls, only to find that home is changed. There is no hero's welcome for him, just a scar and a dog who recognizes an old friend's scent.

Baseball is kinder. Homeward-bound mates are greeted with high fives, fist-bumps, cheers, and thumps on the back. Every man is a hero, even if he reached on an error and just trotted the bags as the result of someone else's swinging for the fences. The collective undertaking, perversely isolated in individual encounters between pitcher and batter, runner and baseman, is revealed in its full shared glory.

Though his own condition was more complicated, Odysseus conveys the power of this sacred sharing. Soon after arriving unnoticed, Odysseus and his son Telemachus, one of the few initiates, secretly plot to rid Ithaca of Penelope's presumptuous suitors and restore order. They are gathering weapons in the dark, their way lit by Athena. Telemachus quails and sees disturbing visions. His father quiets him with a memorable admonition: "Be silent; curb your thoughts; do not ask questions. This is the work of the Olympians."[61]

The philosopher Hubert Dreyfus, reflecting on the exchange, finds the message applicable more generally. "[W]hen things are going at their best, when we are the most excellent versions of ourselves that we can be, when we are, for instance, working together with others as one, then our activity seems to be drawn out of us by an external force. These are shining moments in life, wondrous moments that require our gratitude. In those episodes of excellence, no matter the domain, Odysseus's voice should ring through our heads."[62]

Here, the Greek concept of excellence — *areté*, which can also mean virtue or valour — is conjoined with the keenest of desire, to make home whole again. The longing that underwrites this excellent venture is a fragile property, however. We entertain nostalgia at our peril. Does anyone think to ask what Penelope wants? Her faithfulness is legendary, but what quandaries of longing cross-hatch her soul?

Nostalgia in baseball is ineradicable. It is officially a pastime, not a sport. It is played on fields, in parks, at yards. The history of the game is the history of America caught in its idealized, glowing, and therefore false self-image.

The tendency has been criticized many times, though without much effect on the prevailing trends past-ward. Critic David McGimpsey, for example, has noted the fatal tendency in baseball writing to elegy and eulogy.[63] Mentions of baseball in "high" culture, especially the literary kind — Walt Whitman, F. Scott Fitzgerald, Marianne Moore, Jacques Barzun, Robert Coover, Don DeLillo — are collected and treasured like silver-edged trading cards, the sterling literary-provenance proof of seriousness. The baseball novel, almost inevitably suffused with some version of the aforementioned glow, thus creates an auratic swirl of commodified baseball-desire; it becomes the ultimate souvenir hat.

Despite the cogency of this critical foray—which was delivered, I should say, as a talk among the baseball faithful, including several baseball novelists, at the Cooperstown Baseball Hall of Fame—the dialectical force of baseball ideology folds its energy back into the dominant narrative. McGimpsey is a fan, after all, or he wouldn't be thinking and writing so cleverly about baseball. He also cared enough to submit his paper to an academic conference about baseball. No dummy, he performed his own dialectical maneuver by citing a scene from *The Simpsons*.

This is not the most famous baseball-themed episode of the animated comedy show. That honour belongs to "Homer at the Bat," the 17th episode of Season Three (February 20, 1992). After making a rash bet, billionaire robber-baron Montgomery Burns, that nostalgic graduate of Yale College, hires a side of professional ringers to take on the beer-league team that features Homer and the other duffers of Springfield. Roger Clemens, Wade Boggs, Ken Griffey Jr., Steve Sax, Ozzie Smith, José Canseco, Don Mattingly, Darryl Strawberry, and Mike Scioscia all appear as themselves. Each is eventually carried out of contention by a series of unlikely events, including spontaneous insanity and freak injuries. (In 2017, this tale was "inducted" into the Hall of Fame in Cooperstown.)

No, the episode McGimpsey cited was "Brother's Little Helper," the second outing in Season 11 (October 3, 1999). By this stage, as many critics noted, the show had developed a form of narrative eccentricity in which linear connection was almost entirely absent, and opening sequences might contain a fistful of *non sequiturs* and abrupt segues. The key incident in the episode involves Bart Simpson's theft of a tank (a reference to a contemporary news item), which he drives destructively through town on his way to blast his school into nothingness. Instead, he shoots down by mistake a satellite belonging to Major League Baseball.

Inside the satellite, revealed as a surveillance device, there are detailed accounts of everyone's actions. Mark McGwire appears and stuffs the documents under his hat. To Bart, who is gaping, he admits what is going on: "You're right. We have been spying on you, pretty much around the clock." To the others gathered at the crash, he asks, "Do you want to know the terrifying truth, or do you want to see me sock a few dingers?" The good people of Springfield know their own interests better than any critic. "Dingers!" they shout. "Dingers!"

In a weird, gratifying footnote, McGwire's team, the St. Louis Cardinals, was later investigated by the U.S. Justice Department and F.B.I. for hacking the computer records of the Houston Astros in search of a competitive advantage.[64] Life, art, etc.

But the overall patterns here are never settled. Nostalgia is just as often acquired by accident, and even instantly, rather than experienced as the scours and lashes of years away from home.

We tend to misplace it, adopting the music of our older siblings or even parents as the soundtrack of *weltschmerzlich* indulgence. Clothes get recycled along with a wholly anachronistic desperation for the times they represent: the 60s, the 80s, and so on, not to be confused with the merely literal decades featuring those numbers: the 60s run from 1963 to 1973, for example, the 70s from 1974 to 1982, and the 80s from 1983 to 1992. Philip Larkin's poem "Annus Mirabilis" (1967) makes the point: "Sexual intercourse began / In nineteen sixty-three / (which was rather late for me) — / Between the end of the 'Chatterley' ban / And the Beatles' first LP."[65]

Woody Allen, likewise, neatly skewers the continental drift towards someone else's past in his *Midnight in Paris* (2011), in which young literary aspirant Gil Pender (Owen Wilson) longs to be part of the 1920s Paris scene that featured Picasso, Cocteau, Porter, Hemingway, Fitzgerald, and Stein. By way of a magic chariot, in the form of a vintage Peugeot automobile, he is able to visit and find success there—only to fall for a love interest of that world who longs, in turn, for a different past. She wants to be part of the same city's 1890s vogue, the Belle Époque of Guy de Maupassant and Proust. Nostalgia is revealed in this structural irony as a form of self-cancelling restlessness, the temporal equivalent of the inability to sit quietly in one room, which Pascal considered the path to all of humanity's problems.

Gil's attempted novel, about a man who works in a nostalgia shop, opens with these lines, which enchant Gertrude Stein: "'Out Of The Past' was the name of the store, and its products consisted of memories: what was prosaic and even vulgar to one generation had been transmuted by the mere passing of years to a status at once magical and also camp." A store that sells memories sounds like something out of Philip K. Dick's "We Can Remember It for You Wholesale" (1966; adapted for film, twice, as *Total Recall*, 1990 and 2012). There, Earthly immiseration has made implanted memory a cheap alternative to actual vacations off-world—until something goes badly wrong on Mars. I won't spoil it for you; make your own memories. But a machine for generating memories! How wonderful and diabolical at once! But of course that's exactly what a *souvenir* is, what the word literally means. What do we seek when we haunt the long rows of memorabilia shops that line the street right outside the Hall of Fame in Cooperstown? It's a capture and keep mission, a sortie for mental prisoners.

I was never a baseball trading-card geek, so I don't have the traditional story that belongs here, about how my mother took my shoebox of carefully collected and sorted miniature biographies and consigned them to the trash. She did that very thing to my painstakingly constructed multi-level Dungeons & Dragons layouts, however, so I still have a version of the complaint to cherish. The only time I ever had a baseball-card collection it came by accident, and that was maybe instructive.

I was at a baseball game one summer night near the Annapolis Valley campground where our musty, canvas-topped trailer was parked for a few weeks. Once again, our parents thought that time spent wandering around what amounted to a bare field, or else cooped up in the tented portion of the trailer as the heavy Nova Scotia rain descended outside, counted as a vacation. I remember being terrified of the wooden latrines, rickety structures reeking of ancient urine that were also infested with huge daddy longlegs spiders that seemed to move towards me with evil intent every time I had to use the toilet. The camp's proprietor, a short, nut-brown bald man who went every day in just shorts and sneakers, called them his *vashroomps* in what he fancied was a comical German accent. I developed a fierce, silent hatred for this malevolent, sun-darkened imp, who would cry out, to no one in particular, "I must go clean my vashroomps," and then, somehow, always leave them with an intact population of fist-sized spiders.

As always, the baseball game was a respite from the boring routines of camp life, the toast routinely burnt on the Coleman stove, the hot water that needed to be heated each night to wash the Bakelite crockery, the endless hours with no stimulus or amusement except comic books and the uncertain attentions of other kids. The only daily treat was a waiver of my mother's usual categorical ban on sugared cereal. We got packages of miniature cereal boxes that could be opened on the side panel, like knocked-over cardboard cabinets. You could pour milk right into the box, and have it soak up the throat-tightening sweetness of Frosted Flakes or Cap'n Crunch.

My brother Steve and I had walked over to the game. I don't remember anything about it as a game. I may even have toted along a kung-fu comic book of some kind to stave off boredom. As we climbed down from the little bleacher, sliding into a muddy hump behind the field, I saw a half-crushed box. It turned out to contain a substantial cache of baseball cards, some of them a little stained but mostly intact. I confess it here: this was 1974, I was 11, and I didn't even think about trying to locate the rightful owner. I scooped up the cards and walked on as if they were mine.

It was a pretty good collection. Mets ace Tom Seaver was one of the prize items, and there were lots of journeymen whose names and faces I can no longer recall. What I do remember is that the cards provided new purpose to our daily existence. Now we had something other than candy on which to splurge our measly allowances. I made the collection a group possession, and we bought slick wallets of new cards, with that dusty, hard gum whose hard corners would hurt your soft palate as you attempted to render its resistant squareness into a chewable mass. I felt no genuine attachment to these players, or the cards that I had, in effect, stolen. But they oozed a kind of baseball gravitas that stays with you. The handsome male faces, clean-shaven college-boy types alternating with emergent weirdos sporting Serpico moustaches; the nicknames; the pocket biographies and lifetime stats rendered in boxes of tiny type; the serio-comic "action" shots of some cards, with players winding up to throw or assuming a batting stance with a grim simulacrum of gameface.[66]

I loved those cards. I don't know where they went. I don't blame my mother. They just went. They were not mine, but the memories are. Magical, yes. Camp, yes.

And it will surprise nobody if I say that, on the now vanishingly rare occasions when I taste Frosted Flakes, I am flung backwards in time whether I like it or not. I feel the hot, soapy water on my hands as I wash green ceramic cups in a plastic tub set on the picnic table. The colour of my mother's gold wedding band as her hands tanned in the sun. My cool, striped Hang Ten t-shirts, brought from California, and knee-length shorts made of cut-off jeans, the edges frayed with a pin. My scuffed North Star sneakers. Chocolate milk made with powder in a can whose top you had to pop with the back end of your spoon. Mosquito bites and the smell of oily *Off*. Skin peeling across my nose. A hacked-off bowl haircut executed by some talentless air force functionary at the B/X back in Summerside.

And the spiders. Always the spiders.

Proximity

As WE SAW IN A previous section, it is another truism among baseball people that part of the appeal of the game lies in the relative normality of the players' bodies, the visibility of their faces, the lack of bulky protective equipment. As players seem to grow in size and power, there are still miniature powerhouses like Dustin Pedroia or José Altuve who give hope—baseless, of course, but that's the nature of hope—to smaller athletes everywhere. Marcus Stroman, the talented Toronto pitcher of diminutive stature, has a clothing line emblazoned with the logo *HDMH*: height doesn't measure heart. This makes these players' almost superhuman feats of baseball grace and prowess all the more indigestible.

I recall reading a *Sports Illustrated* story about former Baltimore outfielder Brady Anderson, he of the long sideburns. Anderson said he was constantly being challenged in bars to compete in parking-lot foot races. He didn't *look* fast, you understand. He just looked normal—whatever that means. So Anderson regularly drank for free, because *of course* he kicked other guys' asses in these impromptu sprints. They didn't have a chance. He's a Major League outfielder! But you can imagine the mutters as these semi-inebriated mooks handed over their cash to the bartender. *He doesn't look fast...*

I should say that this issue of appearance should be separated from another one, which is more in the way of the
world. Some years ago I found myself standing next to Jack
Morris at a sprawling downtown bar. In fact, I wasn't really
next to him, because the veteran Blue Jays pitcher, then late
of the Twins—and on his way to help the Jays to their first
World Series title—was surrounded by a half-dozen of the
most beautiful women I have seen in my life. Depending on
your aesthetic notions, Morris may or may not count as handsome. I just remember thinking that he looked pretty awful
that night, with his lopsided face, big out-of-date moustache,
and light blue Dad jeans. But there is no arguing with aura:
glamour, as John Berger argued in his *Ways of Seeing*, is "the
quality of reflected envy."[67] Morris, objectively dumpy and
even undistinguished, glowed with that unmistakable light
of fame, money, and success.

The flip of this scene might be one, actually the same story
repeated many times, described to me by a former student
who used to work as a hostess in a lively rooftop nightclub
near the centre of Toronto. She is a ballplayer herself, one of
those talented young women who are forced to play college
fastpitch because there is no varsity hardball for women. Her
job was to cast a skeptical eye over the little crowds on the
other side of the velvet rope. Sometimes musicians or actors
came in, getting the celebrity free pass. Also athletes. But saddest of all were the young players, rookies who were languish-
ing deep in the bullpen or the platoon depth chart, who would
try to breast the velvet threshold by brandishing their own
cards. (These were not collectible cards but plastic ID flashes,
on lanyards, which they used to get into the locker room at the
stadium.) *See, I'm a professional athlete! Really, I am!* Come back
when you're famous, meat. Come back when we can recognize your face in the world, not just depicted on a card.

The background operation here is a primal one: recognizing the uniqueness of a face and, sometimes, a gait or

characteristic movement. Is that...? Is he...? Athletes don't make their living with their faces the way actors do, but they know how important recognition can be. It is the moment when a player becomes real, in the world, actually a human being and not just a moving image seen from the stands or viewed on television. That's why it's so interesting to sit in seats near a baseball dugout, where you can see the grimaces of failure after a strikeout, hear the swearing voices, sometimes even get a player to respond to your heckle or cheer.

But there is still a barrier, baseball's version of the theatrical fourth wall. Fans are not allowed to breach the barrier between audience and play—at least not physically. You can yell as loud as you want, but you had better do it from your side of the magic barrier. Otherwise, you will be ejected like the threshold-contaminating garbage that you are, expelled from the scene, the drama, the play.

This is surely why any close encounter with a professional athlete is so memorable for ordinary fans, the ones who aren't sportswriters or stadium workers. When I was a kid living in a Winnipeg suburb as my father toiled through another navigation course, the neighbourhood grapevine informed us one day that Bill Frank, an outstanding offensive tackle with the hometown Blue Bombers, was a nearby resident. Canadian Football League salaries are such, especially in the recessed 1970s, that it is more like a blue-collar union than an elite roster of bling-sporting superstars. Plus, offensive linemen are notoriously unspectacular members of the gridiron fraternity. Frank was one of these, a quiet Colorado native who probably liked frigid Manitoba winters more than some of his American teammates.

Word came one summer night, as we were just hanging around doing the usual nothing, that Bill Frank was having a barbecue. Not a party barbecue, just him grilling some steaks for the family and sitting at a picnic table in the shared part of the housing block. We ran, biked, and skated over that way, excitement building the whole way. Why? Bill Frank was huge, a mountain of a man, 6'5" and about 275 pounds — actually not at all big by today's standards; but still, in 1974, probably the largest human I had ever seen up close.

He was going to eat a steak that was, one kid claimed, *three inches thick and as big as a dinner plate*. We gathered at a short, respectful distance from his picnic table, the nine-year-olds of a townhouse project in Westwood, and watched, awestruck, as Bill Frank put away a piece of prime Alberta cowflesh closely resembling that description. That was it. He ate it; he seemed to enjoy each bite; we watched; then we left, buzzy with the spectacle. Bill Frank died in June 2014, a member of the Canadian Football Hall of Fame, eulogized as an exemplary, unsung hero. Nobody mentioned his appetite for grilled steak, but I'll always remember that dry summer night in Winnipeg, 1971.

Wayne Gretzky shook my hand at the Hockey Hall of Fame one time, and did a wink-and-point thing at me in response to a "joke" I made about the relative merits of Los Angeles and Edmonton. I also told him that we both got married on the very same July day in 1988. This was undoubtedly an unanswerable remark; not even the wink this time. The little shopping-coupon newspaper in the small town where I got hitched, Markham, Ontario, carried a story with the headline: "Local couple marry on same day as Great One." I'm sorry to report that, despite this unusual osmotic sanction of near-greatness, the marriage didn't last.

Arnold Palmer gave me a golf ball after a skins game played at Glen Abbey that same summer. Woo hoo!

The day that Roberto Alomar celebrated his Hall of Fame induction at the SkyDome — July 31, 2011, if you're keeping score — it happened that my regular seats were right on the aisle down which he trotted to enter the playing field. He gave me a high five, stretching his already too-tight electric blue suit. Yes, I have since washed the hand, because I'm not

11 years old any more. But I did spread the high five around the section a bit.

In 1991 I was sitting on the verandah of the Otesaga Hotel in Cooperstown, New York. This is a grand resort hotel in the old style, with gorgeous brickwork and colonial columns, overlooking the 18th hole of the golf course, and a little marina on the southern shore of Lake Otsego, James Fenimore Cooper's legendary "Glimmerglass." I was a sessional instructor at the time and could never have afforded to stay at the hotel. No, I was sharing a motel room down by the working marina on the less grand side of town with my buddy Jim Davidson. So I settled for having a gin and tonic on the verandah, which is known for its rocking chairs and air of general elegance.

I had given a paper earlier that day, and was feeling relieved and even a little pleased with life. The verandah was nearly empty. I looked around as a man walked out from the little door leading to the lobby. He strolled over to where I was sitting and gazed out over the lake. We looked at each other and smiled without saying anything, "two sportsmen taking their ease," as a character says in DeLillo's *Pafko at the Wall*.[68]

Then I realized: it was Hank Aaron. He ambled off before I could invite him to share a drink with me, but I think that's just as well. Silence is sometimes louder than words, smiles more binding than wine.

These next ones don't really count, because they were not fan-driven. In the 1990s and early 2000s I made a few television appearances on a sports talk show that had a greater-than-usual tolerance for variety in its guests. That was cool, and I enjoyed it. We talked about sports and politics, culture and sports, that kind of thing. There were writers and minor rock stars and, sometimes, exceptional athletes.

So I sat in a chilly little TV studio every now and then, orange with that old-fashioned pre-HD makeup, and talked

233

or argued with: Georges Laraque, a huge defenceman from
the Montreal Canadiens, among other teams, known as
one of the most dangerous fighters in the NHL; Ferguson
Jenkins, long-legged and soft-spoken, legendary pitcher and
first Canadian inductee into the Hall of Fame, who looked
like he wished he'd stayed at home; Chris Bosh, new to the
Toronto Raptors, gawky and uncomfortable on camera;
charming Damon Allen, then the Toronto Argonauts' starting quarterback, who after the show offered me a ride to the
subway in his convertible, parked over by the Canadian Tire;
and a host of lesser lights whose names and faces can no longer fire the relevant neurons in my aged brain.

One notorious episode of this show, of which I was a helpless participant, featured Wesley Snipes, who was dressed
like he was still on the set of *Blade 2* and acted like he was
being investigated for tax evasion. Oh, that's right, he was
being investigated for tax evasion.

The show was eventually cancelled, but not before an episode that paired Canadian Prairie politician Preston Manning
with adult-film veteran Ron Jeremy. In his memoirs,
Manning wrote that he assumed Jeremy was just a mouthy,
washed-up hockey player. Nope, a mouthy, washed-up porn
actor. I was not present that day, nor was I in the studio for
Spike Lee, Duane "The Rock" Johnson (then a wrestling
freak, now a comedy genius), Gene Simmons of Kiss (then
and now, just a freak), Vince Carter, or Pink. I doubt Pink
would have offered me a ride to the subway after the show. I
doubt she drives her own car.

And so: a final encounter that was not an encounter of
real proximity, but has had lasting effects on my life. During
that same posting in Winnipeg in the first years of the 1970s,
the Montreal Expos Triple-A farm team was the short-lived
Winnipeg Whips. They played just one-and-a-half seasons
in the Manitoba capital, finishing second-last and then last
in the International League in 1970 and 1971. They had

been moved by the big club from Buffalo, where they'd been called the Bisons—a name that, you might have thought, could easily be retained in any move to the Western plains. Buffalo would re-launch the Bisons, a club founded in 1886, some years later; they have been a Blue Jays Triple-A affiliate since 2013, after a stint in the Mets system.)

But no, the Winnipeg side became the Whips, and Montreal mounted a big publicity campaign to overcome their sub-par play and the fact that the Whips, as members of the International League, were over a thousand miles away from the nearest rival club, the Toledo Mud Hens. High-level pro ball was a novelty in Winnipeg, and my father was excited to take us to games. The publicity effort was in full-court press, and coincided with my mother's decision that I should open my first bank account. The Bank of Montreal leveraged their biggest star, Rusty Staub, to make the whole campaign run. Staub, in his prime, was one of a new breed of power-hitters, a superb player who would go to the Mets in 1972 in a blockbuster trade. A sophisticated, wine-loving New Orleans native, he had embraced Montreal enthusiastically, learning French and proudly bearing the nickname "Le Grand Orange"—like "Rusty," a reference to his bright red hair.

So, along with my baby-blue plastic-covered pass, hand-inked entries of my tiny allowance savings, and a sense of awesome adult responsibility, I got a free membership in the Rusty Staub "Grand Orange" Fan Club—actually officially known as the Young Expos Club. There was a pin, a membership card, a certificate suitable for framing (this never happened), a signed letter from the man himself (likewise), and a patch to sew on my GWG jean jacket.

"It all gelled," Staub said later of his time with the Expos. "I travelled across the country. I went into every major city there was in all the provinces. I spoke for baseball and for the Expos and for baseball in Canada. We had that Young

Expos Club with the Bank of Montreal. The first year, we had 25,000 children. The second year it was 75,000 and then the third we had over 150,000 children in the program across the country. To be able to do that and have a real part in it was very fulfilling, like I was doing something above just being a player."[69]

Staub would return to the Expos eight years after his trade to the Mets, as a 35-year-old sometime pinch-hitter. He was clapped out, overweight, no longer fast with the bat anymore. Sixty thousand Expos fans gave him a standing ovation that turned his legs to jelly.

There are only a few chartered banks in Canada, so my decision on where to open an account was not a large-choice-set problem. But I say truthfully that I started saving with the Bank of Montreal because of baseball and Rusty Staub. And I'm far from the only one — Montreal *Gazette* sportswriter Mel Cowan, for one, had exactly the same experience, though in his case much closer to actually seeing the big Canadian Hall of Fame hitter in action.[70] I never did, and the Whips were not much more than a colourful disappointment, despite strong fan support and excellent early-70s merchandise.

I'm with the bank still. These days I get investment reports instead of sew-on patches. There are no passbooks. There are no Expos either.

You can still get a hat with their logo. I have one.

Justice

I PLAYED, BRIEFLY, IN A Sunday league in the blue-collar college town of New Haven. Besides my pal Stephen and me, I don't think there were any other Yale grad students out there on the field. This was a league for older guys who wanted to get some semi-brisk summer exercise, nothing too strenuous, punctuated by bursts of (as they saw it) good-natured ribbing. It felt a lot like the Sunday softball games on Hampstead Heath played by restless Canadian expats living in London, as described by Mordecai Richler in his novel *Cocksure* (1968). There was the same air of frustrated ambition sublimated into borderline nasty chatter, a common air of a scene that, zooming out, demanded the eye of a satirist.

It was probably abstract, lofty, grad-school thoughts like that which kept me from paying attention to the actual game. The umpire, he of the largest belly, explained the no-talent pitching schema, which involved each batter getting just two pitches. If the pitch was a ball, it was an automatic base on balls; if it was a strike, you were out. This encouraged free-swinging antics that had the virtue of moving the game along and, not coincidentally, glossing over the fact that pitching well is a lot harder than bashing and catching the big ball.

237

I came up, immediately dubbed a ringer because, like Stephen, I had a Body Mass Index somewhere inside the non-obese range and because, to the anxious middle-aged male mind, relative youth and thinness must equal athletic prowess. The truth is that I was not a great hitter, though I possessed, like all the men in my clan, a nice-looking horizontal swat of a swing. It often went horizontal some distance from the ball, but that was simply my cross to bear as I was out there, styling.

There was a lot of "friendly" jawing as I stepped to the plate, some comments on my allegedly skimpy gym shorts and my ephebe's complexion. Yeah, I'm pretty sure none of the hecklers knew the word "ephebe"; this is my version of events. Anyway, I stepped to the plate, assumed the position, and waited for the pitch. It was a high, looping effort that appeared to me clearly outside the strike zone, maybe even destined for the parking lot behind the backstop. So I moved the bat slightly and held back, feeling like I had an easy base.

"Strike," the fat ump yelled. He was actually fat, I'm not just being resentful. "The batter's out!"

Now, I realize that strikeouts are every hitter's nemesis, at any and every level of the game, but this struck me immediately as grotesquely unfair. I had submitted to the two-pitch conventions of the contest, it's true. And I had counted on a judgment call to get me an easy trip to first instead of the dribbling put-out that would certainly have resulted from the piece of sky-high nonsense I'd been fed by the pitcher. But you're telling me that was a *strike*? And now I'm *out?*

Even as I was attempting to digest these enormities, the portly umpire advanced a few feet in front of the plate to make an announcement. "For those not familiar," he chubbily intoned, "it is always recommended that you swing at the pitch." My sense of outrage and unfairness deepened. If this was so, why were there *two* pitches allowed? What could be the point of the second pitch? Who dreamed up this

cockamamie game anyway? And by the way, that was no
fucking strike, Santa Claus. Check your eyes, Burl Ives. No
whine before its time, Orson Welles. I don't know what that
means, I just made it up.

That was my only at-bat of the game, a five-inning affair
that was nevertheless long enough to witness me being
replaced in the lineup the second time through by a much
older man who hit a triple. Our side lost.

Baseball is a game that teaches us much about justice, but
usually by way of its absence. Yes, we seek to record account-
ability with every passed ball or error, every run earned or
unearned. But the game itself is so shot through with contingencies and near-misses that it is instructive mainly in a
negative fashion. You may hope for a fair strike zone, and
you may sometimes be rewarded. But don't count on it. The
sadly iconic image of a hitter returning to the dugout shaking his head is not just a portrait in futility, or an opportunity for home-town jeering; it is also a physical enactment of
disgust with the ways of the universe, where a willing and
sincere participant in the drama can be undone by perfidy,
deception, near misses, and the basic human error of the man
behind the plate.

Perhaps someday the umpire's strike-zone calls will be
replaced by a disembodied version of the pitch-tracker or
zone-scan technologies now used by television commentators. These projected grids define the actual strike zone,
across the face of the plate and between the letters and the
knees of the batter. They can show you just how wrong, how
variable and slipshod, an umpire's call can often be. But the
human element of the game is part of its lesson. There's a
reason balls and strikes are not reviewable by instant replay.
It's the same reason that, long before instant replay and still
true now, the one reliable way of getting tossed out of a game
is by questioning the home plate ump's execution of the
strike zone. Players will sail close to this wind now and then,

shouting "Bullshit!" or simply saying "That was not a strike" as they trudge back to the bench. But you can't *argue*. Because that would be to argue with life itself.

Baseball is not a political game, not really, but it holds out some lessons of the basic political dynamic, especially that part of it concerning justice, which is to say the relation of humans to each other under conditions of *moderate scarcity*. For the record, the basic formulation is Hume's, and it is a good one, at least to start with. If scarcity of goods is gross, then there is a chaos of striving for mere survival. We are in a state of nature, and *can't afford* mechanisms of distribution. If there is no scarcity at all, then justice issues do not arise: superabundance solves our human problems. We all sit contented, and *don't need* mechanisms of distribution.

Of course, this version of events ignores those species of goods that are scarce by definition: positional goods (things I can have only if you do not), competitive goods (things that are only available via zero-sum contest), and non-fungible goods (things so closely associated with one act of possession that they cannot be transferred to another). All of these mean we could witness protracted justice issues even under conditions of moderate abundance. And this, *this* is the human predicament as we actually witness it.

Enter baseball. The main good of a win is obviously a positional and competitive good. Winning at sports is a zero-sum game: winner takes all, losers fuck all. That's the point of keeping score. But within the contest are dozens of micro-contests and staged confrontations that bring home more complex lessons. I can have a great individual game, going three-for-four with six RBIs, and my team might still lose. A starting pitcher can be in line for the win with an outstanding six-inning performance, only to get a dreaded no decision when his bullpen blows the save. Judgment calls are everywhere, distributing the goods of strikeouts and hits, stolen bases and snazzy tags, with no regard for cosmic rightness, just the exercise of imperfect human senses.

The game is at once the most fair thing one can imagine, a controlled and regulated match between equal sides using the same rules, and the most unfair experience one can imagine. Say it again: you can do everything right, and still fail. What could be more like life than that? And yet, it is not life at all, but instead a staged performance whose main theme is happenstance.

That's one reason baseball must have its long season, not just in months but in games. (Professional hockey's season is now longer, to nobody's great edification.) Playing 162 games before there is a decision about ultimate winning and losing sounds insane — until you remember that life happens every day, too, one sunrise at a time. An early-season game matters, because all games matter, but it will not make or break a season. Managers always tell their players to break down the season into series: three games with the Orioles at Camden Yards? Try for two, three is a bonus. Stay above .500 and then press the advantage when you can. It's a marathon, not a sprint.

Settling the ultimate matter of winners or losers is thus, necessarily, an imperfect business. A nested postseason of best-of-five and best-of-seven series is a compromise with contingency. It is the best one can do, without an infinite deposit of world enough and time. Roger Angell, writing in the *New Yorker* of the history-making 2016 World Series between the Cubs and Cleveland, said he wished the series could be the best eight of 15, rather than four of seven:

> The Cubs, trailing three games to one in this Series, were facing winter, but now will have a day off and a sixth game, and maybe even a glorious seventh. Baseball does this for us again and again, extending its pleasures fractionally before it glimmers and goes, but, let's face it, this time

a happy prolonging has less to do with baseball than ever before. This particular October handful has served to take our minds off a squalid and nearly endless and embarrassing election—three hours of floodlit opium or fentanyl that can almost erase all thoughts of Donald Trump's angry slurs or Hillary Clinton's long travails. If I could do it, I would make this World Series a best eight out of fifteen.[71]

But then, extend the reasoning: why not the best 11 of 21? Why not the best 19 of 37? Hey, I have an idea—let's play 162 games, one almost every day, and *then* decide! Oh, right.

Justice will out, even if it is not the result some of us desired. That is the nature of the game, also the nature of justice. The game is democratic, in the sense that it does not distinguish between individuals even as it rewards their virtues and actions in a decidedly uneven manner. Here, even the connection between reward and individual is a contingent one—as it should be. Baseball does not allow the distortions of *entitlement*, where individuals claim conquest based merely on who they are, or where they have been born, rather than what they have done. Baseball teaches that entitlement is a spurious error of self-congratulation. There is wisdom in the saying that an entitled person is one who "was born on third base and thought he hit a triple."

In baseball, the only way you get to third base is to actually hit the triple. Well, of course that is not quite true. You can be batted over, you can steal, you can advance on an error. But that's all part of the game's spirit of justice. The one thing you cannot do, ever, is be born there.

There is, naturally, democracy within the game too. Consider this well-known *aperçu* from the diamond philosopher Crash Davis: "Relax, all right? Don't try to strike everybody out. Strikeouts are boring! Besides that, they're fascist. Throw some ground balls—it's democratic."

But speaking of entitlement and justice, I feel like I cannot leave this particular inning without saying something about cheating. We all know that players cheat, in ways big and small. Cheaters, as a previous section indicated, can actually be tolerated as marginal costs on the game, negatively reinforcing the norms of good play. But there is a special case of cheating that seems worth mentioning: what the English writer Stephen Potter brilliantly codified as "gamesmanship."[72]

In his series of serio-comic works, ostensibly the clandestinely circulated volumes of a secret society of gaming intellectuals, Potter outlined a dizzying array of schemes, stratagems, gambits, and feints designed to allow players to get "one up" on the other fellow. These tactics all depended on the *prima facie* commitment of players in competitive games to be good sports, or at least not openly hostile enemies. Subjects ranged from actual games such as tennis and snooker to social game-analogues on the order of dinner-table conversation or participation in academic life (obviously a rich field of study there).

Potter's original book, phrased deadpan as a sort of scholarly treatise, concerns (as the subtitle had it) "the art of winning games without actually cheating." It offered various schemes of subtle undermining, implied challenges to sporting ethics, and sample "parlettes," or little chunks of dialogue, meant to put your opponent off his game. A typical gambit is "the flurry," a series of delaying actions and displays of incompetence designed to make an opposing player feel flustered and anxious. A key rule is to "play against your opponent's tempo," either speeding up or slowing down the game depending on what your opposite number prefers.

Other core tactics include "limpmanship" (feigning injury to arouse sympathy), "nice-chapmanship" (being more sporting than the other fellow, in order to demean him), and "the hamper," a tactic with primary (game-specific) and secondary (personal) dimensions. The hamper plants an unwelcome thought in the mind of the opponent, perhaps concerning his golf swing or romantic life, which keys on the Taoist notion that "conscious flow is broken flow." As soon as I start thinking about the mechanics of my swing, I can't swing any longer. Here is a sample parlette during a game of snooker:

> Gamesman: "Look ... may I say something?"
> Layman: "What?"
> Gamesman: "*Take it easy.*"
> Layman: "What do you mean?"
> Gamesman: "I mean—you know how to make the strokes, but you're stretching yourself on the rack all the time. Look. Walk up to the ball. Look at the line. And make your stroke. Comfortable. Easy. It's as simple as that."

As Potter says, "the advice *must be vague*, to make certain it is not helpful."[73] A further example exploits the sequence of Praise-Dissection-Discussion-Doubt, as the experienced gamesman offers to analyze the *successful* golf swing of his partner. Soon, the layman can no longer walk without second-guessing his motions, let alone unleash a good golf swing. "I often think the possibilities of this gambit alone prove the superiority of games to sports," Potter remarks, "such as, for instance, rowing, here self-conscious analysis of the strike can be of actual benefit to the stroke maker."[74]

The whole exercise, while comical, depends on a key piece of wisdom: if you "break the flow" of an opponent you have taken away a good deal of his or her power. Baseball is not as obvious a site of this as the one-on-one games that figure in the Potter universe, especially golf, tennis, and billiards, but it retains many possibilities of flow-breakage. A pitcher who alters his motion when runners are on base — the stretch versus the windup — can minutely court the balk and make both the batter and the steal-seeking or hit-and-run-hungry runner stutter and stall. A little hitch in the leg-lift does a lot of work.

One of my favourite non-Potter executions of Potter-style tactics occurs in a novel called *The Liar*, by English actor, memoirist, and broadcaster Stephen Fry. Recounting the life experiences of a prodigious liar, the sublimely mendacious Adrian Healey, Fry's book describes a cricket match in which Healey's side is outgunned by another prep school. After a taunting challenge to continue a close match, not to mention an unexpected bet placed in his favour by a future mentor, Healey decides to stop playing fair. "You won't cheat will you, sir?" one of his youthful players anxiously asks. "Cheat? Good heavens. This is an amateur cricket match amongst leading prep schools; I'm an Englishman and a schoolmaster supposedly setting an example to his young charges. We are playing the most artistic and beautiful game man ever devised. Of course I'll cunting well cheat."[75]

The resulting debacle involves subtle intimidation, false solicitude to a dangerous bowler, and a few other cheating-not-cheating moves that Potter devotees will immediately recognize as gamesmanship of a high (low) order. A talented player is reduced to tears as a result of repeated assurances from Healey that he is *not* cheating. Confidence, that essential milk in the cake of athletic success, is soured and clotted. Healey's team carries off the win, and some incidental proceeds from the bet.

This is all very English and even a bit fey. But is it cheating? Not in the usual sense. But it was a deliberate breach of the sporting contract that is nevertheless allowed within the contract. And that is a political lesson as well as an ethical one. You don't have to break the rules to take advantage of the game. The game tolerates cheaters; worse, though, is that it accommodates sly dealers. And worse still, sometimes the latter people are the umpires.

Stephen Potter's wisdom about gamesmanship was acute, and not just on the level of tactics. He is a philosopher of failure. "The value of gamesmanship as a training for the British citizen, and for young people in particular, is shown not only by the special qualities it enhances among those who habitually find themselves on the losing side," Potter remarks late in the original book. "If it is true that the typical Britisher never knows when he has lost, it is true of the typical gamesman that his opponent never knows when he has won."

In other words, this is failure executed with an elegant combination of grace and guile. "The true gamesman knows that the game is never at an end… And the good gamesman is never known to lose, even if he has lost."[76]

Thus the state of baseball, fairness, cheating, democracy, and everything in between. Justice? Sometimes, maybe, if everything falls into place. More often, well, you know the lesson: *There ain't no justice.*

Not coincidentally, less than a week after the Cubs fulfilled Angell's wish and won that most excellent Series, using just the seven games granted them and every other team, the slyly mendacious Donald J. Trump, a gauche yet effective practitioner of lying and gamesmanship who probably doesn't know the word "fey" (or "ephebe"), was elected the next president of the United States. Historians may recall that so comprehensive was his disdain for "losers" that he refused to admit he would abide by the results of an election if he lost. "I'll keep you in suspense," he said.

Who among us has not felt the inclination, when things are bad, to blame it on "a global power structure," a conspiratorial league of omnipotent elitists, including Alec Baldwin, as Trump did? Usually, we then wake up and realize that the truth is less wild and a lot more boring: we are just losing at something.

Trump made it clear that he could not lose the 2016 U.S. presidential election. As his campaign more and more resembled a flaming airplane crash, his protests that the game is rigged grew louder and more desperate. "He either denies that he failed or he argues that he was cheated," Ryan Lizza noted in the *New Yorker*. "Trump is either victorious or victimized, but he is never a loser."

In the same magazine, satirist Andy Borowitz posted an imaginary news item with this headline: "Trump Warns Hillary May Rig Election by Getting More Votes."

This wasn't a mere psychological quirk, it was a fundamental ethical defect that sets a bad example for children and idiots everywhere. The consequences for politics are significant: Trump's comments and actions undermined the Republican Party's integrity, the validity of electoral process, and the idea of democracy. His promise to jail Hillary Clinton if he won made even staunch conservatives compare him to a raving tinpot tyrant from a banana republic.

Worse, though, his attitude mocked the idea of human endeavour itself. "You can't win if you don't play," the lottery ads say. You also can't lose. The essence of engagement is that both possibilities must be live ones. Otherwise there are no stakes and no legitimate outcomes. It means nothing to win if you do not at the same time, and by the same logic, risk losing.

Being a loser doesn't mean being a good loser, that coded insult for someone who doesn't try hard enough. But neither does it mean being a sore loser, which is a condition just a few steps away from Trump Tower. Hate losing, avoid cycles of self-defeat, but accept loss as the price of being in the game.

Trump aroused appalled fascination because he was the pure creepy-clown avatar, the Donald McDonald of world-swallowing competitive attitude. In a bizarro twist, he had no concept of zero, like an ancient Greek mathematician. The resulting two-step paradox goes something like this: (1) everything, no matter how nuanced or complex in fact, must be reduced to a winner-take-all contest; and (2) just as I never apologize, I never lose.

If the latter trait destroys the idea of honest effort, the former impoverishes life. Baseball again: we enter the field of play accepting that the game is zero-sum, and we will be here — or the players will — until the matter is decided, even if it takes two days, 25 innings, and more than eight hours. A player can turn a year older during a single game (this happened to Yankees first baseman Mark Teixeira in 2015).

But comprehensive zero-sum thinking makes us all less virtuous and more unhappy. Being a loser offers another deep moral lesson: all games matter, but not everything that matters is a game.

But then Trump won, and all was undisturbed in the world of his imagination. Democratic? Just? Well, this is a book about baseball, not politics. You decide.

Late

OUR TIME TOGETHER GROWS LATE, my friends.

Lateness—that bane of throws and guests and gestures. The man who was late, in Louis Begley's novel of the same name (1993), is a child of European refugees who doesn't quite fit in with the Ivy League and Wall Street scions among whom he works. His story is told, post-mortem, by his long-time friend Jack, a true East Coast patrician reflecting on the bare inappropriateness of someone from New Jersey who never quite fits into the social scene he has conquered. A late letter destroys any chance for happiness in Ben, our severely flawed protagonist. His protracted bout of loneliness in Geneva, the loneliest of civilized cities, sees him indulging every impulse known to man. A Monte Cristo cigar, an expensive sweater, a swan dive into the famous weir that bridges the Rhône River in the heart of the city.

"How did it get so late so soon?" Dr. Seuss asks. "It's night before it's afternoon. December is here before it's June. My goodness how the time has flewn. How did it get so late so soon?" You might well wonder. Baseball, the game that refuses the tyranny of the clock, still knows lateness all too well: late tags, late innings, late swings (you can't catch up to the fastball, can you, late in life). "It is never too late to be what you might have been," George Eliot said, in what might be considered an Aristotelian mood. But is that correct? Sometimes, surely and alas, it is simply too late.

Why bother with lateness? Only because it is the familiar trope of human disappointment. The action not performed in time; the witty rejoinder composed only after the fact, a product of *l'esprit de l'escalier*; the athletic feat that just misses because the split-second decision to execute was just another split second behind success. How much of failure is lateness, the inability to be on time?

Begley's man who was late, Ben, is out of step and out of sorts. To be a refugee is somehow always to be unmeshed from the gears of comfort. The novel is, I think, a deliberate homage to *The Late George Apley* (1937), one of John P. Marquand's early-century bestsellers, now mostly forgotten. The novels share, for part of their narration, scenes in Boston and Cambridge, the rearing-ground of the American establishment. Apley is a man who has been forgotten by time, a conformist with late-blossoming notions of freedom that are sadly out of place, and therefore doomed. Ben is his spiritual twin a generation later, in a new post-war America. Marquand reminds us that even those to the manor born may find themselves out of sync; their burdens are subtle and full of muted sorrow. Begley's novel rings changes on the aspirant narrative of late-century America. How can you hope to fit in when even those who appear to fit in actually don't?

And of course we are all late sooner or later, lately here but now gone. The final lateness is that one, the state beyond simple tardiness.

There is something about baseball that prompts these mortal thoughts. Not every time I see a game, but reliably enough to be worth mentioning. Sitting in the stands, the innings growing late, how can one not think about the world outside the idealized confines of the game? I know I do, anyway; I am suddenly overcome with a heavy mantle of existential awareness—not dread, exactly, just cold knowledge. The crowd goes on roaring, the vendors hawking their wares, the PA system pounding out its insensate barrage of loudness. Inside my tiny bubble of consciousness, the thing that makes me myself, I am seized with an irresistible conviction of inevitability.

Football and hockey leave no room for such reflection; baseball seems positively to invite it. The game is not a respite for mortality; rather, a controlled reminder thereof, like a tragic play. Here comes a reliever, in a slow stroll from the outfield bullpen. The manager has ambled out to the mound to make a change. A pitcher, spent and maybe disgraced, walks head down to the dugout. Maybe he rates a cheer, maybe not. He is headed for the shower, not the tomb; but the drama is as sombre as the darkest scene in Shakespeare.

Hitters are retired at the plate, punched out. On-base runners, stranded by their flailing teammates, are said to have "died." The ball, that magic pill of action, is declared dead over and over in a single game.

Actual deaths at the ballpark are mercifully rare—though two researchers recorded some 900 baseball-related deaths in a 2008 reference book, *Death at the Ballpark*, at all levels of play.[77] A reviewer noted two qualified thoughts of uplift while surveying this catalogue of human fragility.

First, Jon Mooallem wrote, "It's weirdly moving, if not exactly consoling, to learn just how many of baseball's casualties made the play before expiring."[78] Yes, it's true: a surprising number of players used their last breaths to make the requited play, even, as in one case, completing a throw to first after being fatally struck in the throat. Second, "Take it as an indicator of just how much time Americans have spent on and around baseball fields over the last century and a half— of what baseball means to us," Mooallem eulogized. "We've managed to die on the diamond in so many crazy ways only because it's one of the places we've done the most living."

I'm not at all certain that's comforting, or even moving, but I will work on thinking so. A sharp foul ball can kill: it has done so, though not as frequently as you might imagine. Fastballs to the head are, likewise, extremely rare in the lethality department. Lightning plays a large, literally flashing role; so does the odd outcome of *commotio cordis*, the shocking body-blow that can literally stop your heart. In amateur games, running after fly balls and into traffic is regular peril. Sometimes, discretion is the better part of gameplay.

Baseball is life. That is the point. And in the midst of life, we are in death. Of course we are. What else?

Heartbreak

"IT BREAKS YOUR HEART," Bart Giamatti wrote in the most-quoted passage of *Take Time for Paradise*. "It is designed to break your heart. The game begins in the spring, when everything else begins again, and it blossoms in the summer, filling the afternoons and evenings, and then as soon as the chill rains come, it stops and leaves you to face the fall alone."

In the manner of a preacher or a certain kind of poet, Giamatti continues the passage by making the same point again, in rhetorical elaboration: "You count on it, rely on it to buffer the passage of time, to keep the memory of sunshine and high skies alive, and then just when the days are all twilight, when you need it most, it stops. Today, October 2, a Sunday of rain and broken branches and leaf-clogged drains and slick streets, it stopped and summer was gone."

More nostalgia? Well, maybe. Romanticism certainly, and no surprise from this expert in English Renaissance literature, whose book, as we know, is a reading of the game as a quest poem with tragic overtones. Maybe the better word is the Portuguese *saudade*, which names that feeling of profound melancholy and yearning that is not quite nostalgia, since we know that returning home is impossible. That consciousness, after all, is part of our thwarted longing, our incurable sadness. Home, like the past, is the inaccessible country.

Whatever the label, I find this short passage moving every time I read it. I picture Giamatti, baggy-faced and ill like the last time I saw him in person, at a New Haven social function. He sits in his study, looking out the rain-smeared window. The fallen leaves do indeed clog the drains at every intersection of the town, creating miniature lakes to make pedestrians leap. There is nothing more autumnal than a college town in the northeast, with football season pushing baseball into the past, the hot, humid days of September, when classes first met, waking to the cool mornings and mounting academic anxieties of October.

Giamatti knew he was dying, I think. A lifetime smoker, he was also overweight and looked far older than his scant half-century. He'd been made commissioner on April 1, 1989. Enjoying the last days before the fall semester at a family house on Martha's Vineyard, he collapsed suddenly with a fatal heart attack. Just eight days earlier he had secured Pete Rose's agreement to withdraw from the game of baseball for life, thus ending the Reds' slugger's drawn-out betting scandal, a blemish on the game. Did the protracted tussle with pugnacious, mendacious Rose hasten the commissioner's end? We will never know. Bart Giamatti was just 51 years old when his personal summer ended on the first day of September in the last year of the 1980s. His classic book appeared in October, a fitting memorial.

I have tried to read this passage aloud on what seemed like appropriate occasions, but this is a cluster of words that, by their very eloquence, seem to refuse easy vocalization. They stick in your throat because your throat won't open.

And so I printed out a copy of the text, and then just left it on the grave when we buried Aunt Linny's ashes in Walpole, New Hampshire, late August of 2016. It was a windy cool day, more fall than summer. We stood around awkwardly, sadly, in postures made self-conscious by the occasion. The small, square hole was deep, and as I knelt down to lower the urn, a heavy translucent vessel made of degradable salt, half-formed thoughts swirled through my preoccupied mind. Salt, I thought: how Biblical! Hmm, this hole is deeper than I thought! I have to stretch. My knees are muddy now. This urn is heavier than I thought! Okay, done. It's done. It's done. Goodbye, Linny. Salt of the earth.

The next time I visited the site, a few days later, the paper with the Giamatti quotation was gone, blown off by the wind or picked up by the conscientious groundskeepers as litter.

Beauty

BEAUTY, ACCORDING TO STENDHAL, IS "only a promise of happiness."[79] But what a compelling and irresistible promise it can be.

What is the beauty of a game? The lines of reaction and grace under pressure. The economy of movement in bodies negotiating space. Elegance as an end in itself, the physical version of Ockham's Razor: what is needed, and nothing more, to achieve the end in view.

Or, if there is something more, the addition is a grace note, a flourish. The way Javier Báez snaps his glove down at second, not even looking, to tag an unwary attempted steal. The way Marco Estrada finishes off a pitch with a slight flap of his hand, his face unmoving as he walks to the dugout, another inning's work done. Alfonso Soriano's way of uncorking a long, smooth throw from the outfield, a miniature essay in torque and mechanics. Rickey Henderson's taunting swagger in the lead-off, exploding into sprinting glory. When he passed the Major League steals record, Henderson ripped the base from its plug in the ground, grabbed a mike, and started talking with the same alacrity he had always brought to the base paths. Fitting, somehow, if a little too showboaty for some.

And then everything is not beautiful but which serves to highlight what is: Pete Rose's bear-like crouch and swat at the plate, muscling the ball into play; Tim Lincecum's oddball long stride and effortful hurl; all kinds of weird pitching moves, in fact, submariners and sidewinders and windmill flingers. And then there are the middle ways: Joe Carter's semi-hunch at the plate, somewhere between the classic form of youngster Bryce Harper and the bizarre but effective stances of Kevin Youkilis, Tony Batista, Craig Counsell, or Moises Alou. The legendary business-like lope of Ted Williams after every home run, first to last, without variation, celebrated by John Updike as the best farewell baseball has ever witnessed. "Like a feather caught in a vortex, Williams ran around the square of bases at the center of our beseeching screaming. He ran as he always ran out home runs — hurriedly, unsmiling, head down, as if our praise were a storm of rain to get out of. He didn't tip his cap. Though we thumped, wept, and chanted 'We want Ted' for minutes after he hid in the dugout, he did not come back."[80]

And now, rising above them all, creating new standards of beauty by rejecting the orthodoxy and its inversions, the Zen archer, the drawn bat-bow execution of Ichiro Suzuki, perhaps the most beautiful player the Major League game has known. Ichiro's grace is of another order, his face and body a combination of stillness and lithe elasticity that brings new style to the North American game.

Ichiro was an immediate power in the field, too; a coiled-spring outfielder whose relatively small frame is capable of generating astonishing power. A seasoned professional when he entered Major League baseball in 2001, he won both Rookie of the Year and Most Valuable Player in the American League. He was a bolt from the blue, just like his trademark fielding assists from right. A week and a half into that season, the first Japanese player to start in a fielding position in the MLB, Ichiro saw Oakland's Terrence Long attempting to reach third from first on a long single to right. He charged the hit, scooped up the ball with exceptional grace and, conceding the single, instead unleashed a laser shot to third.

Long was gunned down easily on the play. The crowd and the announcers went berserk. "The ball came out of a cannon: it was quick and powerful," one said. "It was like Ichiro threw a coin to third base," another offered. "It was like something out of *Star Wars*," a third noted, getting closer to the truth. "It was going to take a perfect throw to get me, and it was," Long himself said later. Ichiro, meanwhile, made no claims to the perfection he had executed in what came to be known as *The Throw*. "The ball was hit right to me. Why did he run when I was going to throw him out?"

Why did he run when I was going to throw him out? Well, dude, because he *didn't* know that. Baserunners would quickly learn to fear the miniature cannon patrolling right field for the Seattle side, just as pitchers who see their ERAs rise like warm dough every time his sliding, sly, cricketer's bat-flash would skip another base hit past their helpless infields. Ichiro's even, metronomic consistency and refusal to philosophize openly about his athletic feats—"It was a fly ball; I caught it" is a representative sample—somehow seemed to envelope him in even greater profundity. The Seattle-based writer David Shields, an eloquent cultural thinker with a strong interest in sports, offered this memorable sketch of the inscrutable gift that Ichiro brought to the universe of baseball: "The tired, wired world we live in seems instantly explicable, knowable, one-dimensional, ceaselessly cacophonous, shoddily made," he said. "Here comes Ichiro: pseudosilent, precise, contradictory, sphinxlike, a cat in a doggy-dog universe."[81]

But Shields also wondered whether his adulation for Ichiro, enough to overcome a basic detestation for television sports, was a form of lily-gilding. "Was I trying to impart philosophic significance to simple athletic excellence? Maybe the words acquired a lyrical glamour as they got translated from Japanese to English?"[82]

There is no error here, in my view. No, what we are witnessing is simply what too-chatty philosophical discourse always has a hard time conveying: the achievement of *wu wei*, the doing without doing. And lest I commit myself the error of being too chatty, I will say no more about it. The beauty of action is its own argument; it needs no discourse.

The churlish Rose, by the way, would mock Ichiro's 2016 surpassing of his professional hit record, racking the latest of 4,257 combined hits. Rose complained to *USA Today* this way: "In Japan they're trying to make me the Hit Queen. I'm not trying to take anything away from Ichiro, he's had a Hall of Fame career, but the next thing you know, they'll be counting his high-school hits." To which a writer at *Deadspin* responded with an article headlined "Ichiro Is the True Hit King and Pete Rose Can Eat Shit."[83] I'm not sure what a Hit Queen is, but no matter how you score this exchange, it's not a label that belongs on Pete Rose—unless you count this record-shadowing whinge as a version of drama-queen behaviour. Two things are clear: (a) Ichiro set this record in some 1,500 fewer at-bats than Rose; and (b) there is little doubt in anyone's mind that, had he spent his entire professional career in MLB, the record would be his, free and clear.

Oh, and (c): later in the 2016 season, Ichiro passed the 3,000-hit mark in MLB stats alone. In his own interview with *USA Today*, Ichiro was sanguine. "I would be happy if people covered it or wrote about [the record], but I really would not care if it wasn't a big deal. To be quite honest, I'm just going out and doing what I do."

Beauty is as beauty does.

One of the most influential accounts of beauty in the philosophical literature is Kant's, in the *Critique of Judgment* (1790). It is an intricate, elegant series of arguments nested inside an intricate, elegant system of human understanding. But certain key phrases stick in the mind of even the most casual student of this text, and Kant's characterization of beauty as "purposiveness without purpose" is one of these.

First, though, Kant argues, against our common relativism, that judgments of beauty are both *necessary* and *universal*. We are never uncertain of them, and we do really think they (ought to) hold for everyone. The standard phrase that "Beauty is in the eye of the beholder" is, in fact, less an endorsement of genuine relativism (for what could that actually be?) and more a matter of peace-making concerning the undeniable fact that we do argue about what is beautiful. We would not do so—and no pacifying bromides would arise—unless we really judged our perception of beauty to be trustworthy and worth defending.

Still, it is hard to pick out beauty except through the act of judgment itself; there is no reliable empirical feature of beauty that we can identify, independent of those judgments themselves. And this is where "purposiveness without purpose" gives us a conceptual handrail. Something is purposive when it conveys to us a sense of its end, or *telos*—that for which it exists. But when we encounter the beautiful, we get a sense of such purposiveness *even as* we are unable to identify any specific purpose thereto. Beautiful things are not *for* anything; they nevertheless convey a sense of importance and direction. This aligns with Kant's idea that the judgment of beauty is *disinterested*—that is, it does not involve my specific interests in pleasure or utility. I am drawn to the beautiful just because it is beautiful, and not for any translatable desire.

One can see how Kant's analysis lent immediate sanction to aesthetic theories of "art for art's sake." This idea, dominant in Enlightenment and Romantic thought, would generate a series of challenges in which we still struggle, about the effectiveness or otherwise of art in arousing ethical insight, political action, or community feeling.

I can't hope to settle these disputes here—or maybe anywhere. But I think the dynamic is similar no matter where
we encounter the beautiful. It is not, in itself, ethically edi-
fying or politically effective. And yet there can be, standing
nearby, ethical and political lessons and opportunities of
substantial force. Beauty hones attention, makes us heed
the world. Art is political even, or especially, when it most
assiduously fights off any standard of value except the aesthetic. A game without ostensible point or purpose can be
the site of protest, or failure, or the raising of consciousness.
Such results can always be judged extraneous to the internal
appeal of the game; they are, nevertheless, made possible by
way of it. Colin Kaepernick's "Star-Spangled Banner" protest, not to mention much of the career of Muhammad Ali,
make no sense otherwise.

Baseball perfectly embodies the aesthetic ideal of purposiveness without purpose. There is no need for the game of
baseball. We can make it serve specific political or cultural
ends, but the game itself will internally resist these, insisting
as always on its complex, lovely patterns of repetition and
difference. The resulting dynamic of purpose and non-pur-
pose generates an eternally deferred form of meaning, the
way all beauty does. What, after all, is the *message* of baseball? At a fundamental level, let's call the game metaphysical,
because why not? Baseball is just baseball, an end unto itself.
The moments of beauty called forth by the game are likewise precious, evanescent, pregnant with significance, and
entirely without purpose. Baseball achieves nothing. That is
why it is so important.

Of course, this purist argument can seem to founder on its
own philosophical pretensions. After all, baseball at the professional level is rife with purpose, profit, ego, and municipal
opportunism. It is far from disinterested as a form of human
activity, and its executors—the players we all revere, at least
from time to time—are servants of goals neither necessary

nor universal. It is a business like any other, a profit-seeking activity employing, or really exploiting, the fleeting athletic talents of a small number of flawed men.

But, but. I want to hold fast to the things within the game, little moments of transcendence that inspired love in the first place and keep us coming back no matter how much we know about the imperfections of the larger scene. One circus catch at second by Dustin Pedroia or Robbie Alomar; a sliding full-body stop at third by Cal Ripken or Brett Lawrie; Derek Jeter diving into the stands to make a foul-ball catch; Sam Fuld or Kevin Pillar stretching flat out or climbing the wall to save a run; Edwin Encarnacion fielding hot shots at first with an insouciance that masks a depth of serene joy only partially communicated by his self-conscious, self-mocking grin. *Success!*

Rilke's canonical poem "The Archaic Torso of Apollo," first published in 1908 ("Archäischer Torso Apollos"), makes the point as well as any piece of writing ever could. Contemplating the remains of a statue depicting the ancient Greek god, the poet considers what is seen and what must go unseen. Here is my favourite English translation, in full, by Stephen Mitchell[84]:

We cannot know his legendary head
with eyes like ripening fruit. And yet his torso
is still suffused with brilliance from inside,
like a lamp, in which his gaze, now turned to low,

gleams in all its power. Otherwise
the curved breast could not dazzle you so, nor could
a smile run through the placid hips and thighs
to that dark center where procreation flared.

Otherwise this stone would seem defaced
beneath the translucent cascade of the shoulders
and would not glisten like a wild beast's fur:

would not, from all the borders of itself,
burst like a star; for there is no place
that does not see you. You must change your life.

You must change your life! Just that, nothing more. That
is the message that fractured beauty brings to the world. The
statue, we are made to see, is a failure, a defective remnant of
imagined perfection. And even so, its demands are insistent
and vivid, a piece of marble infused with a light that opens
up the world. How can we properly respond? Do we have
the capacity to heed its lessons of aesthetics becoming ethics? That is what it calls out in us.

Change how? Change what? Well, recall DeLillo: "The
game doesn't change the way you sleep or wash your face or
chew your food. It changes nothing but your life."

How does the game—any game—do this, exactly? I can't
answer that for you. Only you can do that. There's nobody
else.

Will you fail? Of course you will. Beauty is a stern master.
The thrill of witnessing something without flaw, a perfectly
executed double play or leaping outfield catch, reminds us of
our own earth-bound reality, even as it suggests the heights
which we humans are capable of reaching. There is no perfection without defect. I can't do *that*, but somebody can.

That's how things matter. That's why this thing matters.
Start changing.

After the Game

I DEDICATE THIS BOOK TO the three most devoted baseball fans I have known, all of them taken from us far too early.

Each was a devoted celebrant of the game, and of life. I miss watching games with them, talking about baseball by phone, email, or in person, and, most of all, riding the roller coaster of pennant runs and tough playoff series. They are in my thoughts every time I experience the game, and on almost every other day, too. I wish I'd had a chance to say goodbye, or know which had been the last game we would see or discuss. I hope Linny will forgive me for not cheering for the Red Sox, even now, except when they're playing the Yankees.

Some parts of this book were previously published, in earlier and different forms, in the *Globe and Mail*, *Descant*, *Nine*, *The Idler*, and (no kidding) the *International Journal of Existential Psychology and Psychotherapy*. In several cases, I have reversed or expanded my original views on the subjects. I am grateful for the opportunity to do so here. Sometimes an error can be corrected in life, if not in baseball.

Some portions were likewise delivered as talks in Sydney, Paris, London, Bloomington, Vancouver, Calgary, Toronto, Montreal, and Ottawa; also at the Cooperstown Symposium on Baseball and American Culture, the most excellent academic conference ever. I thank Jim Gates and the staff at the National Baseball Hall of Fame and Museum in Cooperstown for their generous welcomes at this symposium over a period of almost 25 years. Playing town ball on the village green, and then eating a barbecue banquet with a bunch of other nerd-fans, surrounded by the bronze plaques of baseball's immortals, has been a highlight of my recent springs.

A small bit of the text first got aired as part of the 2004 Leacock Debate in Toronto, on the superiority of baseball to cricket. Alison Gordon was my speaking partner then. Audience opinion was divided on whether our arguments in favour of baseball — mostly hers, I should say — were equal to the eloquence of Vern Krishna, Q.C., who defended cricket to hilarious and rational effect. Well, regardless of the official outcome, even if we lost we won — because we got to do it together. Just one of the many ways a fail can bring success.

Many thanks to Tracy Pryce, Dan Wells, Molly Montgomery, Steven Kingwell, Elizabeth Benn, Stephen Marche, Martin Levin, Juan Pablo Bermúdez-Rey, Jonathan Lethem, Misha Barbanel, Daniela Rupolo, Avie Bennett, Nate Charlow, Charlie Mathewson, Lauren Bialystok, and several players from the Hermenaut Squad for illuminating my sense of baseball or saving me from error. Special thanks to Bruce Montgomery, my father-in-law, for sharing a love of baseball on the radio. Red Sox games always sound mythical when pulled out of the hilltop air in the old dining room at Cady House in East Alstead, New Hampshire.

And I guess I should just say: obviously the Toronto stadium will be always be the SkyDome to me. I find it repulsive that the only statue out on the main fan concourse depicts a corporate egomaniac. Sanity demands that we stop short of toppling this aesthetic and moral outrage, Saddam-style; but we can always avert our eyes — and wait for the Joe Carter or Robbie Alomar bronze that fans deserve.

Postscript: I'm writing these words on the morning of October 20, 2016. Yesterday, the Blue Jays lost Game Five of the American League Championship Series to the Cleveland side. The Jays' bats were mostly silent, as they had been in the first three losses of the series. It was José Bautista's 36th birthday yesterday, and he got a hit; but no runs were scored by Toronto. The Cubs tied up their series against the Dodgers over in the National League and, like many fans, I'll transfer my allegiance to them now.

Post-postscript: Now writing from a hotel room in Dallas. The Cubs went on to win the NLCS in six, and then—as everyone knows—the World Series in seven, including a crazy, beautiful, extra-innings Game Seven. Another curse bites the dust. I watched in the hotel bar, along with my instant new friends Jeff and Cathy, and it was perhaps the finest single game of baseball I have ever seen. All the elements: big hits and ties, a rain delay, and great plays in the field to save the day, beauty and error and game-changing actions that seemed to happen in an instant. I would say that I wish every game could be that way, but that is just not so: it was the game of a lifetime, 1908 shattered on a warmish night in Cleveland, 2016.

It has been unseasonably warm all over this fall, almost summery. But for me and every other fan summer is now gone and the boys of that season are leaving town for their homes elsewhere. The weather has turned suddenly colder. *Wait till next year*, sports fans like to say. The future is an undiscovered country where we all get to be winners—until we don't.

But to fail is not to fear. The game will still be here when we, like summer breezes, are all gone...

Endnotes

1   I thank my friend and former student, Eli K. P. William, science-fiction writer and longtime resident of Tokyo, for this example.

2   Don DeLillo, *Pafko at the Wall* (New York: Scribner's, 2001); originally published in *Harper's Magazine* (October 1992). As mentioned, this novella forms the first long part of DeLillo's *Underworld* (New York: Scribner's, 1997). I will use the stand-alone book version as my source for citations.

3   It's probably not the done thing to acknowledge your own failure in a footnote, but I have to consider my attempt at a philosophical study of performance, genius, perfectionism, and music, *Glenn Gould* (Toronto: Viking, 2009), a book that might be considered to have warning-track power only. But sometimes you have to swing for the fences to see if you can reach them. Music is an abstract art that lies beyond the boundary; it will always outpace prose. And even for Gould, there was no such thing, finally, as the perfect performance.

4   Shi Davidi, "Happ joins company of Blue Jays legends with 20-win season," *Sportsnet News* (23 September 2016); http://www.sportsnet.ca/baseball/mlb/happ-joins-company-blue-jays-legends-20-win-season/

5   Paciorek is a baseball-stats hero for this stellar, one-time-only performance. See Benjamin Hoffman, "For the Sultan of Small

Sample Size, a Career Batting Average of 1.000," *New York Times* (30 March 2013); http://www.nytimes.com/2013/03/31/sports/baseball/john-paciorek-baseballs-sultan-of-small-sample-size.html

6   Anthon Wilden, *The Rules Are No Game: The Strategy of Communication* (London: Routledge & Kegan Paul, 1986). In this book and in the companion volume, *Man and Woman, War and Peace: The Strategist's Companion* (London: Routledge & Kegan Paul, 1986), Wilden argues for a theory of play and communication indebted to Lacanian psychoanalysis, Gregory Bateson's semiotic social theory, and the ancient wisdom of Chinese strategist Sun Tzu.

7   Actually, as philosophers know, there is a profound paradox at the heart of the very idea of "following a rule," since any action at all *in language* can be made out to accord with a rule that has simply not yet seen the new instance of an action. See Saul Kripke, *Wittgenstein on Rules and Private Language: An Elementary Exposition* (Oxford: Blackwell, 1982). In its way, this paradox compels a skepticism as profound as those generated by Hume's problem of induction or the doubt concerning mind-independent reality so vividly imagined by Descartes. As with those celebrated challenges, the "solution" here involves either a rejection of some premise of the basic argument or a meta-level acceptance of leaps in the epistemological dark. (For the record: Descartes worried, Hume didn't; the former turned to God for help, the latter turned cheerfully away.)

8   http://www.barstoolsports.com/baseball/showboating-is-only-allowed-if-youre-chris-archer/

9   Ken Fidlin, "Toronto Blue Jays' Jose Bautista 'a f—ing disgrace to the game,' Hall of Famer Goose Gossage says in lengthy tirade," *National Post* (10 March 2016); http://news.nationalpost.com/sports/mlb/toronto-blue-jays-jose-bautista-a-f-ing-disgrace-to-the-game-hall-of-famer-goose-gossage-says-in-lengthy-tirade

10   http://www.si.com/mlb/2016/02/16/new-york-mets-ruben-tejada-los-angeles-dodgers-chase-utley

11   http://www.foxsports.com/mlb/just-a-bit-outside/story/chase-utley-slide-los-angeles-dodgers-new-york-mets-ruben-tejada-broken-leg-players-speak-101115

12   David Lewis, "Scorekeeping in a Language Game," *Journal of Philosophical Logic* 8 (1979): 339-58, at p. 344.

13   I'm not really suggesting this *too* seriously to readers of the current book, but ... the relevant source is Jacques Derrida, "Force of Law: The Mystical Foundation of Authority," Mary Quaintance, trans., *Cardozo Law Review* 11 (1989-1990): pp. 920-1045.

14   Lewis, "Scorekeeping in a Language Game," p. 344. I once mis-scored a high-school basketball game because I was so focused on individual stats that I failed to make the correct adjustment to my own team's total. The referee told me that I could not change the score after the figures had been entered for the quarter, and so I spent the last minutes of the game hoping that my team would *cover the spread of error* I had introduced into the record of the game. They did; nobody beat me up. Not that day, anyway.

15   Don DeLillo, *Pafko at the Wall*, p. 40.

16   Ted Cohen, "There Are No Ties at First Base," in Eric Bronson, ed., *Baseball and Philosophy* (Chicago: Open Court, 2004), pp. 75-76.

17   See David Lewis, "Scorekeeping in a Language Game," and E. J. Lemmon, "On Sentences Verifiable by Their Use," *Analysis* 22 (1962), pp. 86-89. Austin's original article is "Performative Utterances," in his *Philosophical Papers* (Oxford: Oxford University Press, 1961).

18   Donald Hall, "The Art of Poetry No. 43," *Paris Review* (Fall 1991), p. 120.

19   DeLillo, *Pafko at the Wall*, p. 36.

20   If you are not yourself one of those geeks, you might not know that "sabermetrician" is the proud moniker adopted by the quant-happy people at the Society for American Baseball Research (SABR, founded in Cooperstown, New York, 1971), the original and still-dominant organization for serious baseball studies.

21   Matt Yoder, "Mistakes and complaints define TBS's MLB coverage right now," *Awful Announcing* (6 October 2016); http://awfulannouncing.com/2016/mistakes-and-complaints-define-tbs-mlb-postseason-coverage-right-now.html

22   Marshall McLuhan, *Understanding Media: The Extensions of Man* (New York: McGraw-Hill, 1964), p. 326.

23   In a celebrated episode of *The Simpsons* — "HOMR," season 12, episode 9 — Homer discovers that he has been labouring for

years with a crayon in his brain. Once it is removed, he is smart and critical, a new friend to nerdy daughter Lisa, and a conscientious nuclear-safety officer. But he can't bear the pain of being a clever man in a dumb culture, the constant insults to his intelligence, and so he decides to have the crayon re-inserted by Moe the bartender. This is effectively a suicide by Smart Homer in order to bring Dumb Homer back to life. The most poignant detail is the note that Smart Homer leaves with Dumb Homer to give to a distraught Lisa, confessing his weakness. I discuss this episode's philosophical implications in, among other places, Mark Kingwell, "Crayon in the Brain: Machining Happiness in the Time of Homer," *Descant* 37:2 (Summer 2006): 68-87.

24   Adam Schulman, "Aristotle balked, umpires rule," *New York Times* (3 May 1988).

25   John Marshall, "The Answer Guy: Origin of the 'Texas Leaguer' hard to pin down," *Seattle Post-Intelligencer* (19 September 2002); http://www.seattlepi.com/news/article/The-Answer-Guy-Origin-of-the-Texas-Leaguer-1096519.php

26   Scott Ostler, "Talkin' Baseball ... The Can of Corn Is Back on the Shelf," *Los Angeles Times* (1 May 1986); http://articles.latimes.com/1986-05-01/sports/sp-2758_1_teen-agers

27   J. D. Salinger, "Seymour: An Introduction" (1959), in *Raise High the Roofbeams, Carpenters and Seymour: An Introduction* (Boston: Little, Brown, 1991), p. 202.

28   I will have more to say about the distinction between finite and infinite games in later sections of this book. The key discussion of the idea is found in James P. Carse, *Finite and Infinite Games* (New York: Free Press, 2013; orig. 1987).

29   "Baker-Finch can sympathise with Duval," *Golftoday.co.uk* (25 January 2010); the article explores Baker-Finch's professional collapse as compared to David Duval, another brief contender whose game deteriorated to the point of professional failure.

30   Jim Baumbach, "Catching Up With Mackey Sasser," *NewsDay* (8 December 2007); reprinted at https://www.biolateral.com/node/50

31   An excellent discussion of the notion can be found in Edward Slingerland, *Trying Not to Try: Ancient China, Modern Science, and the Power of Spontaneity* (New York: Broadway Books, 2015).

32   *Toronto Daily Star* (17 August 1933).

33   "The Christie Pits Riot and the birth of multicultural Toronto," *National Post* (15 August 2008).

34   Iris Marion Young, "Throwing like a Girl: A Phenomenology of Feminine Body Comportment, Motility, and Spatiality," *Human Studies* 3:2 (1980), pp. 137-15.

35   For more on this version of skilled action, and its opposite, see my essay "Slack Enters the System," *Descant* 43:2 (Summer 2012): 179-89; reprinted in Kingwell, *Measure Yourself Against the Earth* (Windsor: Biblioasis, 2015).

36   See, for example, Dana Stevens, "The Sexy 'Frozen' Moment No One Is Talking About," *Huffington Post* (18 February 2014); http://www.huffingtonpost.com/2014/02/18/sexy-frozen-moment_n_4802792.html

37   The phenomenon, and the term, became the subject of numerous newspaper articles and online commentaries in the summer of 2015. I go on record here in saying that I believe Alison Gordon coined this term, in my hearing, during the summer of 2009, when she and I were crowded into the corner of our metal SkyDome seats by separate posses of heavyset bros sitting—spreading—on either side of us. Whether the usage was original to her or not, I cannot now say; but by using it casually in 2009, she was obviously ahead of the curve.

38   The canonical philosophical account of mental extension is Andy Clark and David Chalmers, "The Extended Mind," *Analysis* 58:1 (1998): 7-19.

39   The most influential study of games and their role in society, especially as coeval with the rise of bourgeois norms of behaviour, is Johan Huizinga, *Homo Ludens: A Study of the Play-Element in Culture* (Boston: Beacon Press, 1971; orig. 1938). In what follows, I trace numerous lines of insight inspired by Huizinga's work.

40   Scott Feschuk, "Counting down the most annoying in video review, by sport," *Sportsnet Magazine* (10 July 2016); http://www.sportsnet.ca/baseball/mlb/counting-annoying-video-review-sport/

41   I deploy this same distinction concerning notions of time, with a more overtly political aim, in "Democracy's Gift: Time, Tradition, Repetition," included in *Measure Yourself Against the Earth*.

42   Quoted in Steve Wulf, "Is This the Year?" *Sports Illustrated* (5 April 1993), p. 36.

43   *The Globe and Mail* (9 April 1993), p. B1.

44   See Higgins, *The Progress of the Seasons: Forty Years of Baseball in Our Town* (New York: Henry Holt, 1989), one of the best memoirs of how baseball and civic life became inextricably entwined. Studs Terkel is famous for commenting that the Cubs were most lovable only when losing. A self-portrait in Cub obsession is provided by William T. Stafford in his story "The Professor and the Chicago Cubs," in *Baseball and the Game of Life* (New York: Vintage, 1990), pp. 109-21.

45   This and all following points regarding the Zorra-Beachville game are taken from "The Old Ball Game: Ontario Crossroads Site of Historic Backwoods Matchup," by Tom Hawthorn, *The Globe and Mail* (4 June 1988), p. A15.

46   See Wilden's *The Rules Are No Game.*

47   Ashis Nandy, *The Tao of Cricket: On Games of Destiny and the Destiny of Games* (New York: Viking, 1989), p. ix. Nandy's view of the issues, with which I substantially agree, is summarized in the following rather complex passage: "I view cricket as [a] medium of self-expression on four planes: traditional English cricket (which is in many ways a reflection of earlier social hierarchies but is also unwittingly a criticism of the values associated with modern industrialism), modern cricket (increasingly an endorsement of the hegemonic, urban-industrial managerial culture and a criticism of the pre-industrial values now associated with defeated ways of life), imported cricket (the cricket which was exported to non-Western societies as a criticism of native life-styles from the point of view of the industrializing West but which, as reconstructed by the natives, brought out the latent function of the game in the West and became a criticism of the common cultural principles of capitalism, colonialism and modernity), and new cricket (the cricket which by its close identification with the industrial-managerial ethos is becoming increasingly an endorsement of the ruling culture of the world and a criticism of the victims of history)," p. xi.

These points will be clarified in what follows. I also discuss them at greater length in an essay called "Keeping a Straight Bat: Cricket, Civility and Colonialism," in Selwyn Cudjoe and William Cain, eds., *C.L.R. James: His Intellectual Legacies* (Amherst, MA: U. Mass. Press, 1995).

48   Nandy, *The Tao of Cricket*, p. 8. Despite its rather unfortunate title, and though occasionally marred by sociological jargon, Nandy's book is the best available full-length treatment of cricket's political implications.

49   *Ibid.*, p. 97.

50   *Ibid.*, p. 7; emphasis added.

51   I am accepting Nandy's version of the useful distinction between the official rules (or, as in cricket, "the laws") of a game and the so-called *unwritten* rules of it. The unwritten rules—here called norms—are the anticipated commitments that make the game's culture what it is. Thus the weight of the well-worn phrase "It isn't cricket": someone saying this is probably not making reference to the rules of the game, but instead to the presumed norms (of good sportsmanship, e.g.) that are thought to underwrite the game. When a culture does not share the norms of a game, it can still play the game within the rules—and may do so very effectively. But James' point here (and mine) is that in that event the game will not remain the same. Indeed it may cease to possess true critical character.

52   Judith Shklar explores our love of exposing hypocrisy in her book *Ordinary Vices* (Cambridge: Belknap, 1984), especially ch. 2. Shklar's suggestion is that "putting hypocrisy first"—considering it the most serious vice, more serious than cruelty, say—leads to misanthropy and a cacophony of accusing and counter-accusing voices.

53   C.L.R. James, *Beyond a Boundary* (London: Stanley Paul, 1963), p. 38 (emphasis added).

54   Charles Ritchie, *Siren Years* (London: Macmillan, 1980).

55   This possibility of remaining a game—a possibility increasingly minor as cricket approaches the degree of professional dominance typical in other major sports—is what animates its critical abilities. If big sport becomes professional sport in the way, for example, pro football and basketball have in the United States, the lines between game and life are obscured. Thoroughly professional sport, in other words, is just life continued by other means: its only difference lies in posting winners and losers, which in itself may constitute a danger. Professional dominance may, of course, be ambivalent. In the pro-football satire *North Dallas Forty* (1979, d. Ted Kotcheff), a

character attacks a coach in a scene that has become famous for expressing the professional athlete's peculiar frustration: "When *we* call it a game, *you* call it a business," he yells at the coach. "When *we* call it a business, *you* call it a game."

56　G.W.F. Hegel, *Phenomenology of Spirit*, trans. A.V. Miller (Oxford: Oxford University Press, 1977; orig. 1807), p. 114 (emphasis added).

57　*Sports Illustrated* (26 October 1992), pp. 40-45.

58　Rachel Brady, "Orioles' Jones says he and outfielder Kim were targets of racial slurs," *The Globe and Mail* (5 October 2016); http://www.theglobeandmail.com/sports/baseball/blue-jays-fans-beer-can-throwing-racial-slur-adam-jones-toronto-rogers-centre-orioles/article32254718/

59　Cathal Kelly, "Jays fans solidify bad reputation with ugly beer-throwing incident," *The Globe and Mail* (5 October 2016); http://www.theglobeandmail.com/sports/baseball/kelly-jays-fans-solidify-bad-reputation-with-ugly-beer-throwing-incident/article32264342/

60　It is only 16 pages long, however, because it's a colouring book. See Marty Noble, *Invisible Mythological Creatures Magic Picture Book* (New York: Dover, 1998).

61　Homer, *Odyssey*, 19.30.

62　Hubert Dreyfus and Sean Dorrance Kelly, *All Things Shining: Reading the Western Classics to Find Meaning in a Secular Age* (New York: Simon & Schuster, 2011), p. 81.

63　David McGimpsey, "That Novel was the Best Hat I Ever Bought: American Fiction and the Baseball Novel as Luxury Souvenir Item," paper presented at the 28th Cooperstown Symposium on Baseball and Culture, Cooperstown, New York (2 June 2016).

64　Mike Axisa, "'The Simpsons' predicts the Cardinals spying on everyone," *CBS Sports Online* (17 June 2015); http://www.cbssports.com/mlb/news/watch-the-simpsons-predicts-the-cardinals-spying-on-everyone/

65　Joshua Glenn offers a comprehensive and somewhat strict scheme for this tendency of Decades to overflow, and undertow, their numerical decades; he is likewise concerned to label carefully a series of generational identities of the kind that lesser, non-hermenautic authors too blithely assume (as in the overworked notions of "Gen-Xers" and "Millennials"). See his "Generations," *Hi-LoBrow* (2 March 2010); http://hilobrow.com/2010/03/02/cuspers/

66   Many fans already know that one of the funniest and best books ever published about baseball is Brendan C. Boyd and Fred C. Harris, *The Great American Baseball Card Flipping, Trading, and Bubble Gum Book* (Boston: Little, Brown, 1973). This indispensable album not only includes more than 250 full-colour reproductions of cards famous and obscure, including such spectacular non-stars as Whammy Douglas, Choo Choo Coleman, Sibby Sisti, and Clyde Kluttz, but also offers a running commentary on the stances, hair-dos, and sad, sad records of journeyman players, all delivered with insouciant after-school wit. The Angels' hard-throwing reliever Ryne Duren, we learn, "wore milk-bottle-thick tinted glasses and used to warm up before each inning by throwing a series of particularly nasty overhand fast balls into the ground in front of home plate, over the catcher's head, against the backstop, and into the stands." Nuke LaLoosh meets the Hanson Brothers ...

67   John Berger, *Ways of Seeing* (Harmondsworth: Penguin, 1972), *passim*.

68   DeLillo, *Pafko at the Wall*, p. 28. This is a moment of stillness in the novella: the speaker, a white middle-class guy taking a break from work to catch the game, is speaking to the young black protagonist who has snuck into the stadium. They will later fight for the magical home-run ball that is the book's talisman and symbol, becoming bitter rivals in a nasty chase scene.

69   Quoted in Richard Griffin, "Expos' Rusty Staub deserves his place in Canadian Baseball Hall of Fame," *Toronto Star* (7 February 2012); https://www.thestar.com/sports/baseball/2012/02/07/griffin_expos_rusty_staub_deserves_his_place_in_canadian_baseball_hall_of_fame.html

70   Stu Cowan, "Another reason to cheer for Rusty Staub," *Montreal Gazette* (7 February 2012); http://montrealgazette.com/sports/another-reason-to-cheer-for-rusty-staub

71   Roger Angell, "Almost There," *New Yorker* (31 October 2016); http://www.newyorker.com/news/sporting-scene/almost-there-world-series-chicago-cubs-cleveland-indians

72   Stephen Potter, *The Theory and Practice of Gamesmanship: The Art of Winning Games Without Actually Cheating* (London: Rupert Hart-Davis, 1947). This was followed by *Lifemanship* (1952), *One-Upmanship* (1952), and *Supermanship* (1958). Only the first two of these, in my view, stand up.

73   *Ibid.*, pp. 44-45.

74   *Ibid.*, p. 58.

75   Stephen Fry, *The Liar* (London: Arrow Books, 1991), p. 303.

76   Potter, *Gamesmanship*, p. 100.

77   Robert M. Gorman and David Weeks, *Death at the Ballpark: A Comprehensive Study of Game-Related Fatalities 1862-2007* (Jefferson NC: McFarland & Co., 2008).

78   Jon Mooallem, "You're Out: The national pastime's shocking death toll," *Slate* (26 May 2009); http://www.slate.com/articles/sports/sports_nut/2009/05/youre_out.html

79   This celebrated *bon mot* of Stendhal occurs in a footnote to a passage in ch. 17 of his *De L'Amour* (1822). The German musicologist and philosopher Theodor Adorno would adapt the adage in his *Aesthetic Theory* (1970) to read that *art* is only the promise of happiness—maybe a more provocative claim.

80   John Updike, "Hub Fans Bid Kid Adieu," *New Yorker* (22 November 1960); http://www.newyorker.com/magazine/1960/10/22/hub-fans-bid-kid-adieu. This may be the single best article ever written about baseball.

81   David Shields, "Being Ichiro," *New York Times Magazine* (16 September 2001); http://www.nytimes.com/2001/09/16/magazine/being-ichiro.html

82   David Shields, *Baseball Is Just Baseball: The Understated Ichiro* (New York: Blue Rider/Penguin, 2012).

83   Patrick Redford, "Ichiro Is the True Hit King and Pete Rose Can Eat Shit," *Deadspin* (15 June 2016); http://deadspin.com/ichiro-is-the-true-hit-king-and-pete-rose-can-eat-shit-1782063120

84   From *Ahead of All Parting: Selected Poetry and Prose of Rainer Maria Rilke*, Stephen Mitchell, trans. (New York: Modern Library, 1995); https://www.poets.org/poetsorg/poem/archaic-torso-apollo